ULTIMATE X-MEN

CRY WOLF

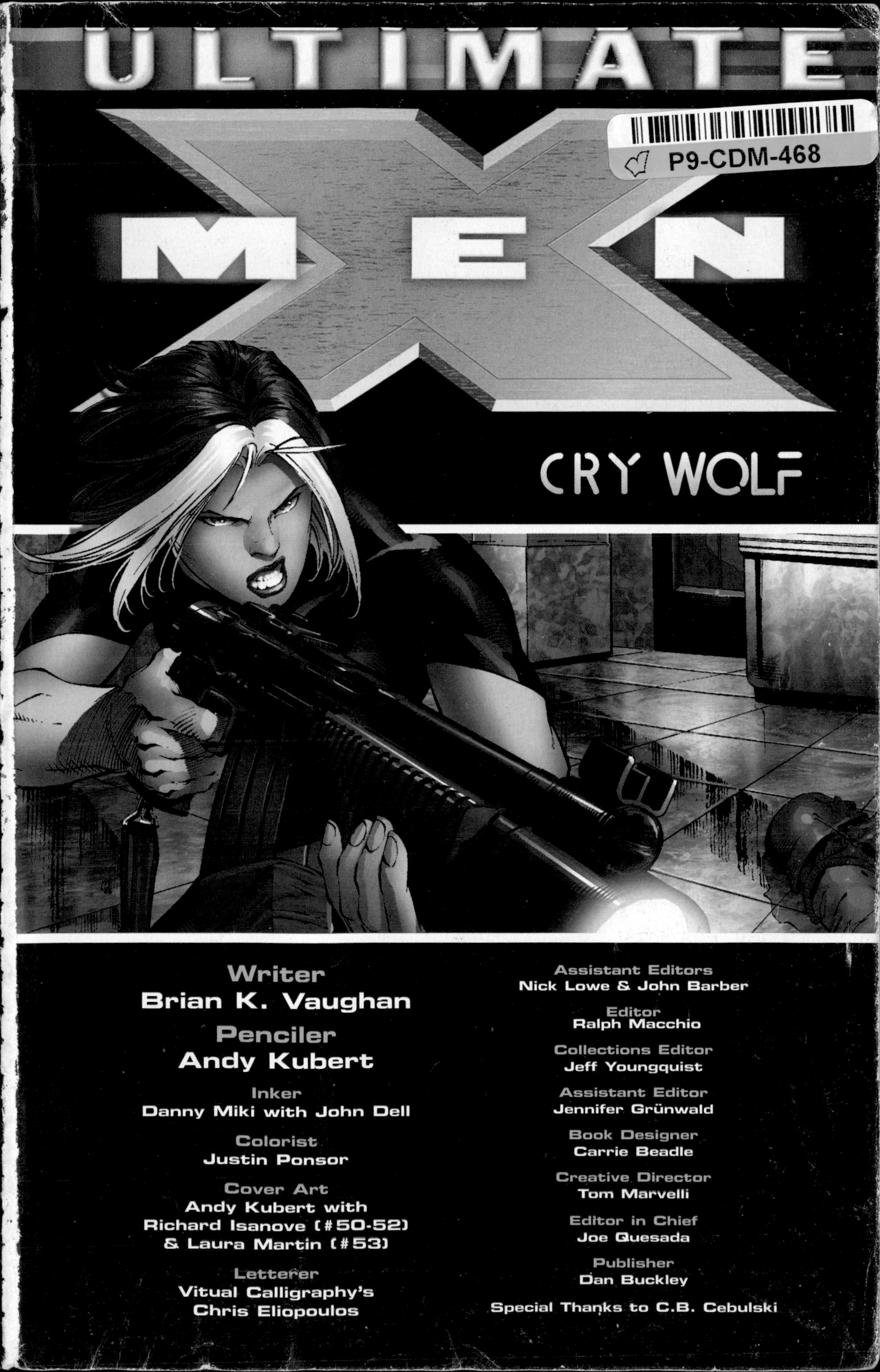

Writer
Brian K. Vaughan

Penciler
Andy Kubert

Inker
Danny Miki with John Dell

Colorist
Justin Ponsor

Cover Art
Andy Kubert with
Richard Isanove (#50-52)
& Laura Martin (#53)

Letterer
Vitual Calligraphy's
Chris Eliopoulos

Assistant Editors
Nick Lowe & John Barber

Editor
Ralph Macchio

Collections Editor
Jeff Youngquist

Assistant Editor
Jennifer Grünwald

Book Designer
Carrie Beadle

Creative Director
Tom Marvelli

Editor in Chief
Joe Quesada

Publisher
Dan Buckley

Special Thanks to C.B. Cebulski

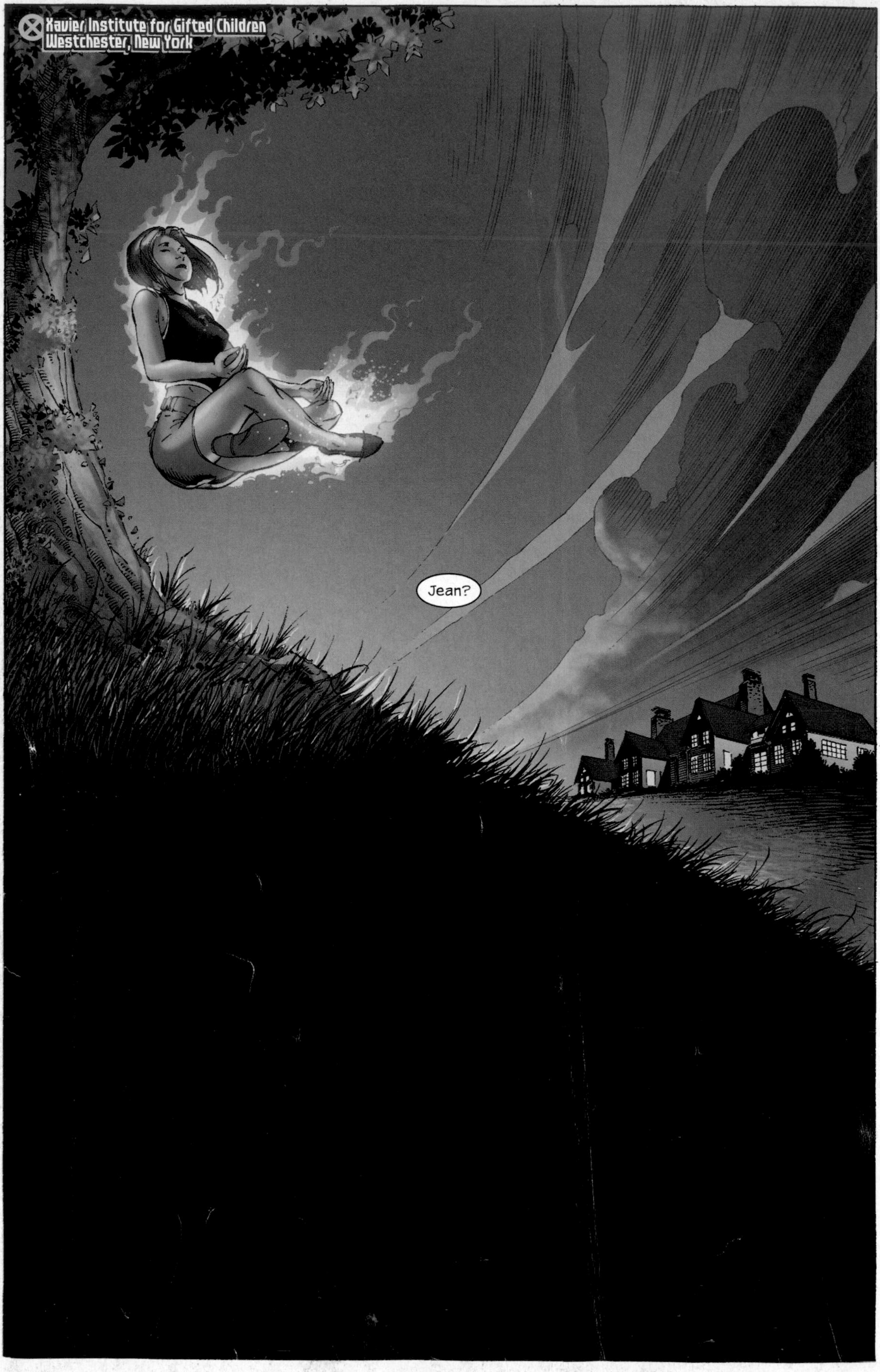
Xavier Institute for Gifted Children
Westchester, New York
Jean?

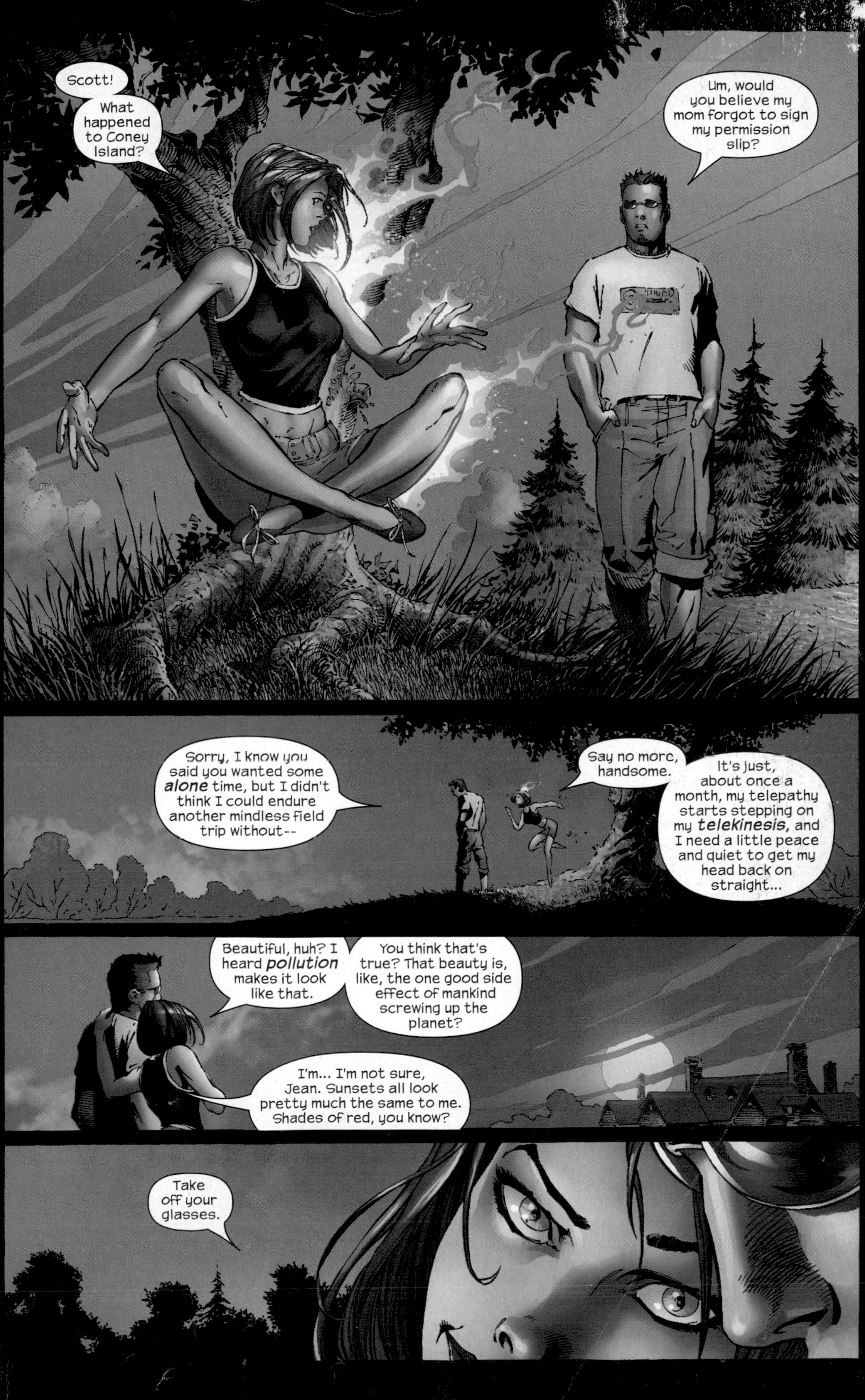
Scott!
What happened to Coney Island?
Um, would you believe my mom forgot to sign my permission slip?
Sorry, I know you said you wanted some *alone* time, but I didn't think I could endure another mindless field trip without--
Say no more, handsome.
It's just, about once a month, my telepathy starts stepping on my *telekinesis*, and I need a little peace and quiet to get my head back on straight...
Beautiful, huh? I heard *pollution* makes it look like that.
You think that's true? That beauty is, like, the one good side effect of mankind screwing up the planet?
I'm... I'm not sure, Jean. Sunsets all look pretty much the same to me. Shades of red, you know?
Take off your glasses.

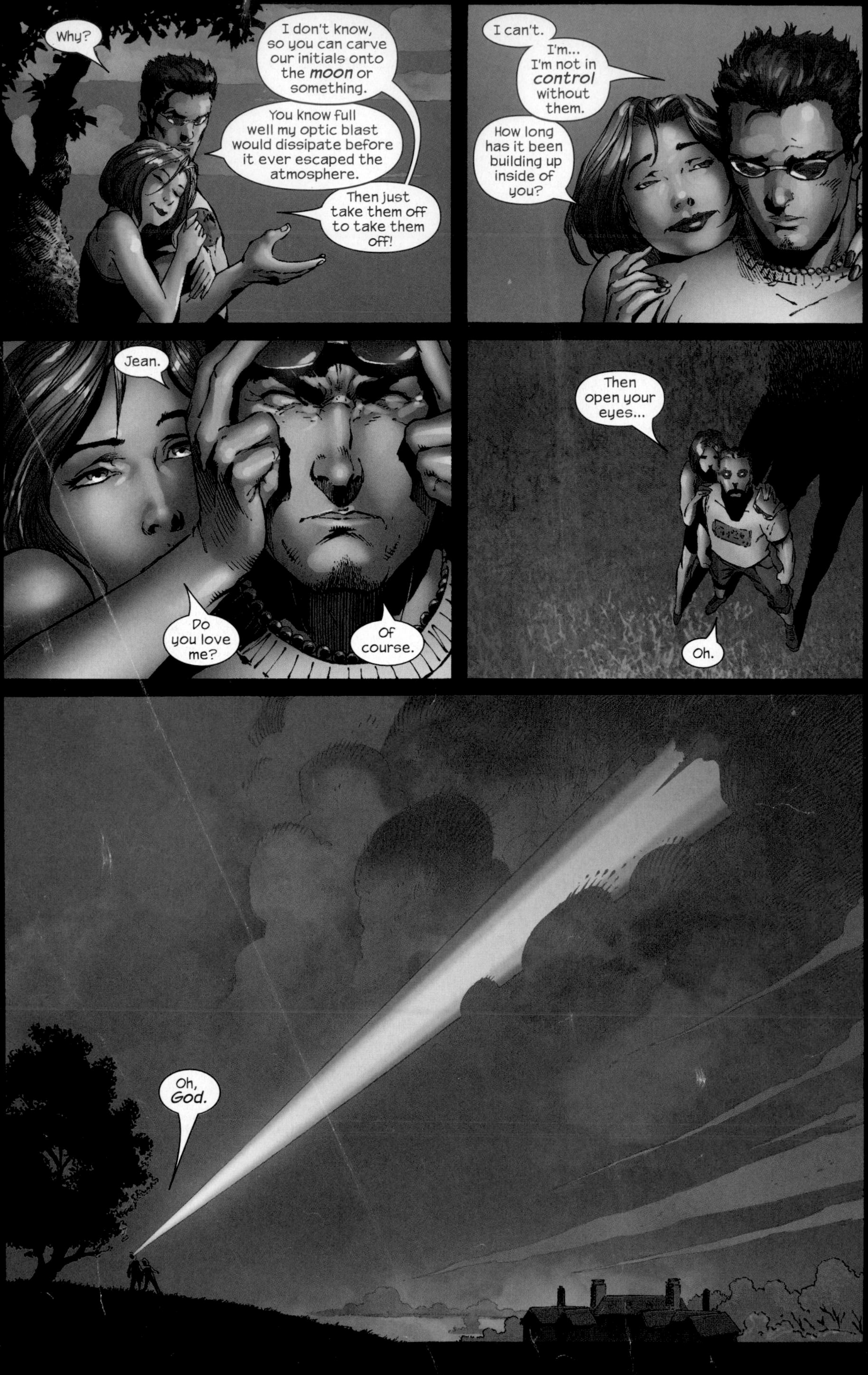
Why?
I don't know, so you can carve our initials onto the moon or something.
You know full well my optic blast would dissipate before it ever escaped the atmosphere.
Then just take them off to take them off!
I can't.
I'm... I'm not in control without them.
How long has it been building up inside of you?
Jean.
Do you love me?
Of course.
Then open your eyes...
Oh.
Oh, God.

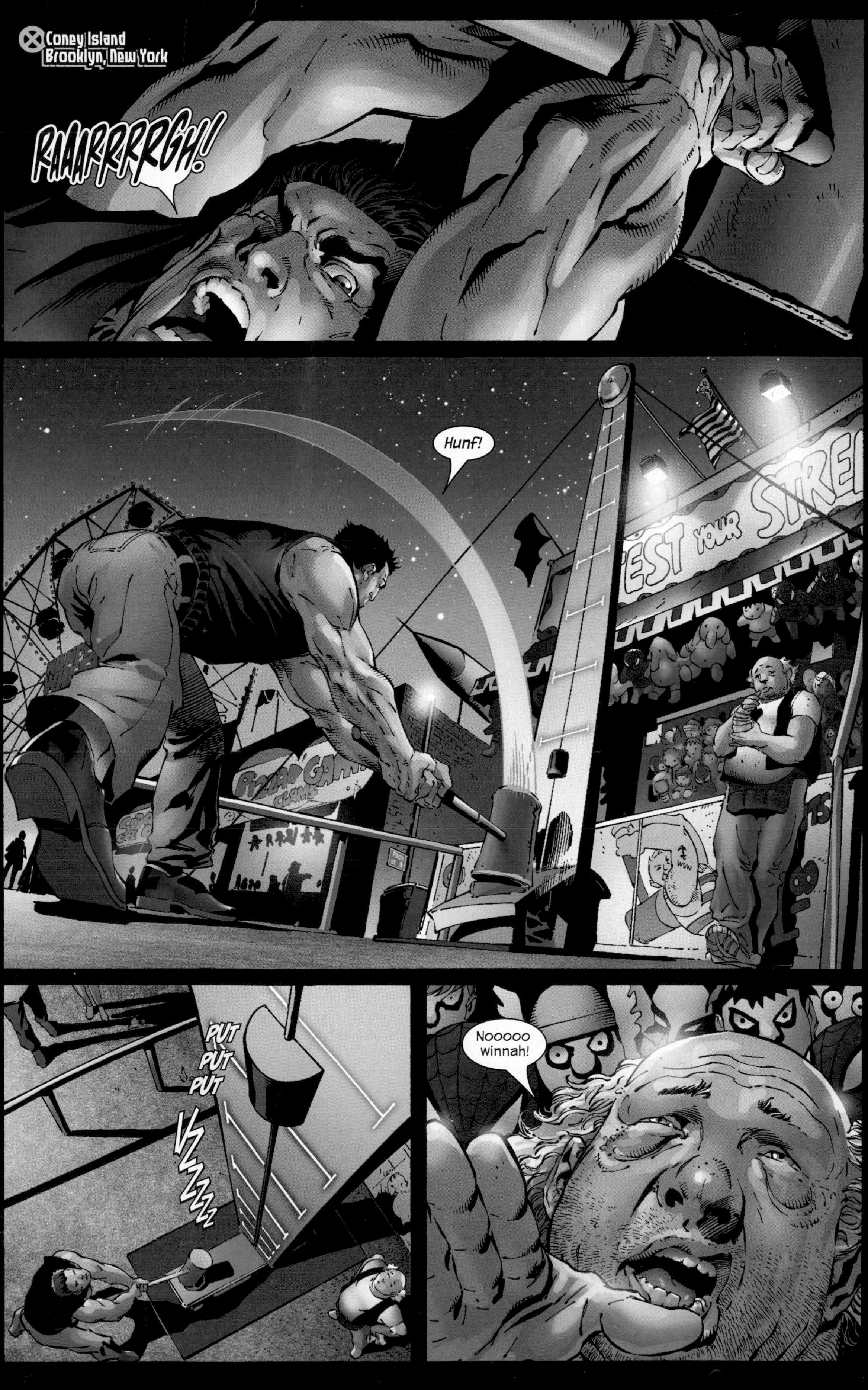
Coney Island
Brooklyn, New York
RAAARRRRGH!
Hunf!
TEST YOUR STRE
PUT
PUT
PUT
VZZZZZ
Noooooo
winnah!

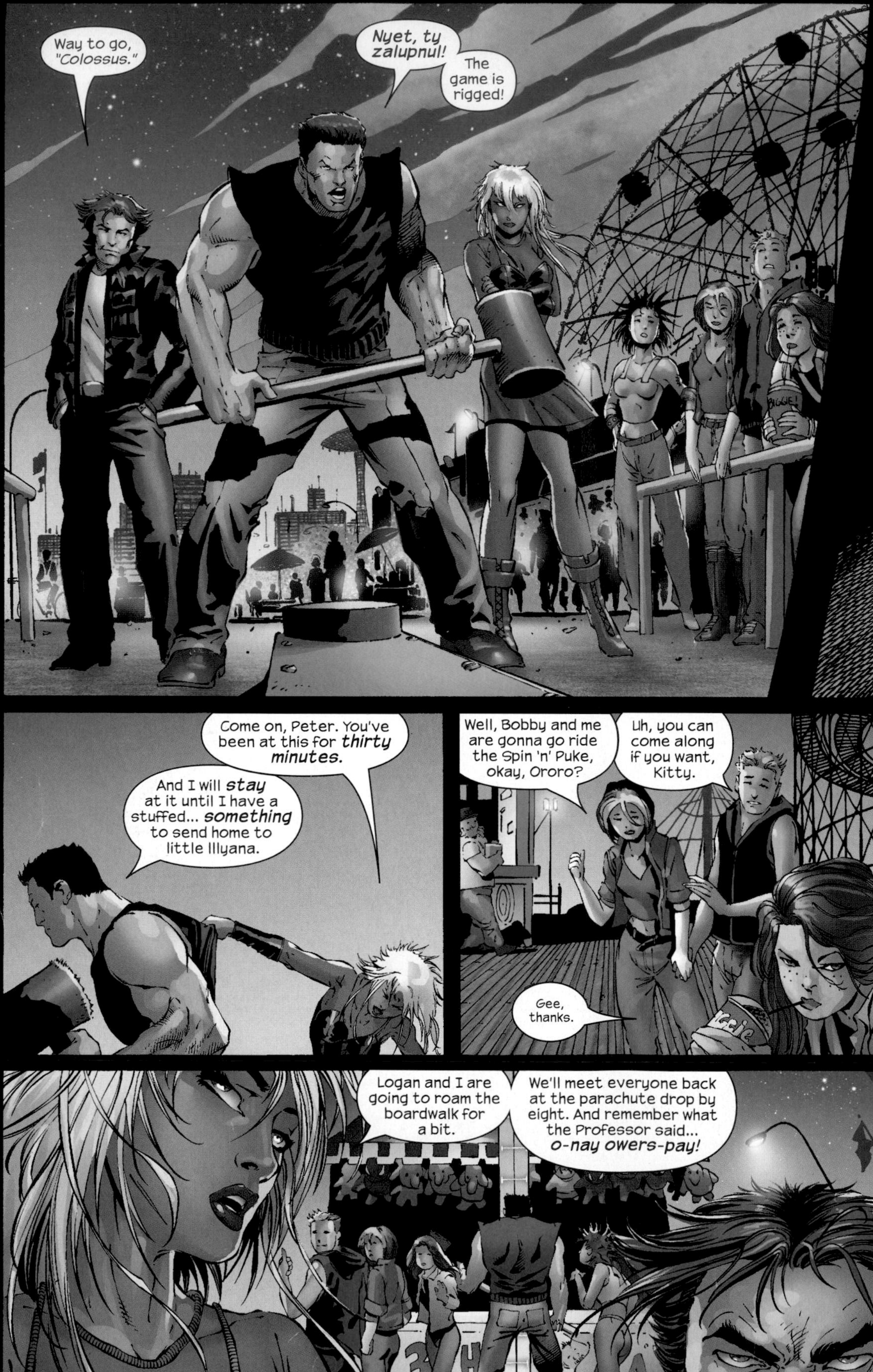
Way to go, "Colossus."
Nyet, ty zalupnul!
The game is rigged!
Come on, Peter. You've been at this for thirty minutes.
And I will stay at it until I have a stuffed... something to send home to little Illyana.
Well, Bobby and me are gonna go ride the Spin 'n' Puke, okay, Ororo?
Uh, you can come along if you want, Kitty.
Gee, thanks.
Logan and I are going to roam the boardwalk for a bit.
We'll meet everyone back at the parachute drop by eight. And remember what the Professor said... o-nay owers-pay!

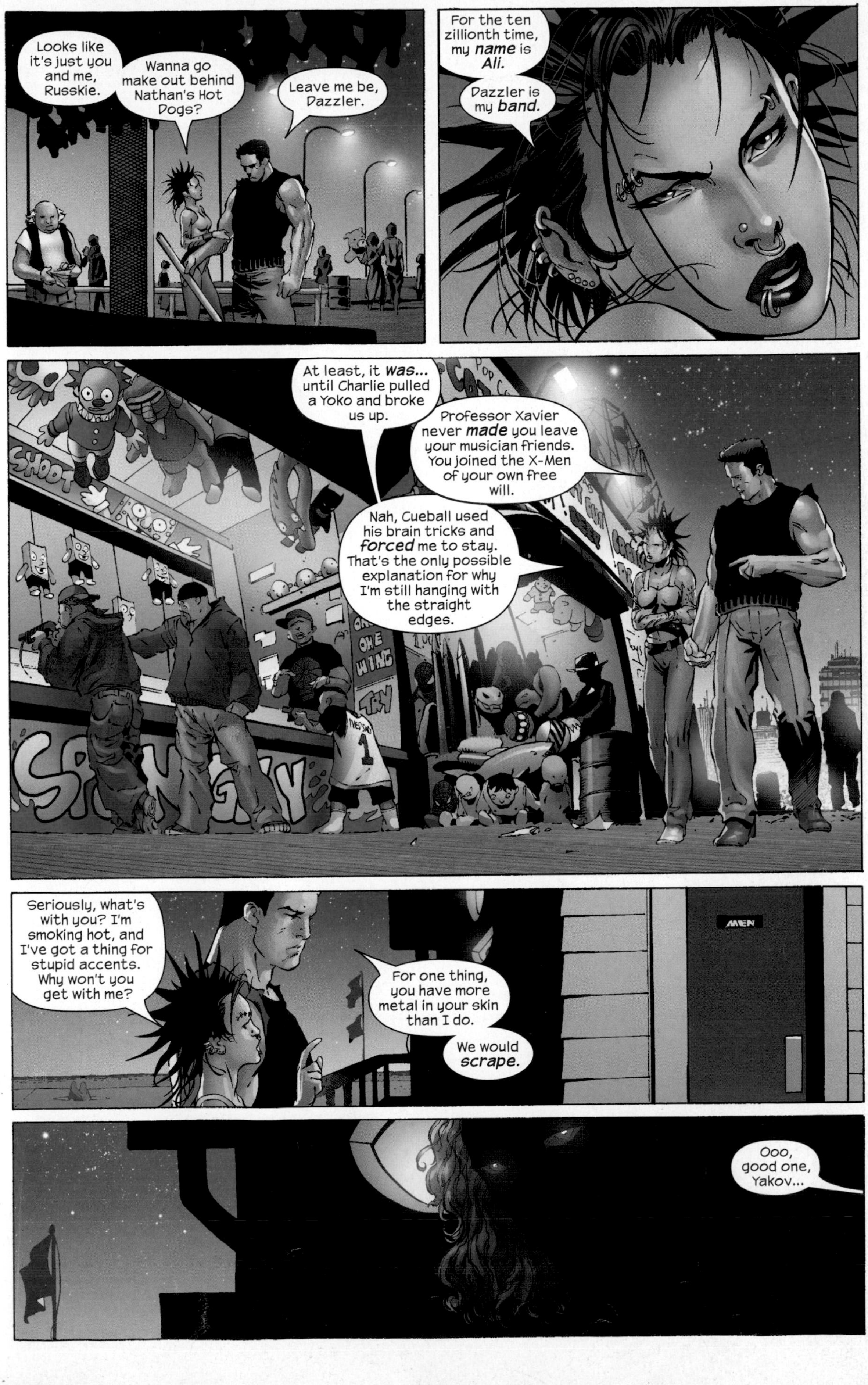
Looks like it's just you and me, Russkie.
Wanna go make out behind Nathan's Hot Dogs?
Leave me be, Dazzler.
For the ten zillionth time, my name is Ali.
Dazzler is my band.
At least, it was... until Charlie pulled a Yoko and broke us up.
Professor Xavier never made you leave your musician friends. You joined the X-Men of your own free will.
Nah, Cueball used his brain tricks and forced me to stay. That's the only possible explanation for why I'm still hanging with the straight edges.
Seriously, what's with you? I'm smoking hot, and I've got a thing for stupid accents. Why won't you get with me?
For one thing, you have more metal in your skin than I do.
We would scrape.
Ooo, good one, Yakov...

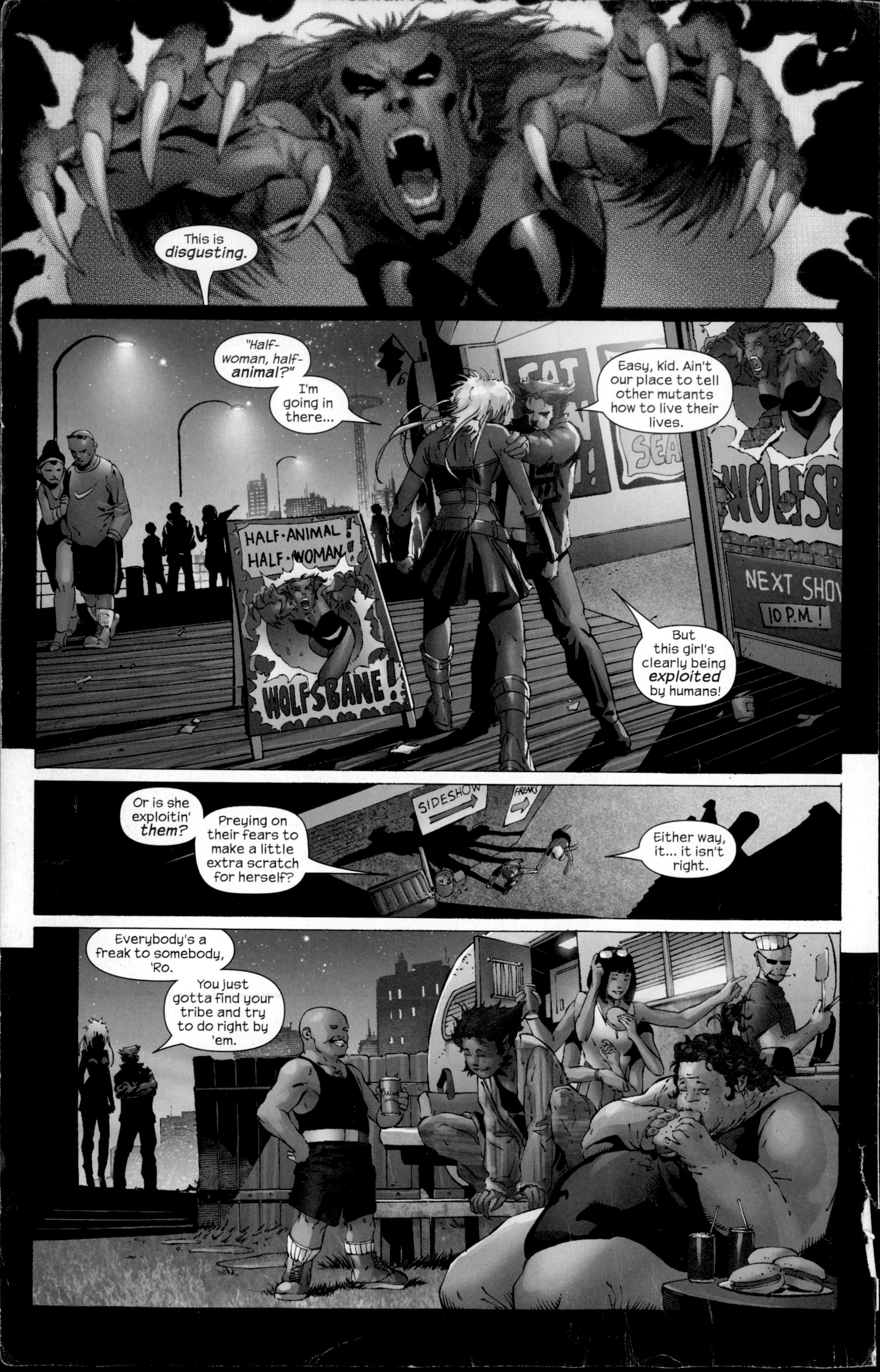
This is disgusting.
"Half-woman, half-animal?"
I'm going in there...
Easy, kid. Ain't our place to tell other mutants how to live their lives.
HALF-ANIMAL! HALF-WOMAN!
WOLFSBANE!
NEXT SHOW 10 P.M.!
But this girl's clearly being exploited by humans!
Or is she exploitin' them?
Preying on their fears to make a little extra scratch for herself?
SIDESHOW
FREAKS
Either way, it... it isn't right.
Everybody's a freak to somebody, 'Ro.
You just gotta find your tribe and try to do right by 'em.

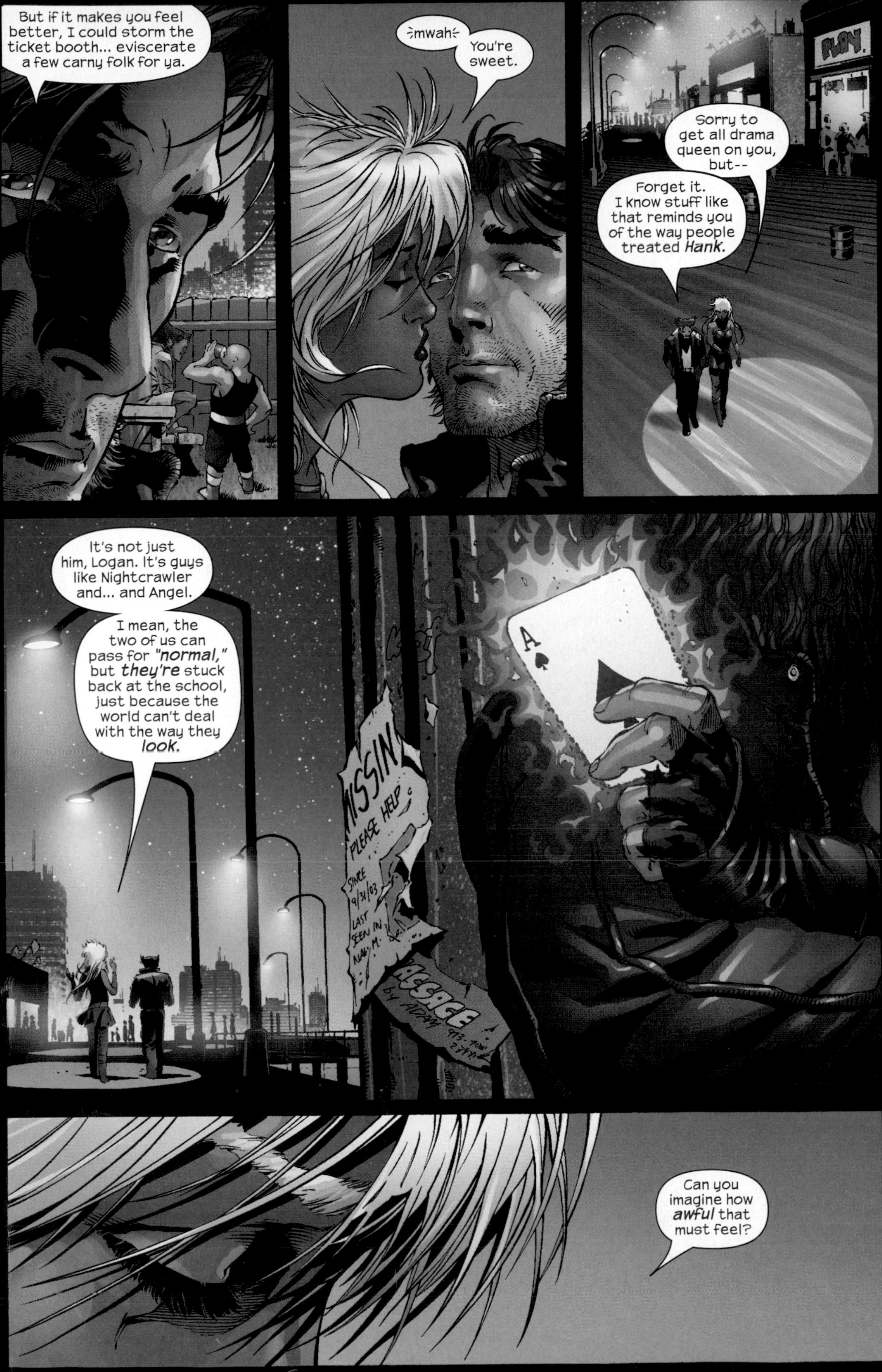
But if it makes you feel better, I could storm the ticket booth... eviscerate a few carny folk for ya.
mwah
You're sweet.
PLAY.
Sorry to get all drama queen on you, but--
Forget it. I know stuff like that reminds you of the way people treated *Hank*.
It's not just him, Logan. It's guys like Nightcrawler and... and Angel.
I mean, the two of us can pass for *"normal,"* but *they're* stuck back at the school, just because the world can't deal with the way they *look*.
PLEASE HELP
Can you imagine how *awful* that must feel?

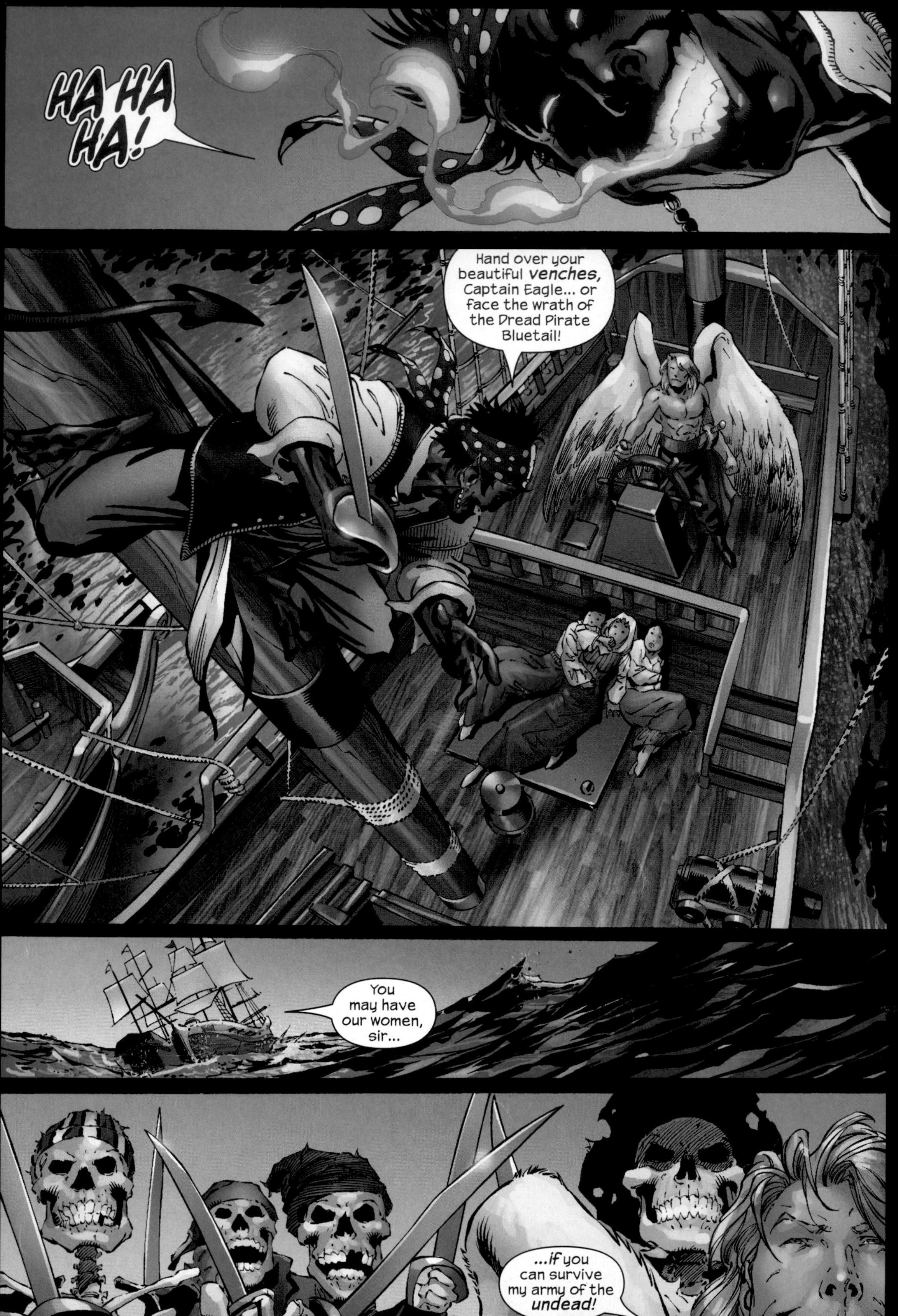
HA HA HA!
Hand over your beautiful venches, Captain Eagle... or face the wrath of the Dread Pirate Bluetail!
You may have our women, sir...
...if you can survive my army of the undead!

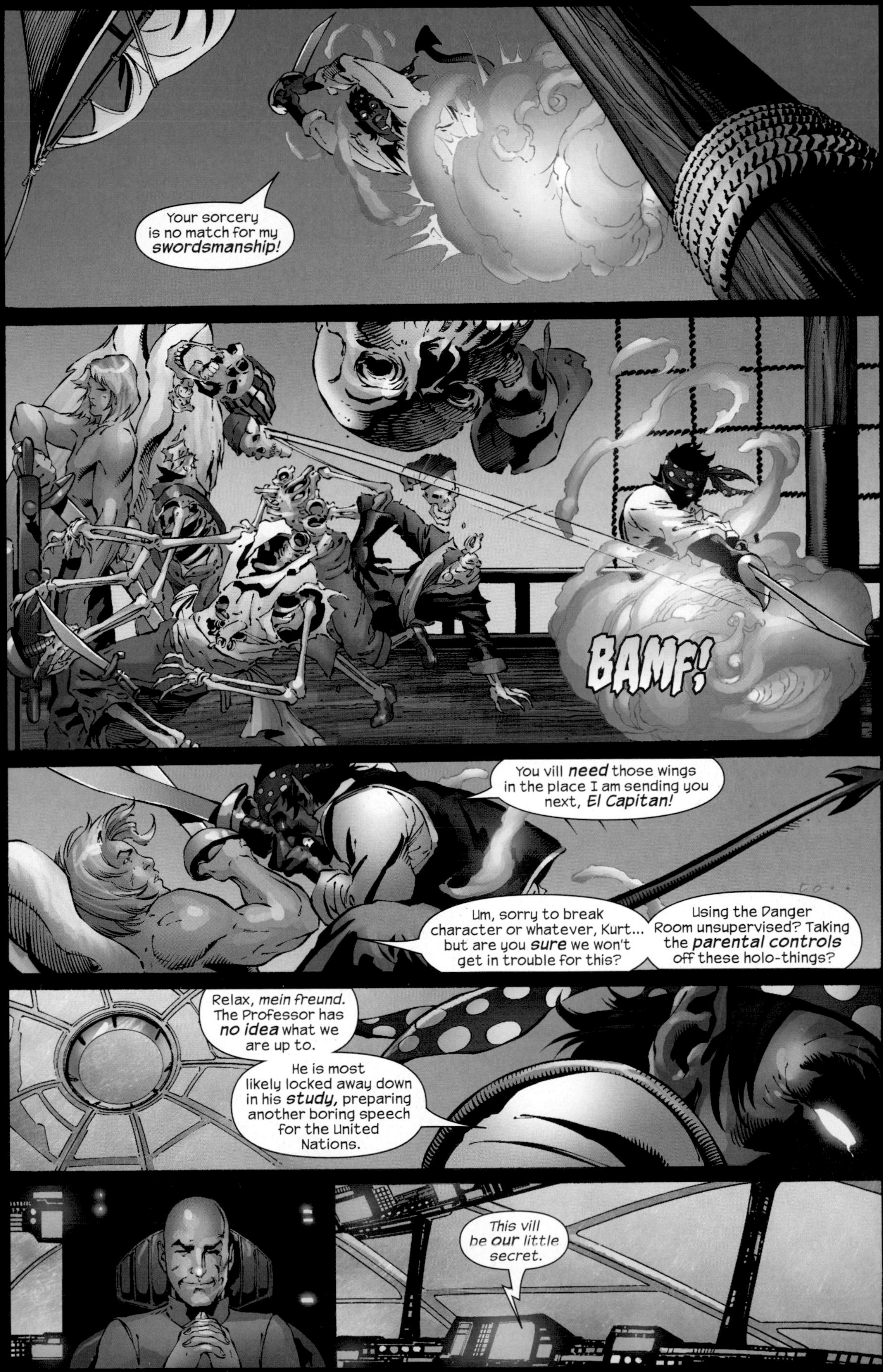

Your sorcery is no match for my swordsmanship!
BAMF!
You vill need those wings in the place I am sending you next, El Capitan!
Um, sorry to break character or whatever, Kurt... but are you sure we won't get in trouble for this?
Using the Danger Room unsupervised? Taking the parental controls off these holo-things?
Relax, mein freund. The Professor has no idea what we are up to.
He is most likely locked away down in his study, preparing another boring speech for the United Nations.
This vill be our little secret.

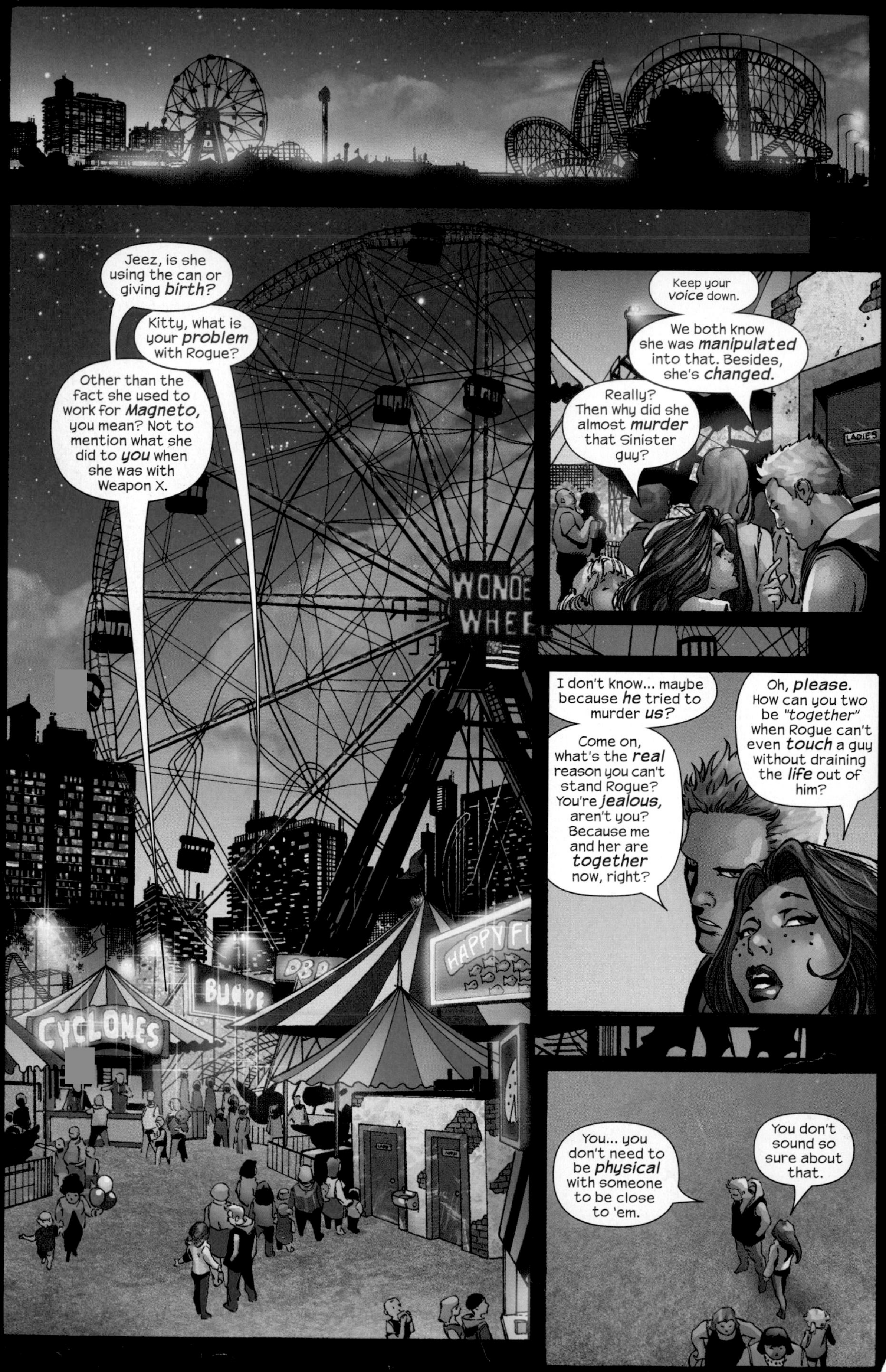

Jeez, is she using the can or giving birth?
Kitty, what is your problem with Rogue?
Other than the fact she used to work for Magneto, you mean? Not to mention what she did to you when she was with Weapon X.
Keep your voice down.
We both know she was manipulated into that. Besides, she's changed.
Really? Then why did she almost murder that Sinister guy?
LADIES
WONDER WHEEL
I don't know... maybe because he tried to murder us?
Come on, what's the real reason you can't stand Rogue? You're jealous, aren't you? Because me and her are together now, right?
Oh, please. How can you two be "together" when Rogue can't even touch a guy without draining the life out of him?
CYCLONES
You... you don't need to be physical with someone to be close to 'em.
You don't sound so sure about that.

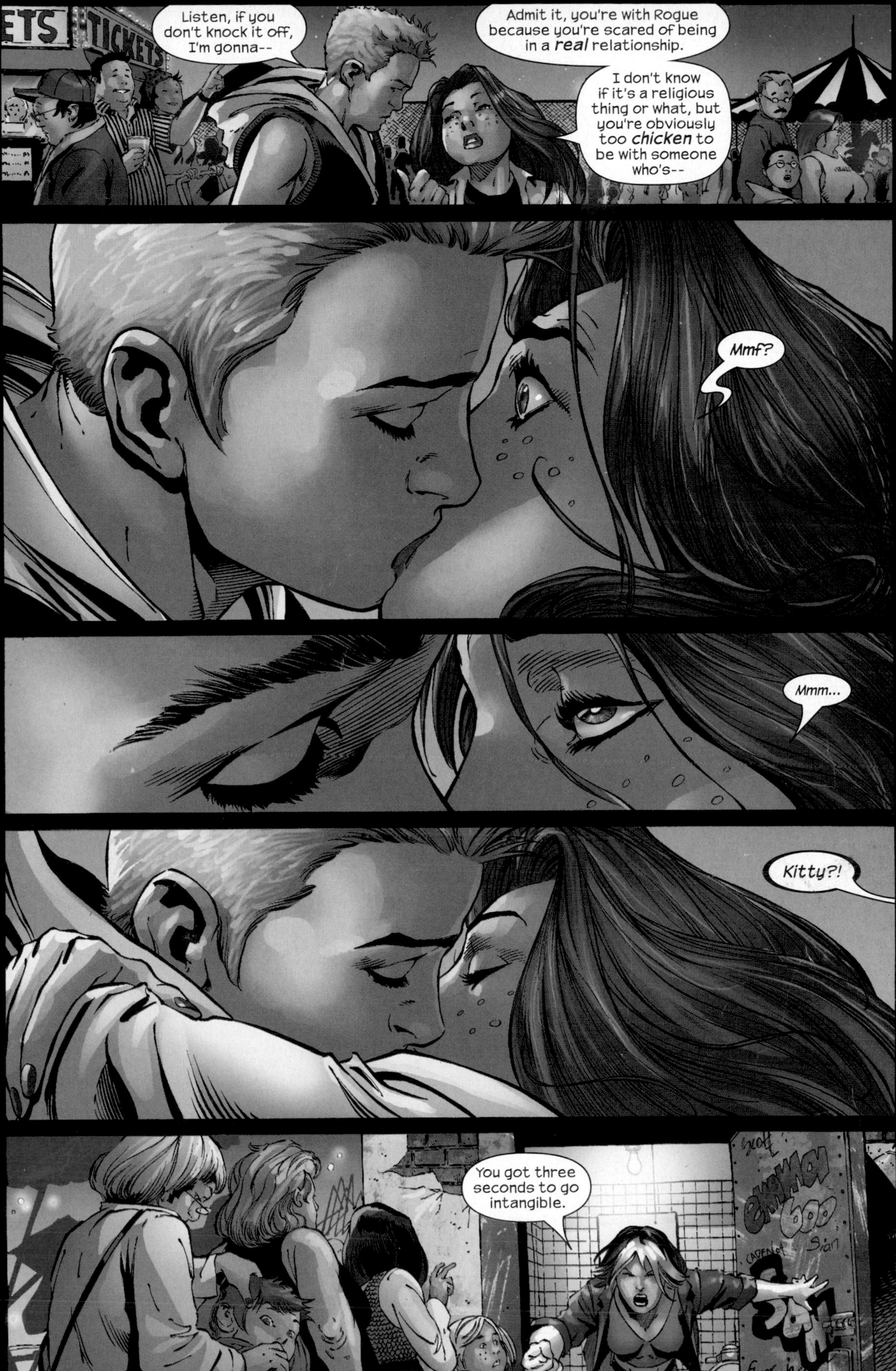

Listen, if you don't knock it off, I'm gonna--
Admit it, you're with Rogue because you're scared of being in a *real* relationship.
I don't know if it's a religious thing or what, but you're obviously too *chicken* to be with someone who's--
Mmf?
Mmm...
Kitty?!
You got three seconds to go intangible.

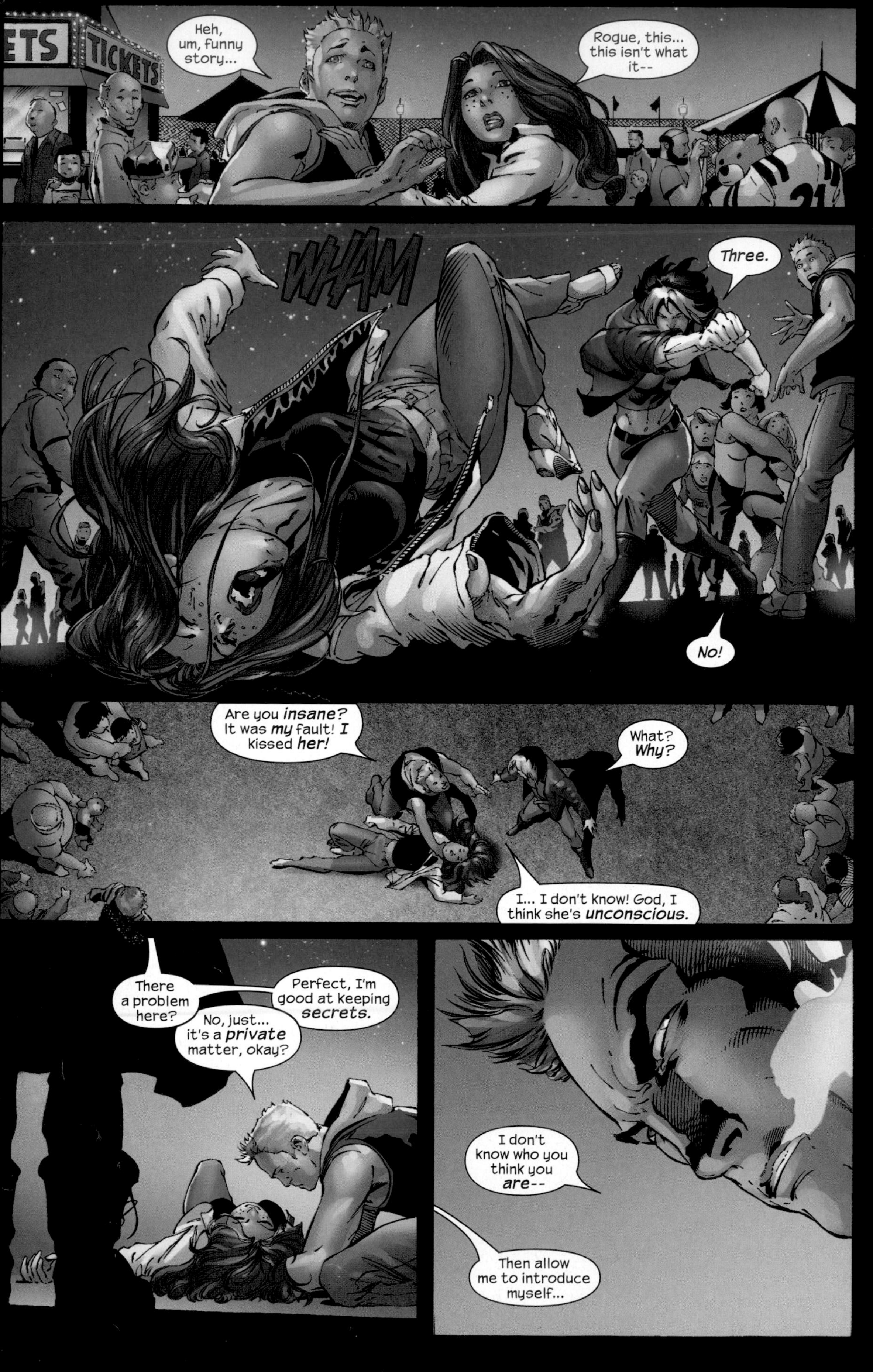

TICKETS
Heh, um, funny story...
Rogue, this... this isn't what it--
WHAM
Three.
No!
Are you insane? It was my fault! I kissed her!
What? Why?
I... I don't know! God, I think she's unconscious.
There a problem here?
No, just... it's a private matter, okay?
Perfect, I'm good at keeping secrets.
I don't know who you think you are--
Then allow me to introduce myself...

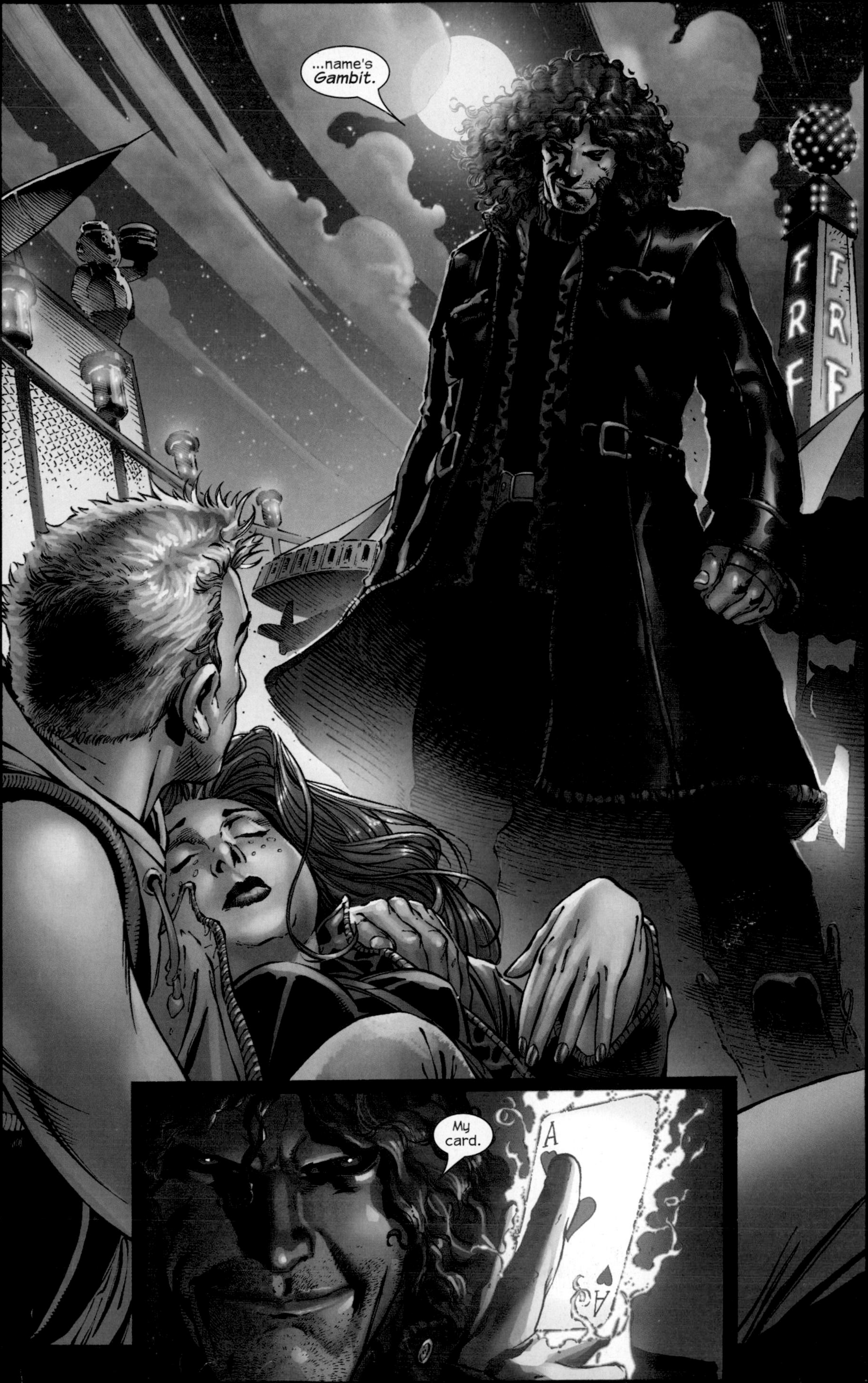
...name's Gambit.
FRF
FRF
My card.

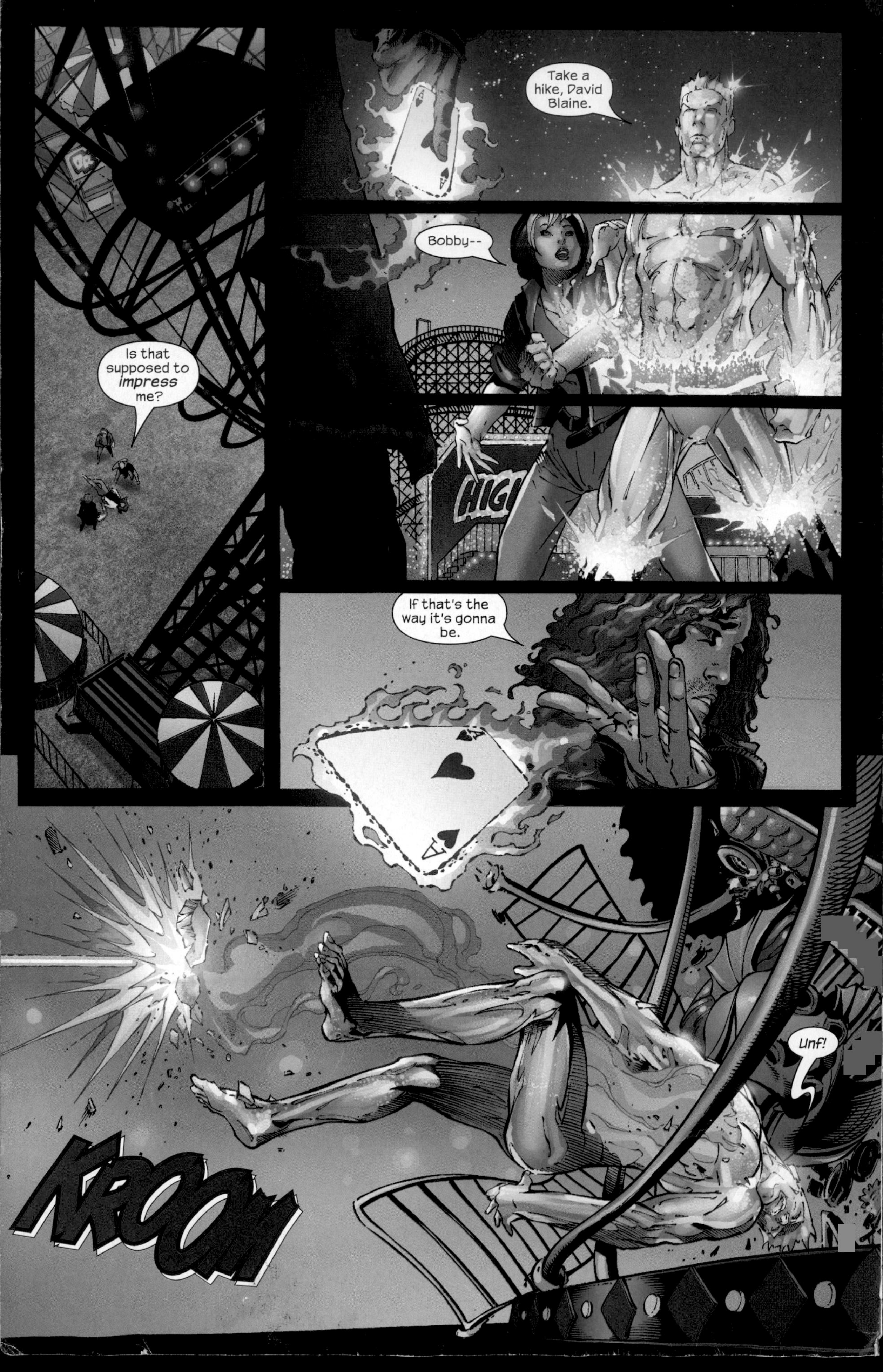
Is that supposed to *impress* me?
Take a hike, David Blaine.
Bobby--
If that's the way it's gonna be.
KROOM
Unf!

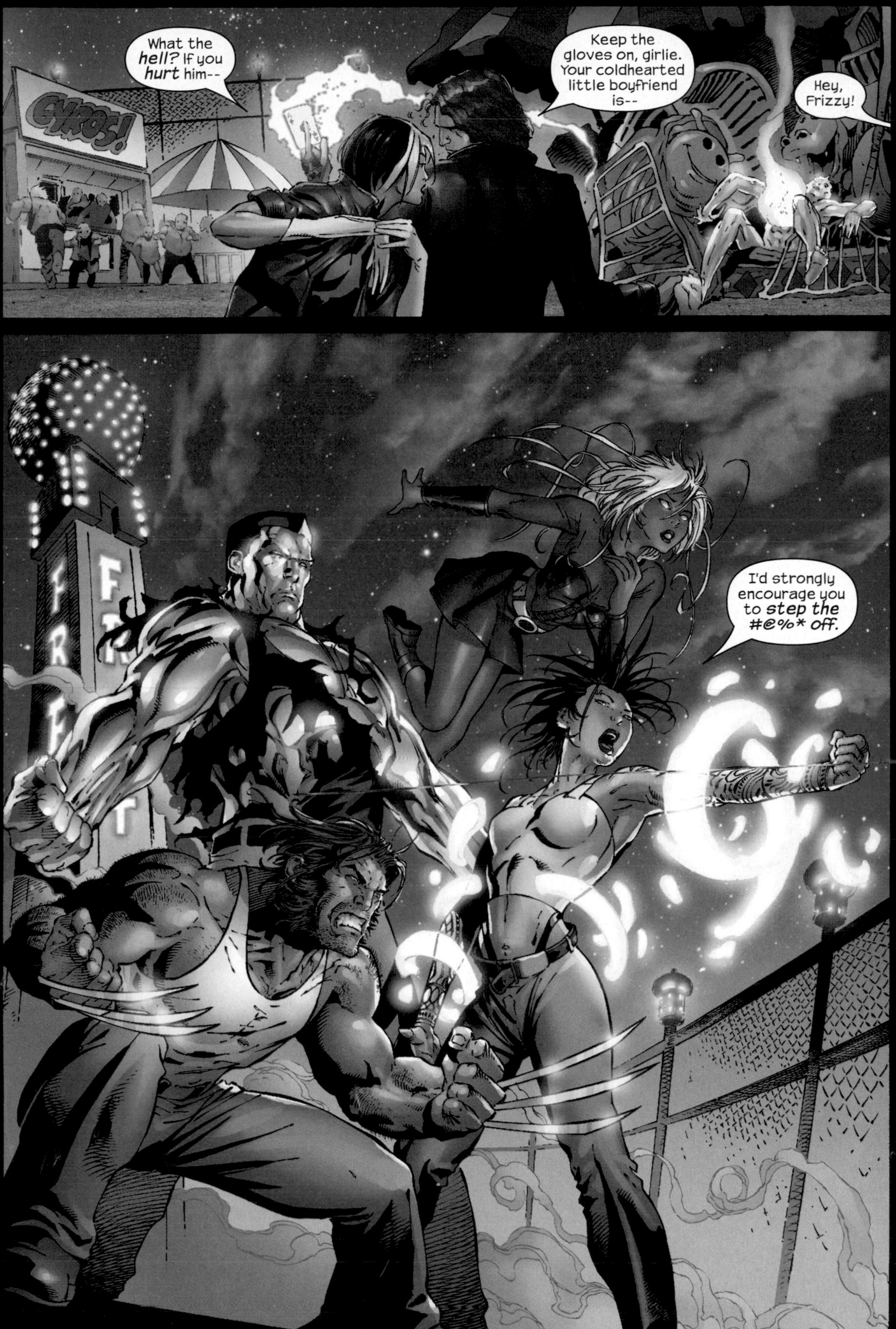
What the *hell?* If you *hurt* him--
GYROS!
Keep the gloves on, girlie. Your coldhearted little boyfriend is--
Hey, Frizzy!
I'd strongly encourage you to *step the #@%* off.*

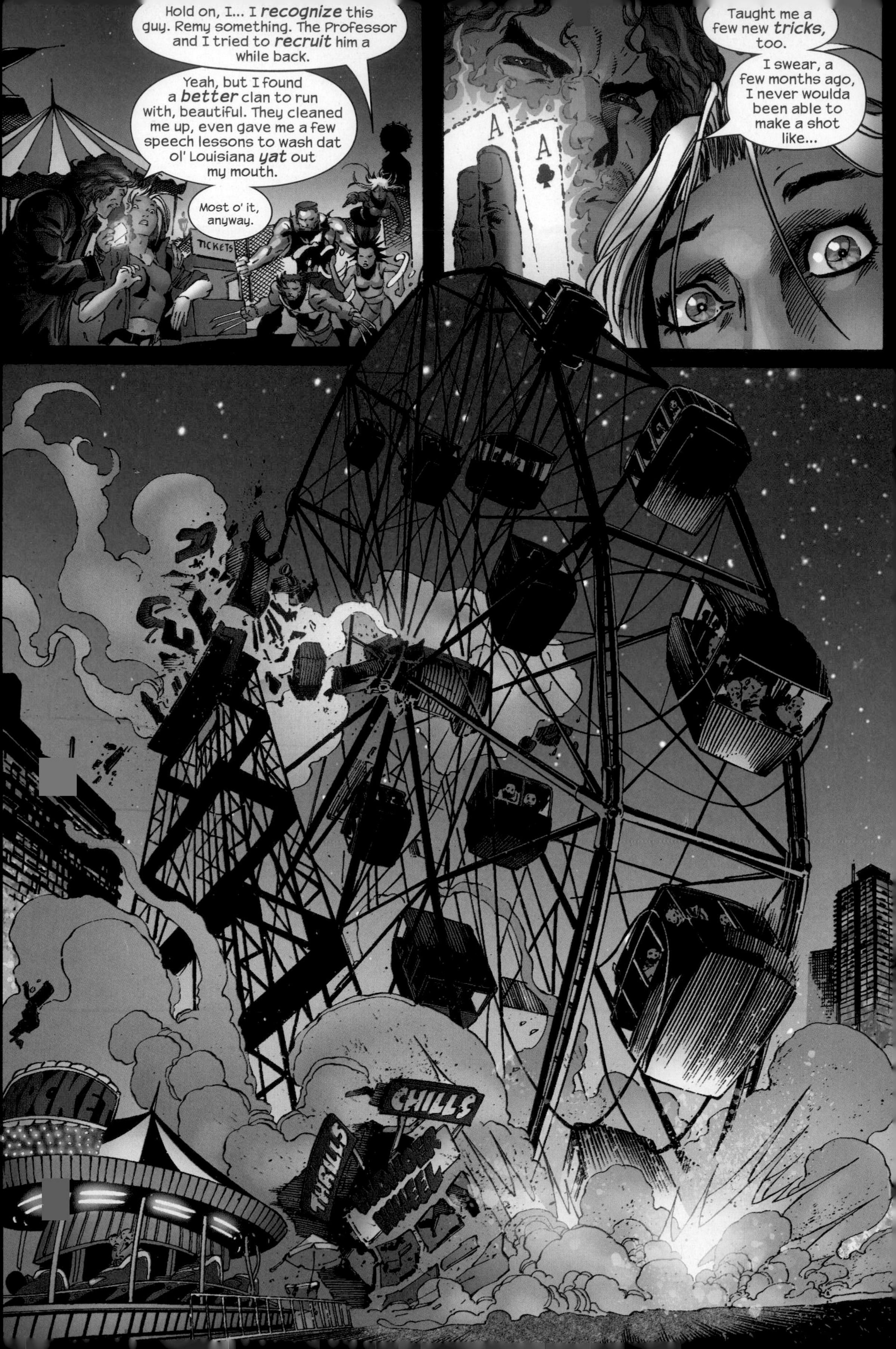
Hold on, I... I recognize this guy. Remy something. The Professor and I tried to recruit him a while back.
Yeah, but I found a better clan to run with, beautiful. They cleaned me up, even gave me a few speech lessons to wash dat ol' Louisiana yat out my mouth.
Most o' it, anyway.
TICKETS
Taught me a few new tricks, too.
I swear, a few months ago, I never woulda been able to make a shot like...
CHILLS
THRILLS

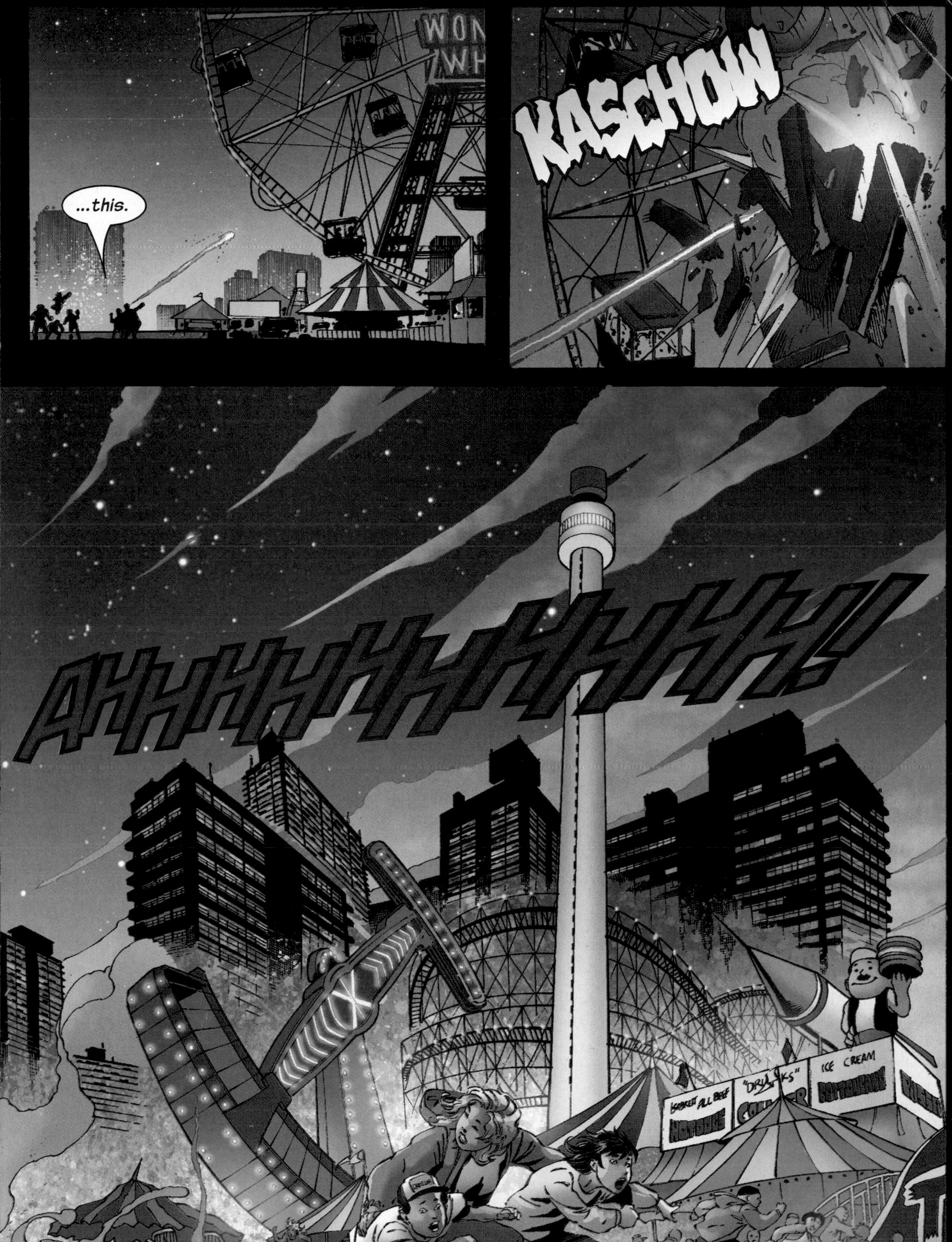
...this.
WON
WH
KASCHOW
AHHHHHHHHHHHHHH!
ICE CREAM
"DRI KS"
ALL BEEF

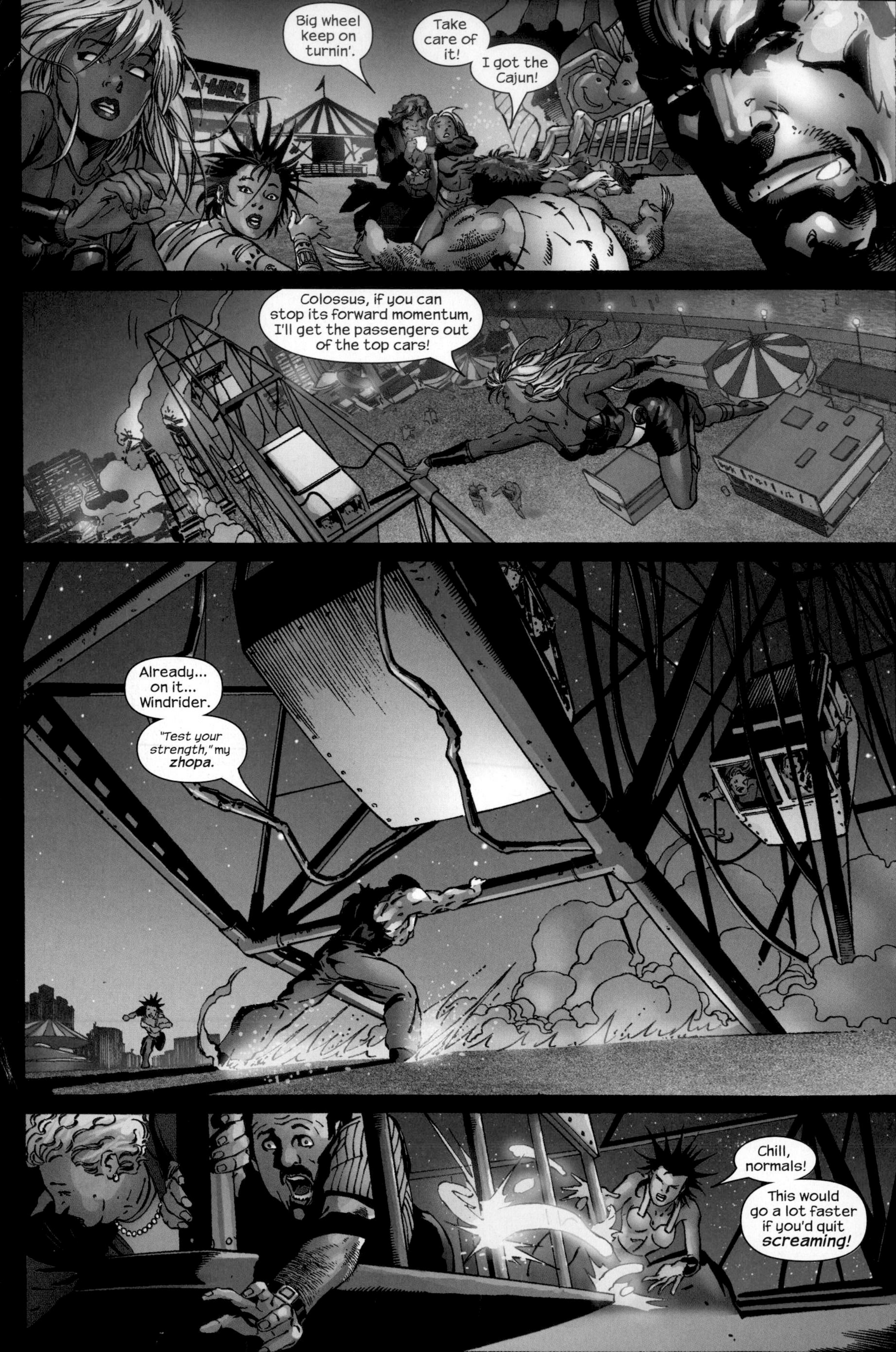

Big wheel keep on turnin'.
Take care of it!
I got the Cajun!
Colossus, if you can stop its forward momentum, I'll get the passengers out of the top cars!
Already... on it... Windrider.
"Test your strength," my *zhopa.*
Chill, normals!
This would go a lot faster if you'd quit *screaming!*

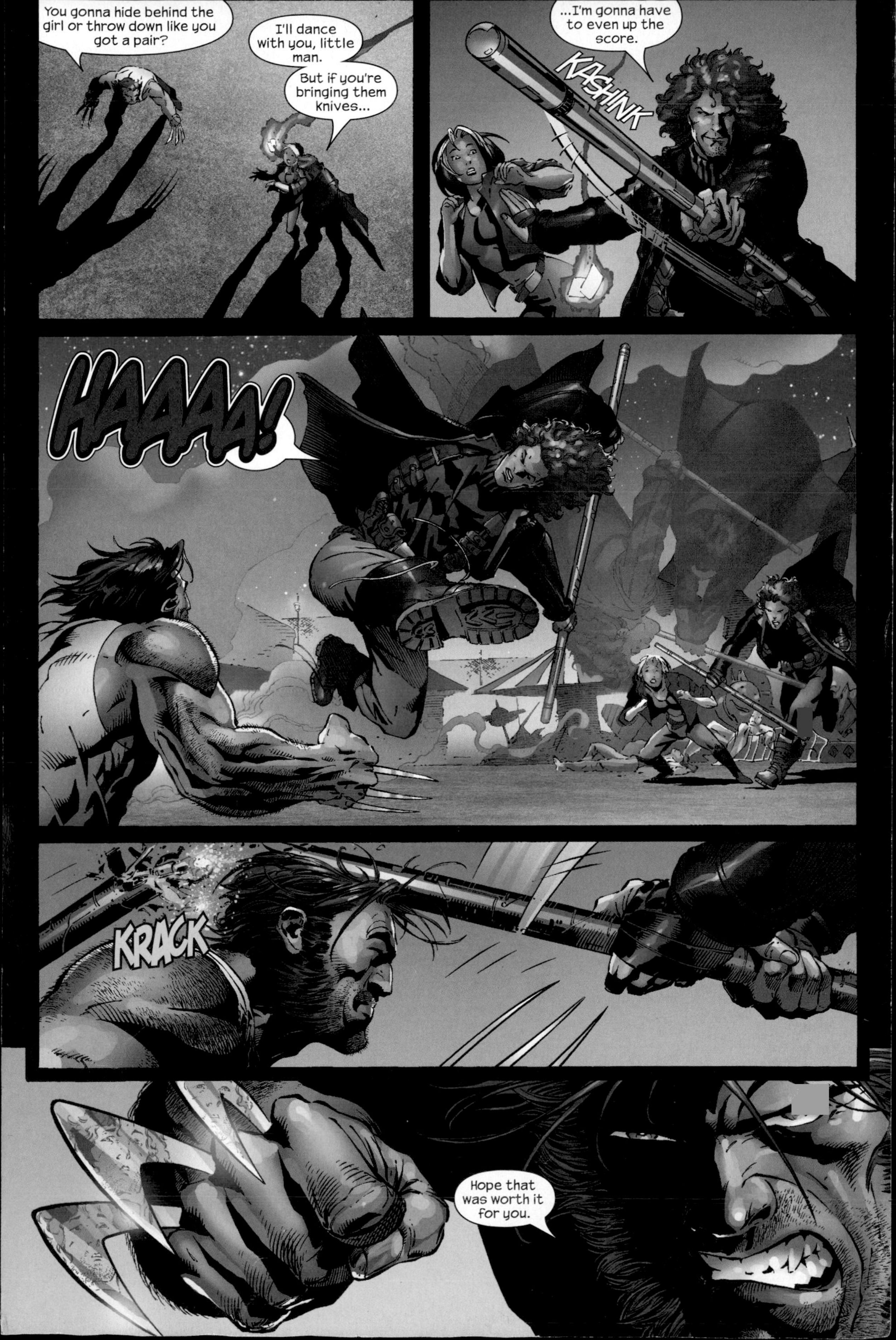

You gonna hide behind the girl or throw down like you got a pair?
I'll dance with you, little man.
But if you're bringing them knives...
...I'm gonna have to even up the score.
KASHINK
HAAAA!
KRACK
Hope that was worth it for you.

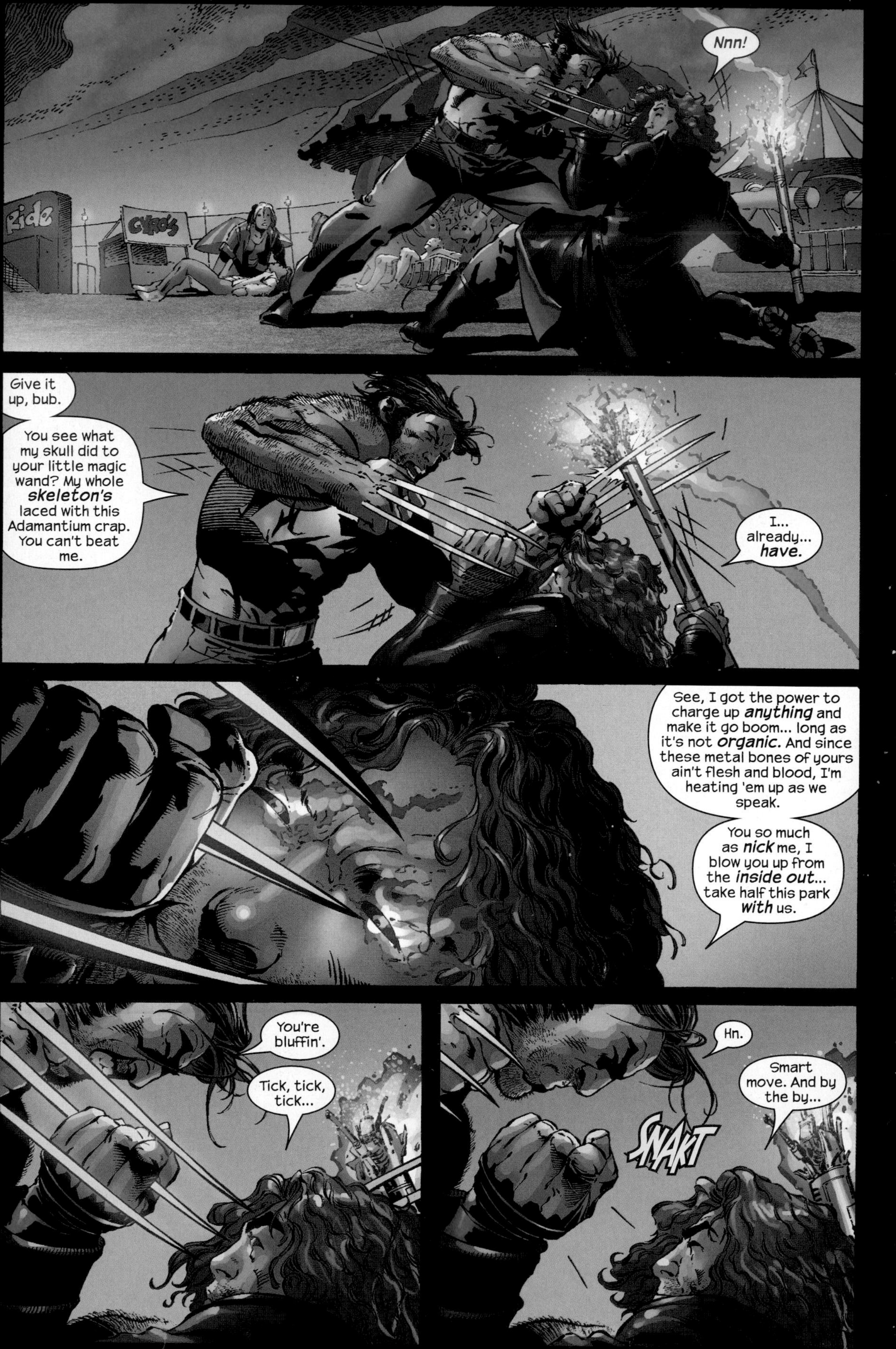

Nnn!
Give it up, bub.
You see what my skull did to your little magic wand? My whole skeleton's laced with this Adamantium crap. You can't beat me.
I... already... have.
See, I got the power to charge up anything and make it go boom... long as it's not organic. And since these metal bones of yours ain't flesh and blood, I'm heating 'em up as we speak.
You so much as nick me, I blow you up from the inside out... take half this park with us.
You're bluffin'.
Tick, tick, tick...
Hn.
SNAKT
Smart move. And by the by...

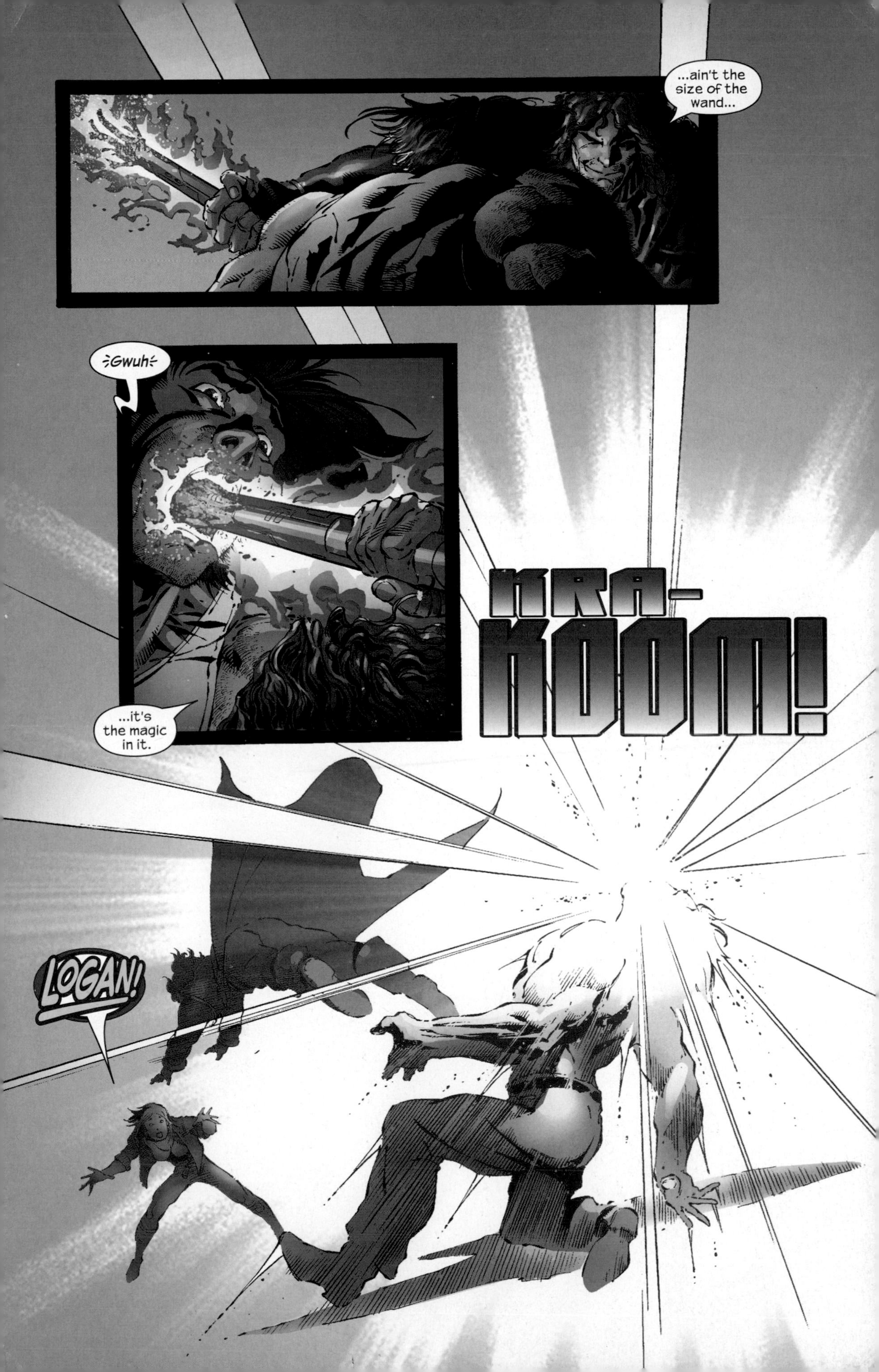

...ain't the size of the wand...
Gwuh
...it's the magic in it.
KRA-KOOM!
LOGAN!

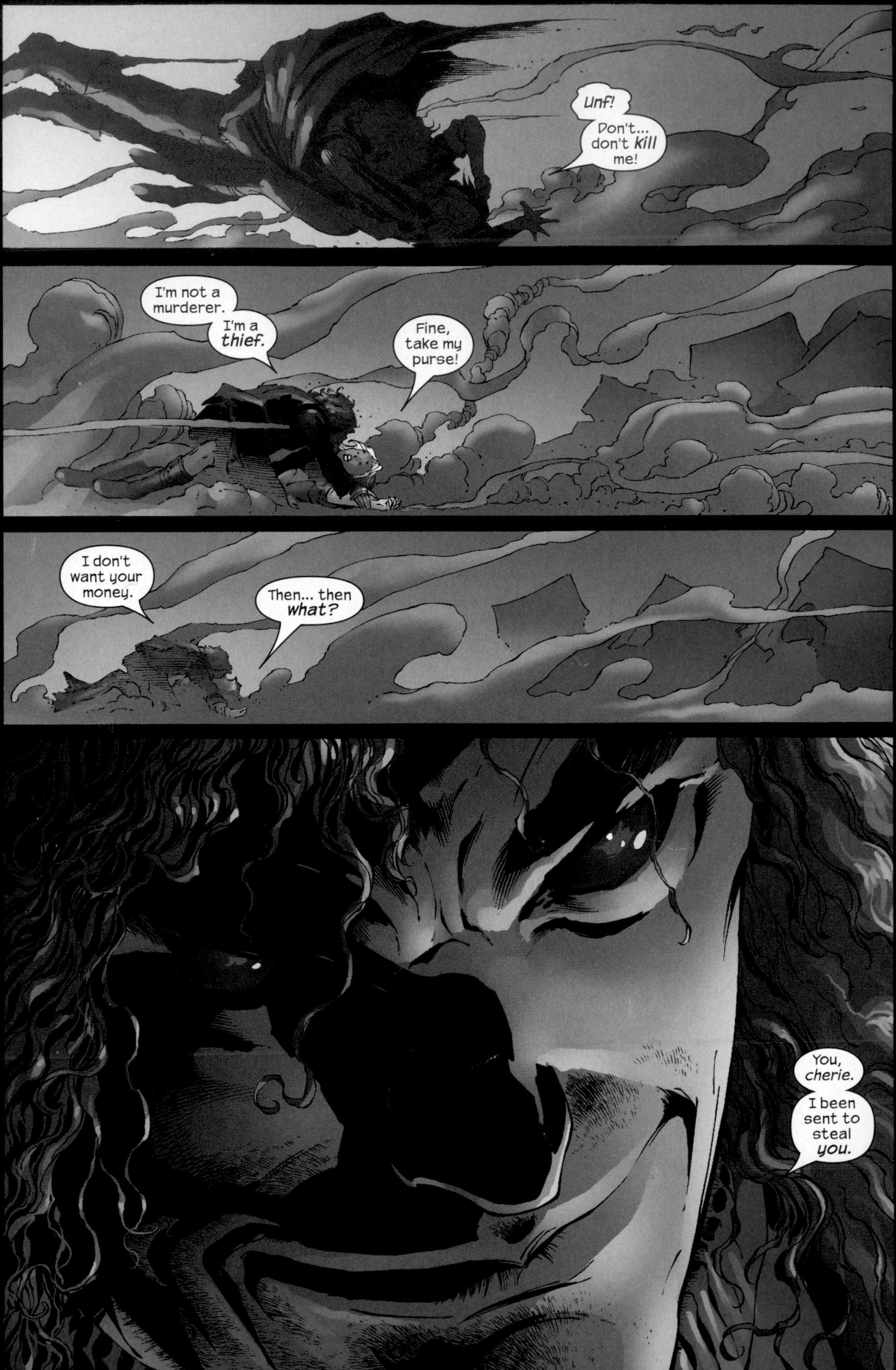
Unf!
Don't... don't *kill* me!
I'm not a murderer.
I'm a *thief*.
Fine, take my purse!
I don't want your money.
Then... then *what?*
You, *cherie*.
I been sent to steal *you*.

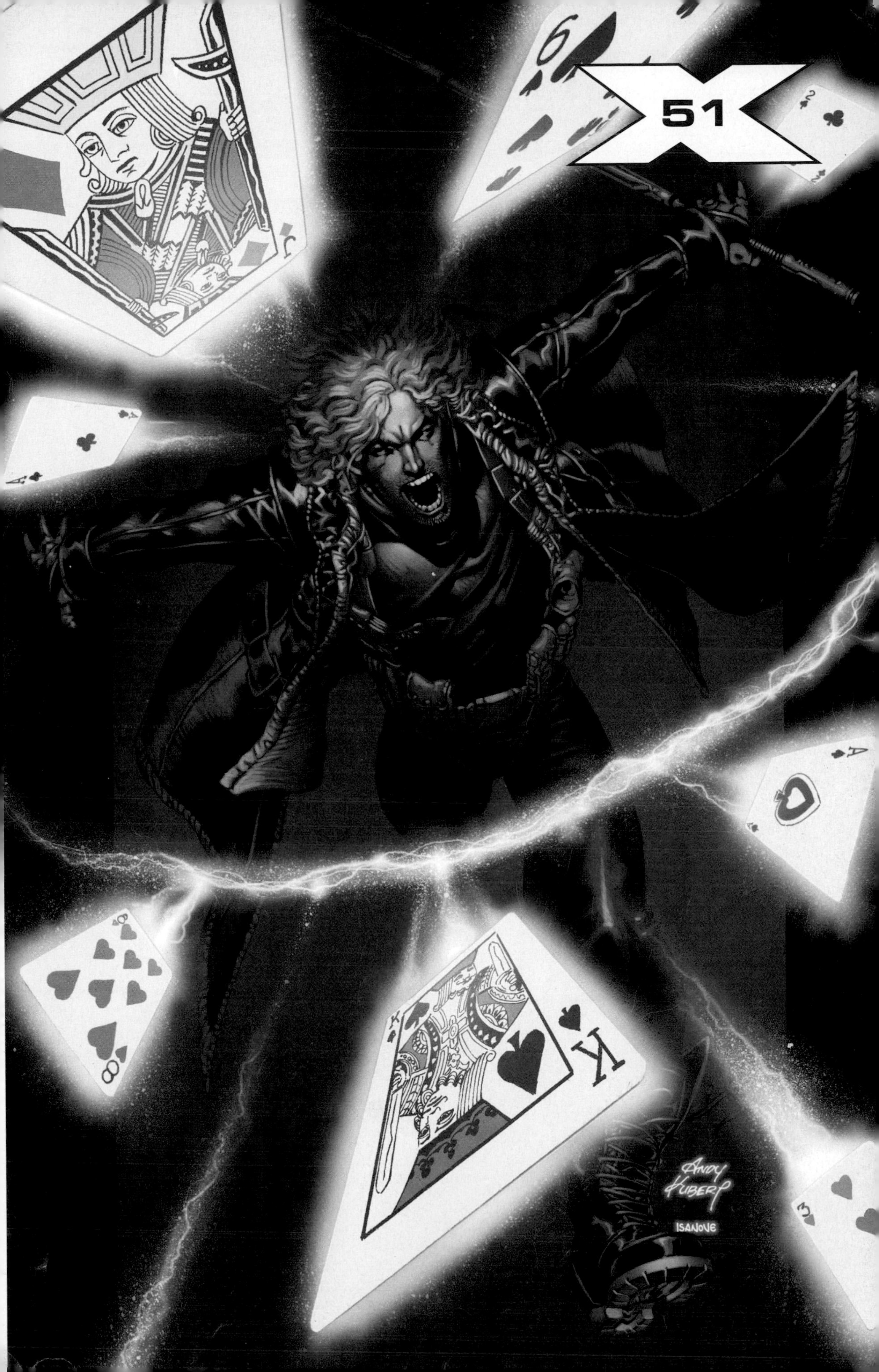
X
51
ANDY KUBERT
ISANOVE

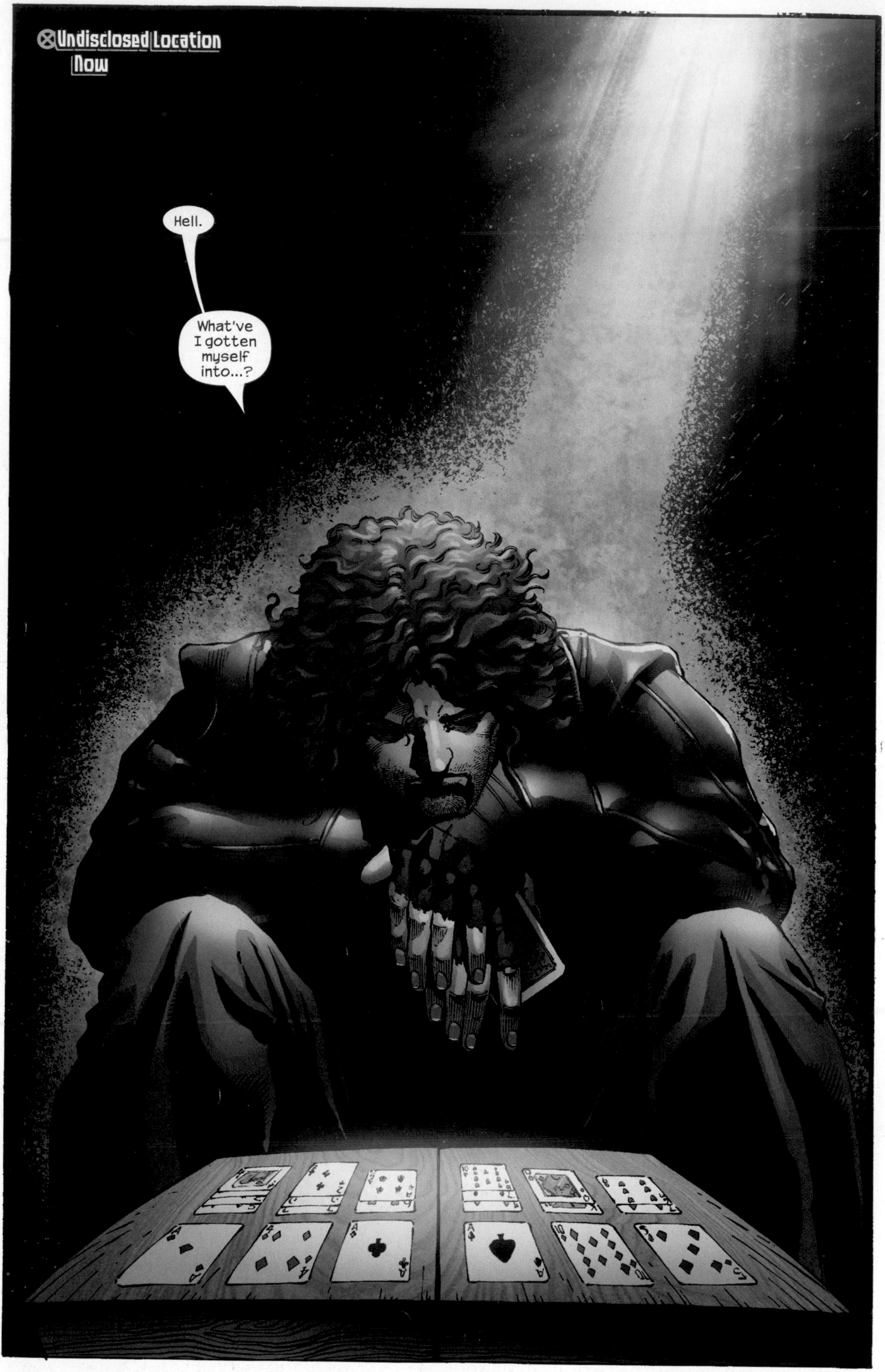
Undisclosed Location
Now
Hell.
What've I gotten myself into...?

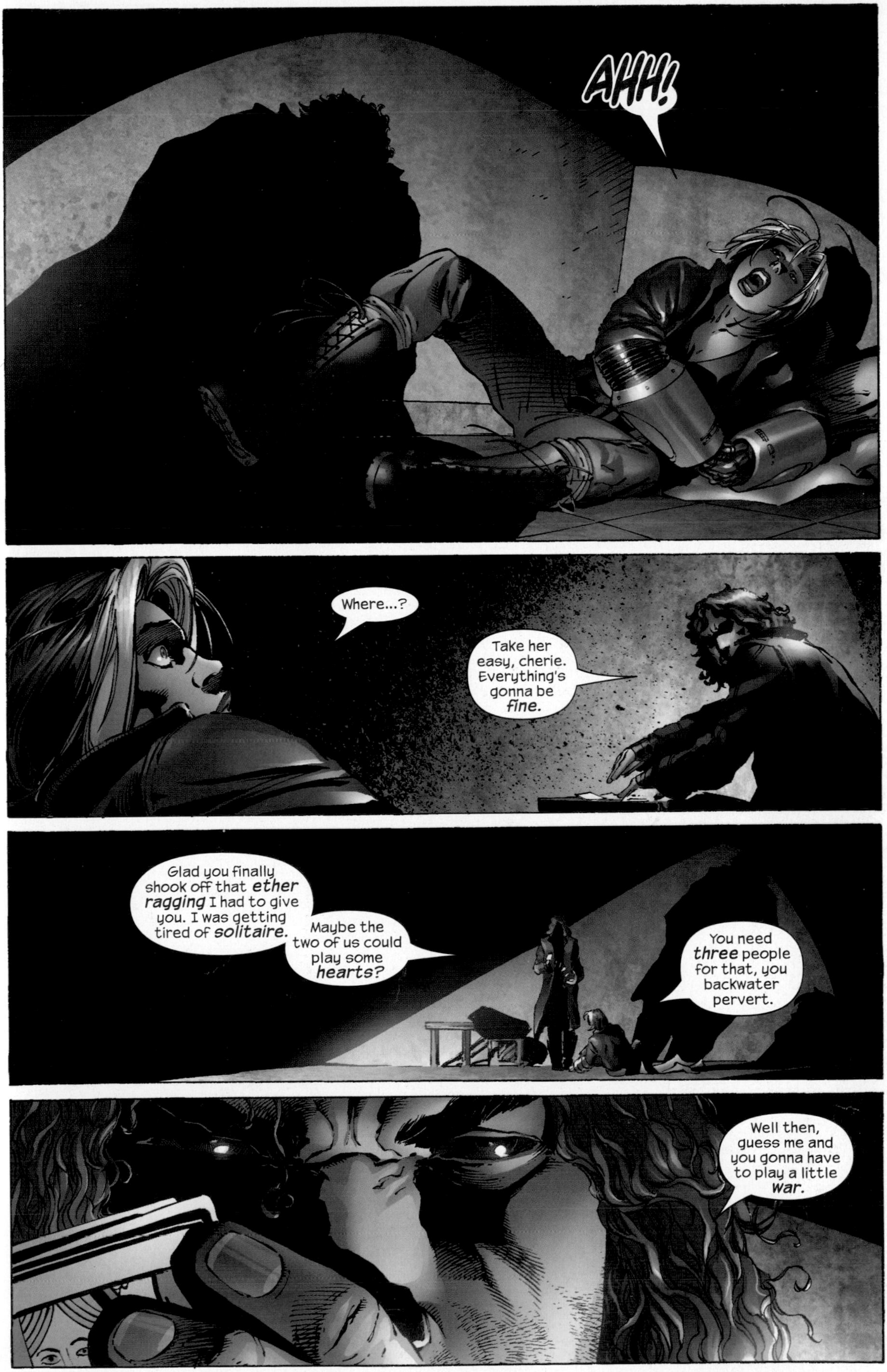
AHH!
Where...?
Take her easy, cherie. Everything's gonna be *fine.*
Glad you finally shook off that *ether ragging* I had to give you. I was getting tired of *solitaire.*
Maybe the two of us could play some *hearts?*
You need *three* people for that, you backwater pervert.
Well then, guess me and you gonna have to play a little *war.*

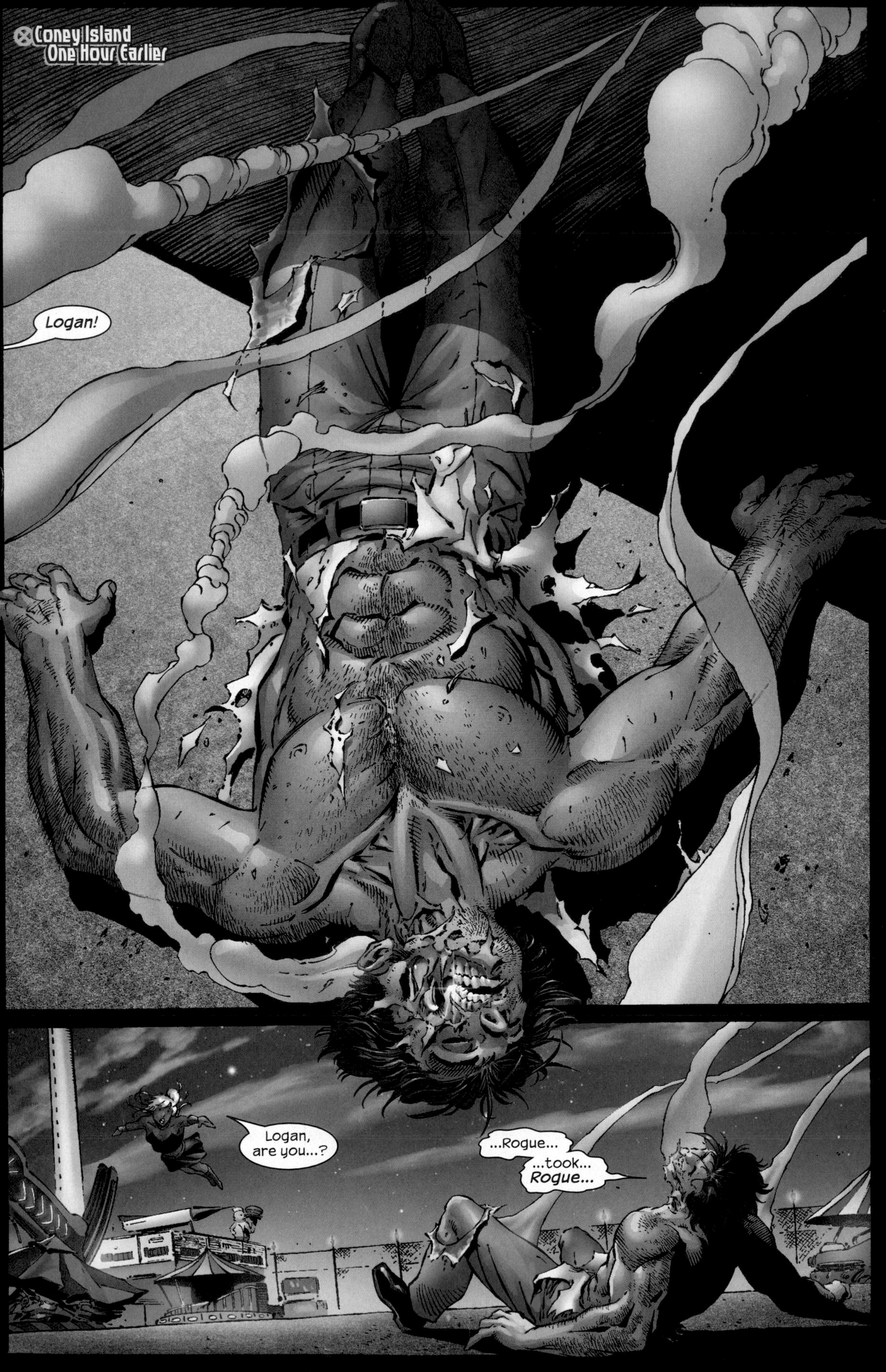
Coney Island
One Hour Earlier
Logan!
Logan,
are you...?
...Rogue...
...took...
Rogue...

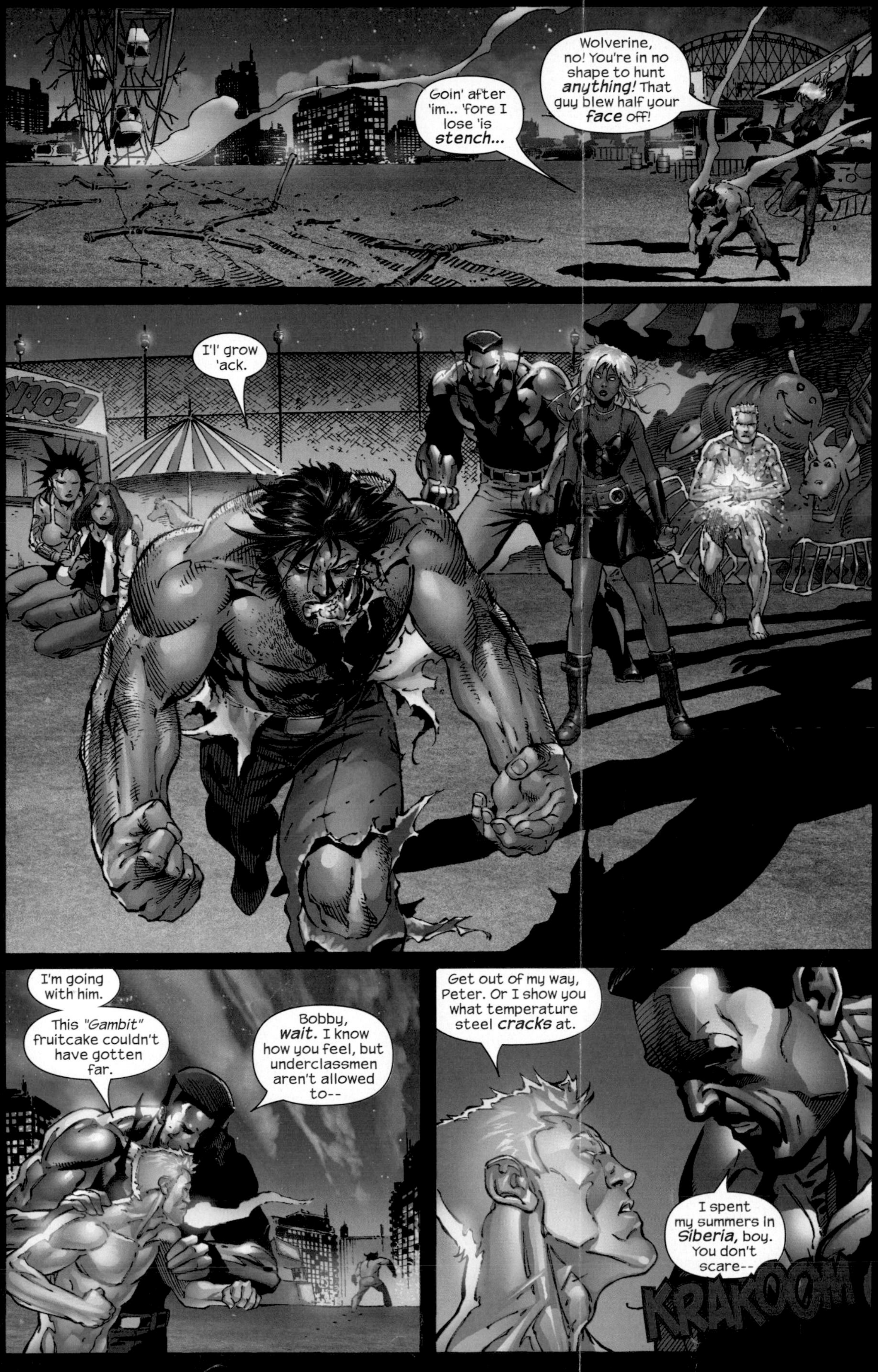
Goin' after 'im... 'fore I lose 'is stench...
Wolverine, no! You're in no shape to hunt anything! That guy blew half your face off!
I'l' grow 'ack.
I'm going with him.
This "Gambit" fruitcake couldn't have gotten far.
Bobby, wait. I know how you feel, but underclassmen aren't allowed to--
Get out of my way, Peter. Or I show you what temperature steel cracks at.
I spent my summers in Siberia, boy. You don't scare--
KRAKOOM

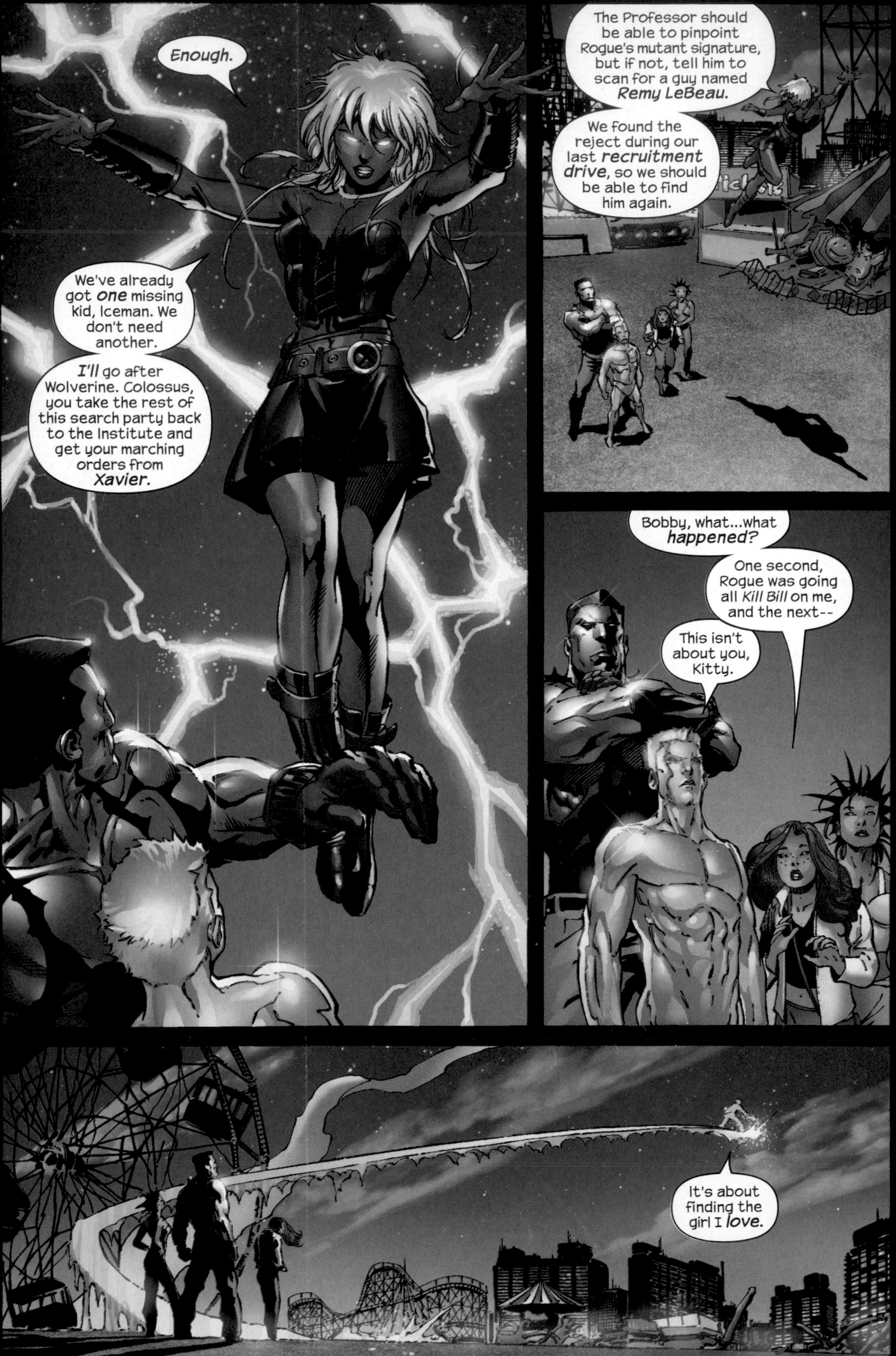
Enough.
We've already got one missing kid, Iceman. We don't need another.
I'll go after Wolverine. Colossus, you take the rest of this search party back to the Institute and get your marching orders from Xavier.
The Professor should be able to pinpoint Rogue's mutant signature, but if not, tell him to scan for a guy named Remy LeBeau.
We found the reject during our last recruitment drive, so we should be able to find him again.
Bobby, what...what happened?
One second, Rogue was going all Kill Bill on me, and the next--
This isn't about you, Kitty.
It's about finding the girl I love.

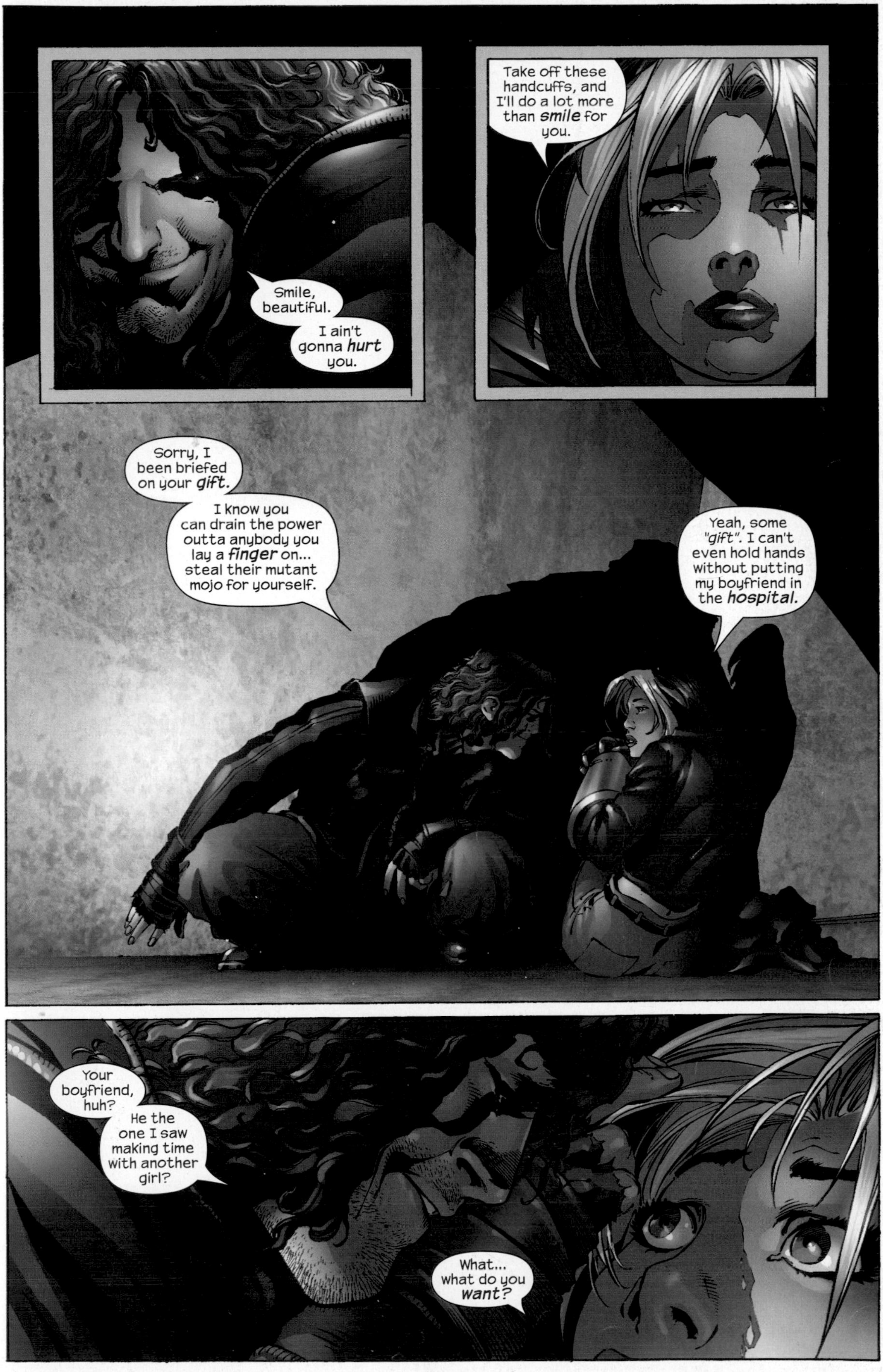
Smile, beautiful.
I ain't gonna *hurt* you.
Take off these handcuffs, and I'll do a lot more than *smile* for you.
Sorry, I been briefed on your *gift*.
I know you can drain the power outta anybody you lay a *finger* on... steal their mutant mojo for yourself.
Yeah, some "*gift*". I can't even hold hands without putting my boyfriend in the *hospital*.
Your boyfriend, huh?
He the one I saw making time with another girl?
What... what do you *want?*

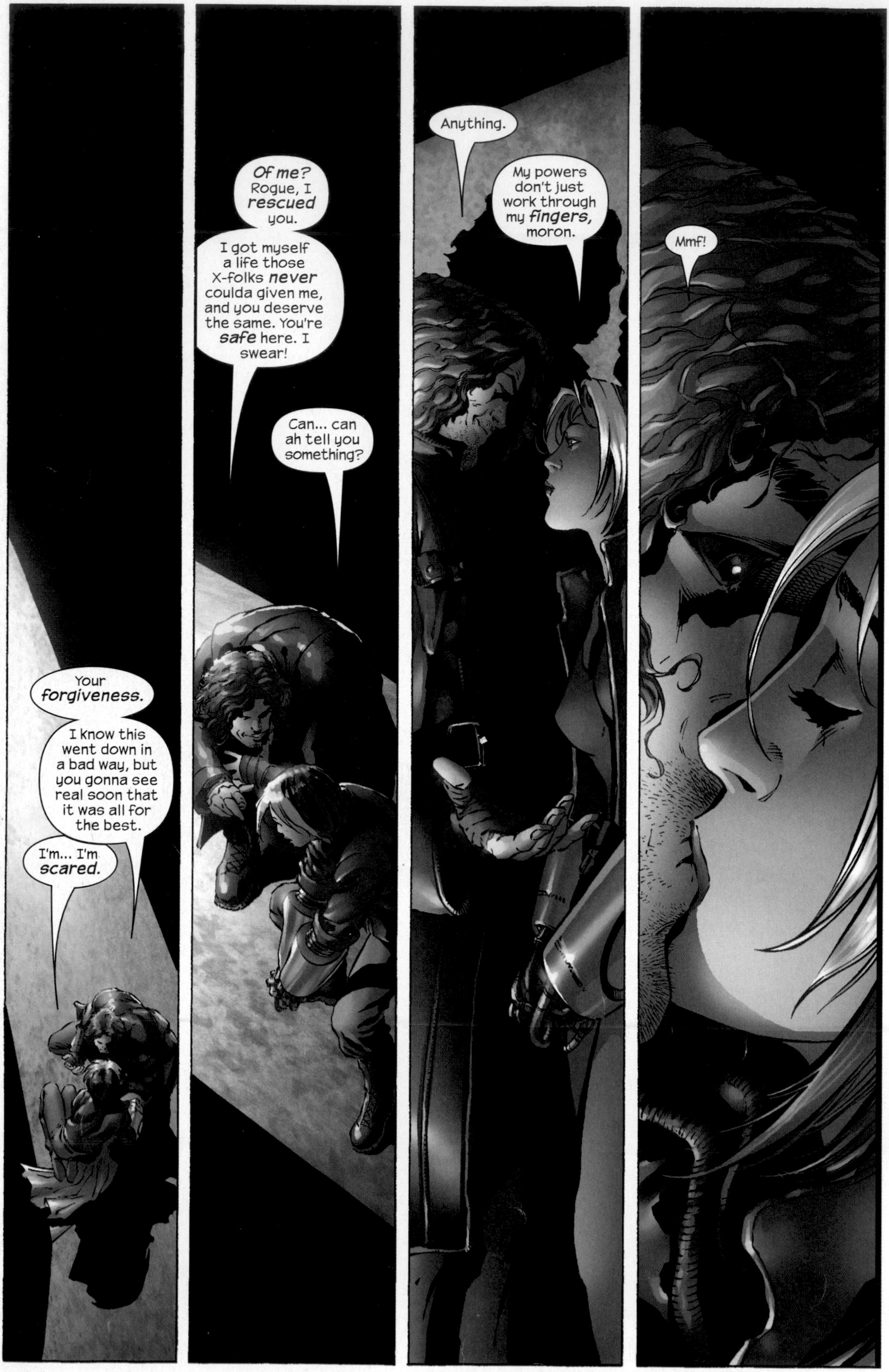
Your forgiveness.
I know this went down in a bad way, but you gonna see real soon that it was all for the best.
I'm... I'm scared.
Of me? Rogue, I rescued you.
I got myself a life those X-folks never coulda given me, and you deserve the same. You're safe here. I swear!
Can... can ah tell you something?
Anything.
My powers don't just work through my fingers, moron.
Mmf!

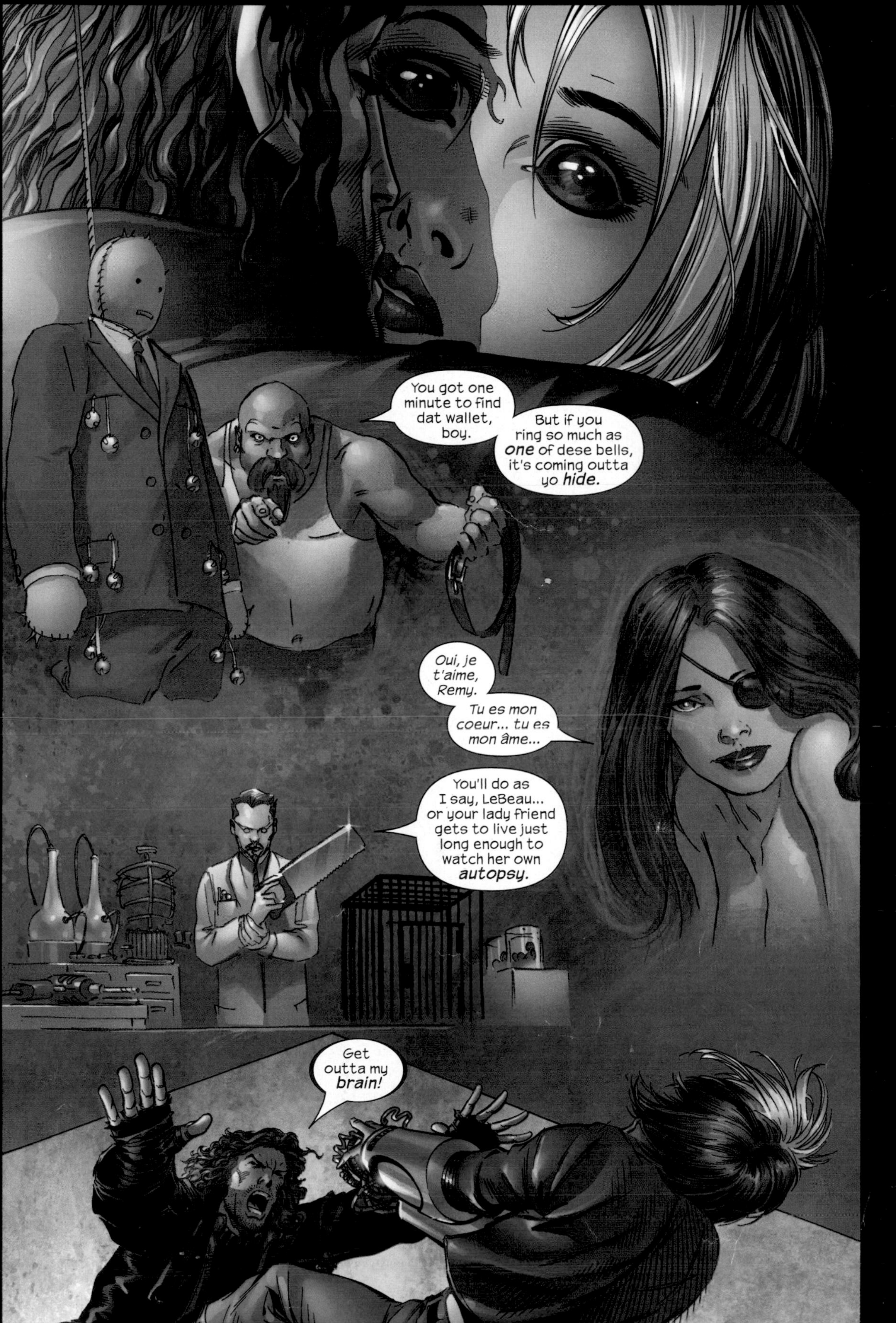
You got one minute to find dat wallet, boy.
But if you ring so much as *one* of dese bells, it's coming outta yo *hide.*
Oui, je t'aime, Remy.
Tu es mon coeur... tu es mon âme...
You'll do as I say, LeBeau... or your lady friend gets to live just long enough to watch her own *autopsy*.
Get outta my *brain!*

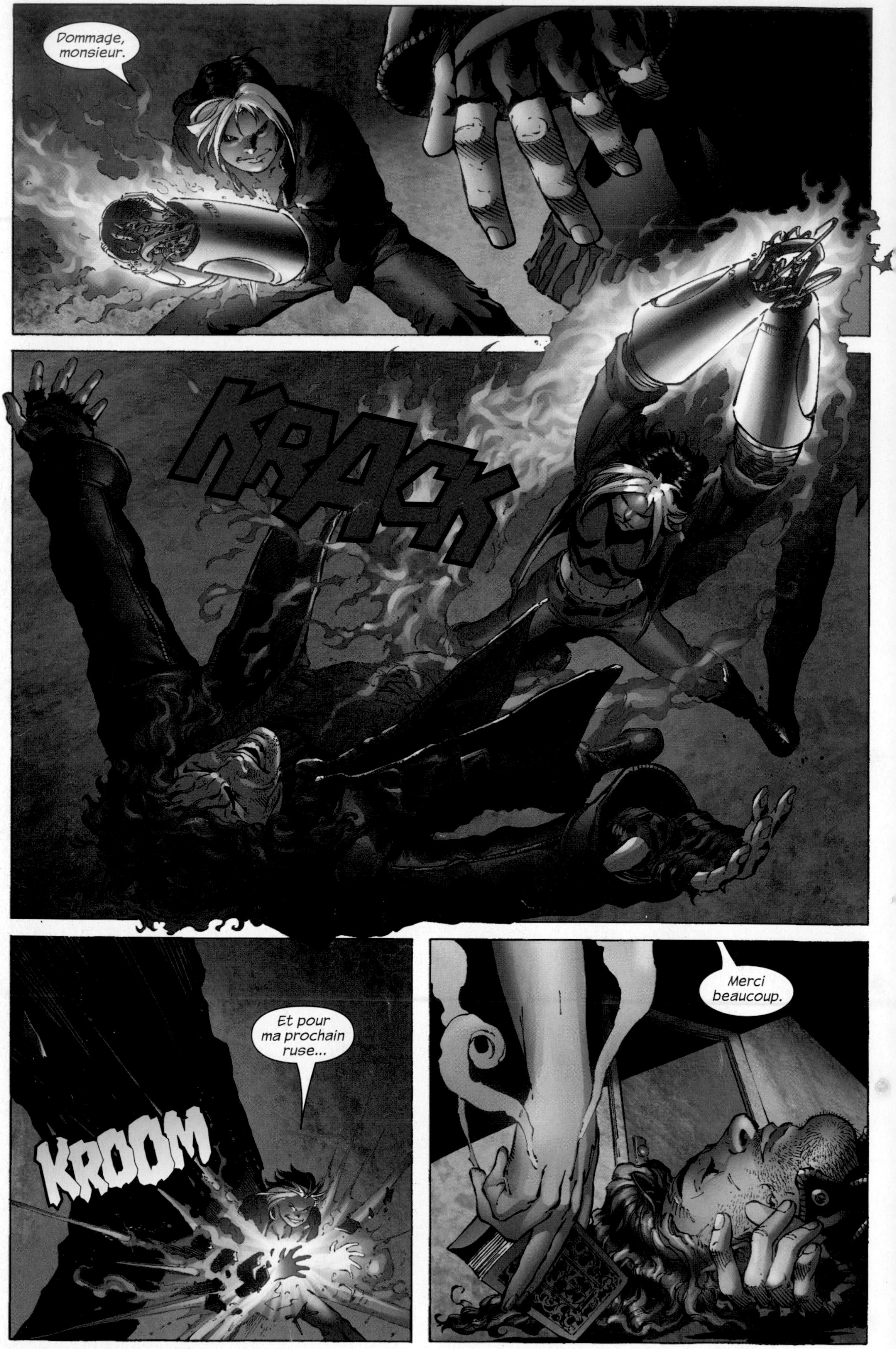
Dommage, monsieur.
KRACK
Et pour ma prochain ruse...
KROOM
Merci beaucoup.

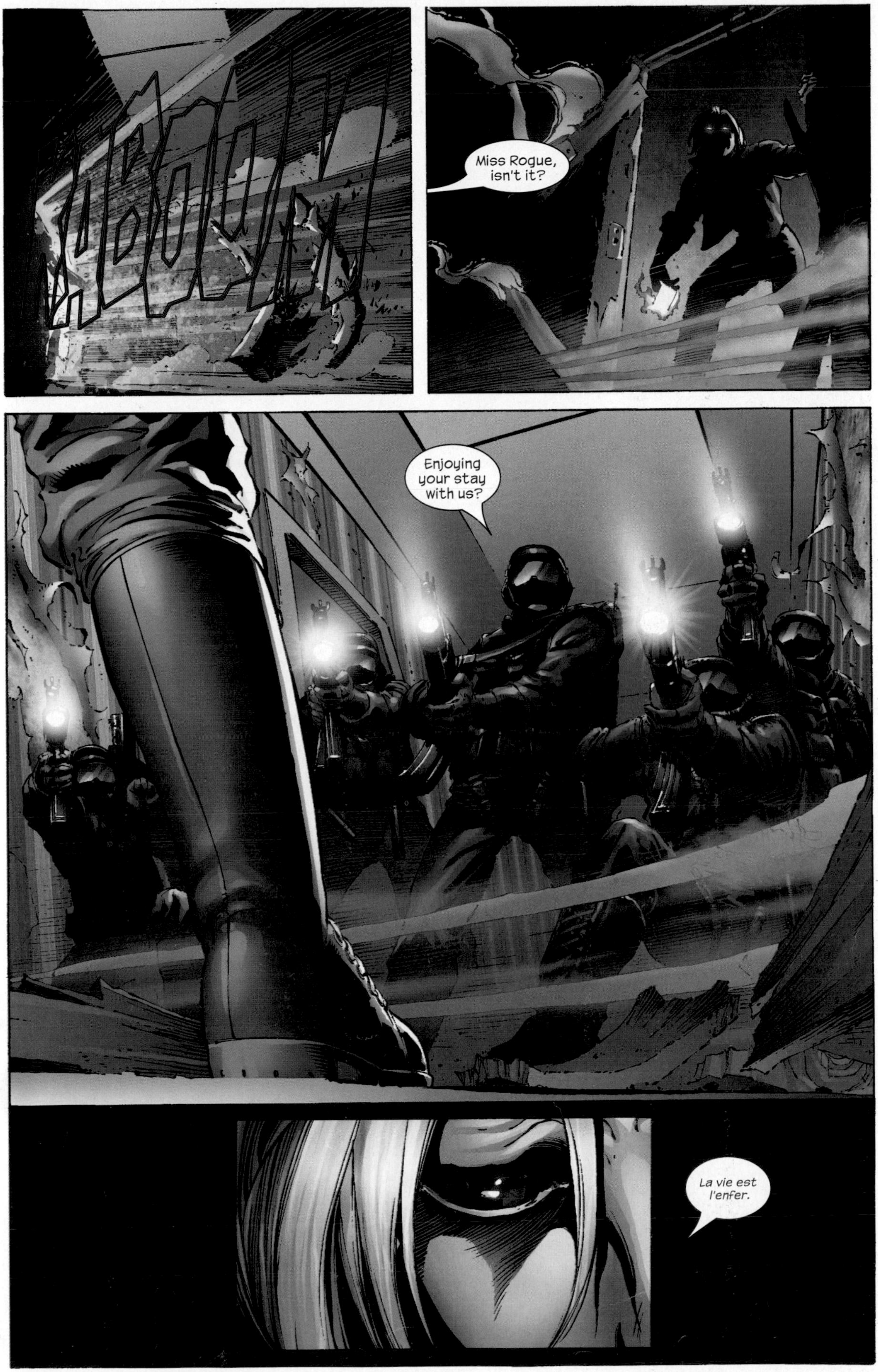
Miss Rogue, isn't it?
Enjoying your stay with us?
La vie est l'enfer.

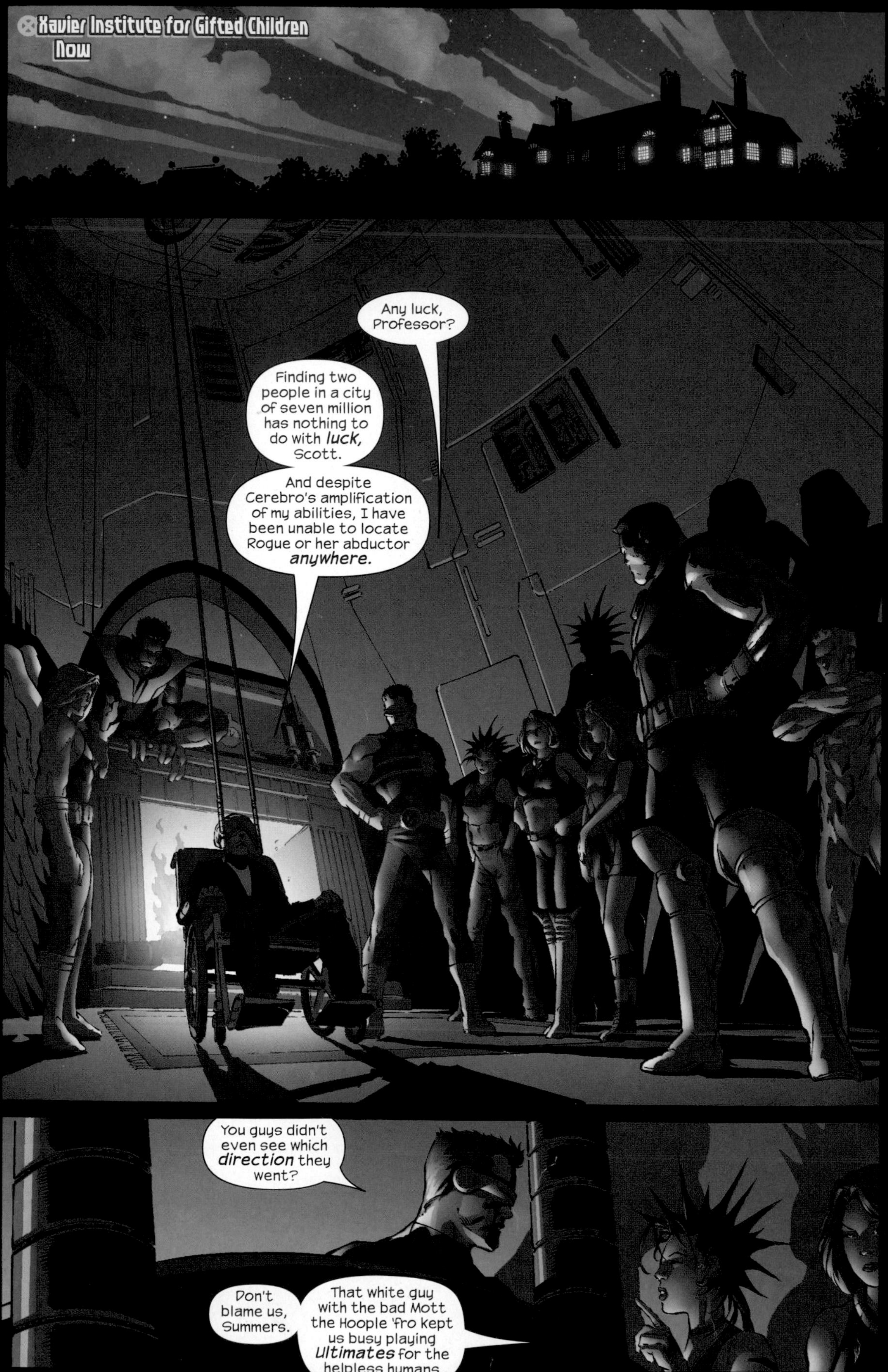
Xavier Institute for Gifted Children
Now
Any luck, Professor?
Finding two people in a city of seven million has nothing to do with *luck,* Scott.
And despite Cerebro's amplification of my abilities, I have been unable to locate Rogue or her abductor *anywhere.*
You guys didn't even see which *direction* they went?
Don't blame us, Summers.
That white guy with the bad Mott the Hoople 'fro kept us busy playing *Ultimates* for the helpless humans.

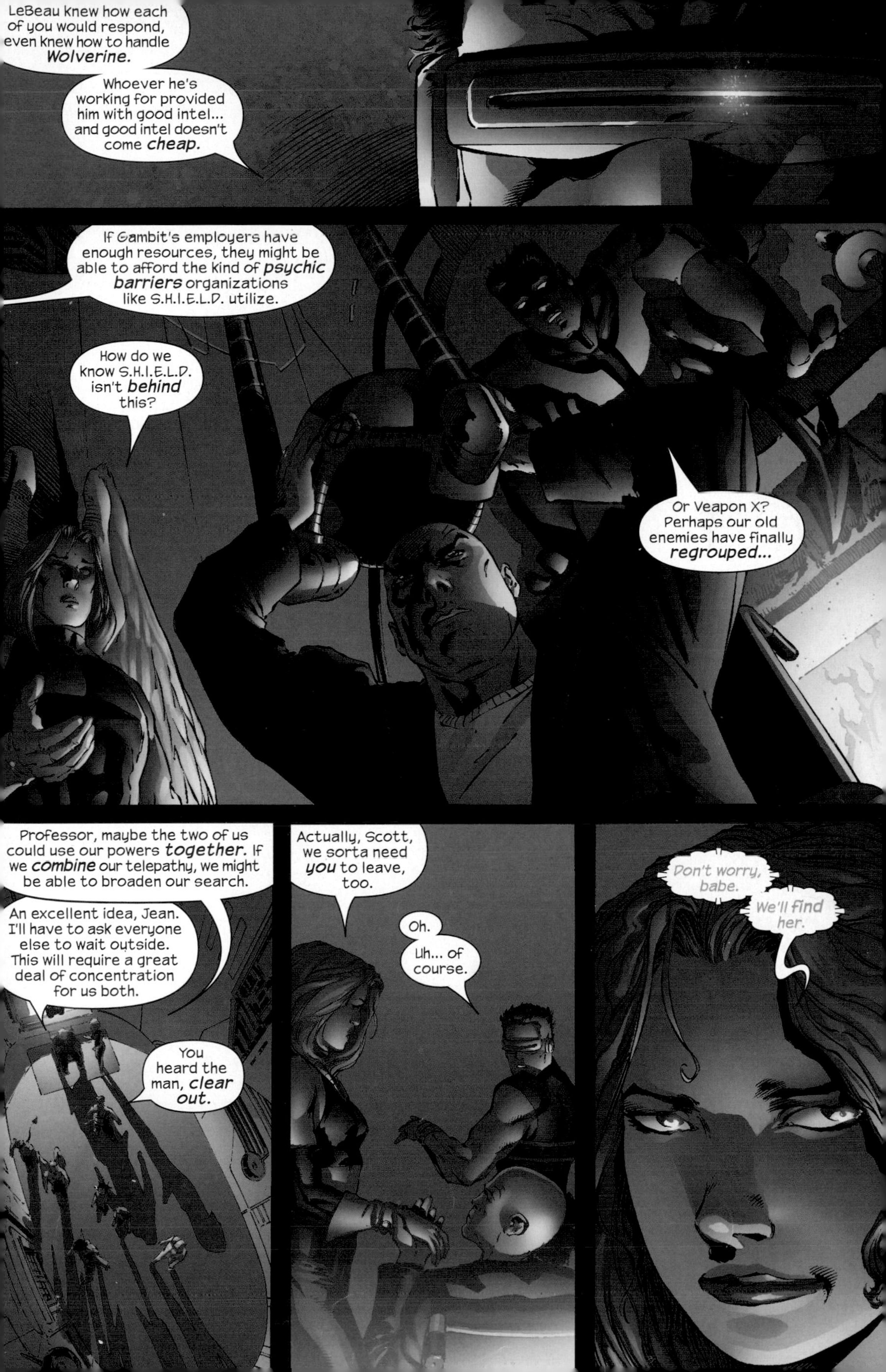
LeBeau knew how each of you would respond, even knew how to handle Wolverine.
Whoever he's working for provided him with good intel... and good intel doesn't come cheap.
If Gambit's employers have enough resources, they might be able to afford the kind of psychic barriers organizations like S.H.I.E.L.D. utilize.
How do we know S.H.I.E.L.D. isn't behind this?
Or Veapon X? Perhaps our old enemies have finally regrouped...
Professor, maybe the two of us could use our powers together. If we combine our telepathy, we might be able to broaden our search.
An excellent idea, Jean. I'll have to ask everyone else to wait outside. This will require a great deal of concentration for us both.
You heard the man, clear out.
Actually, Scott, we sorta need you to leave, too.
Oh.
Uh... of course.
Don't worry, babe.
We'll find her.

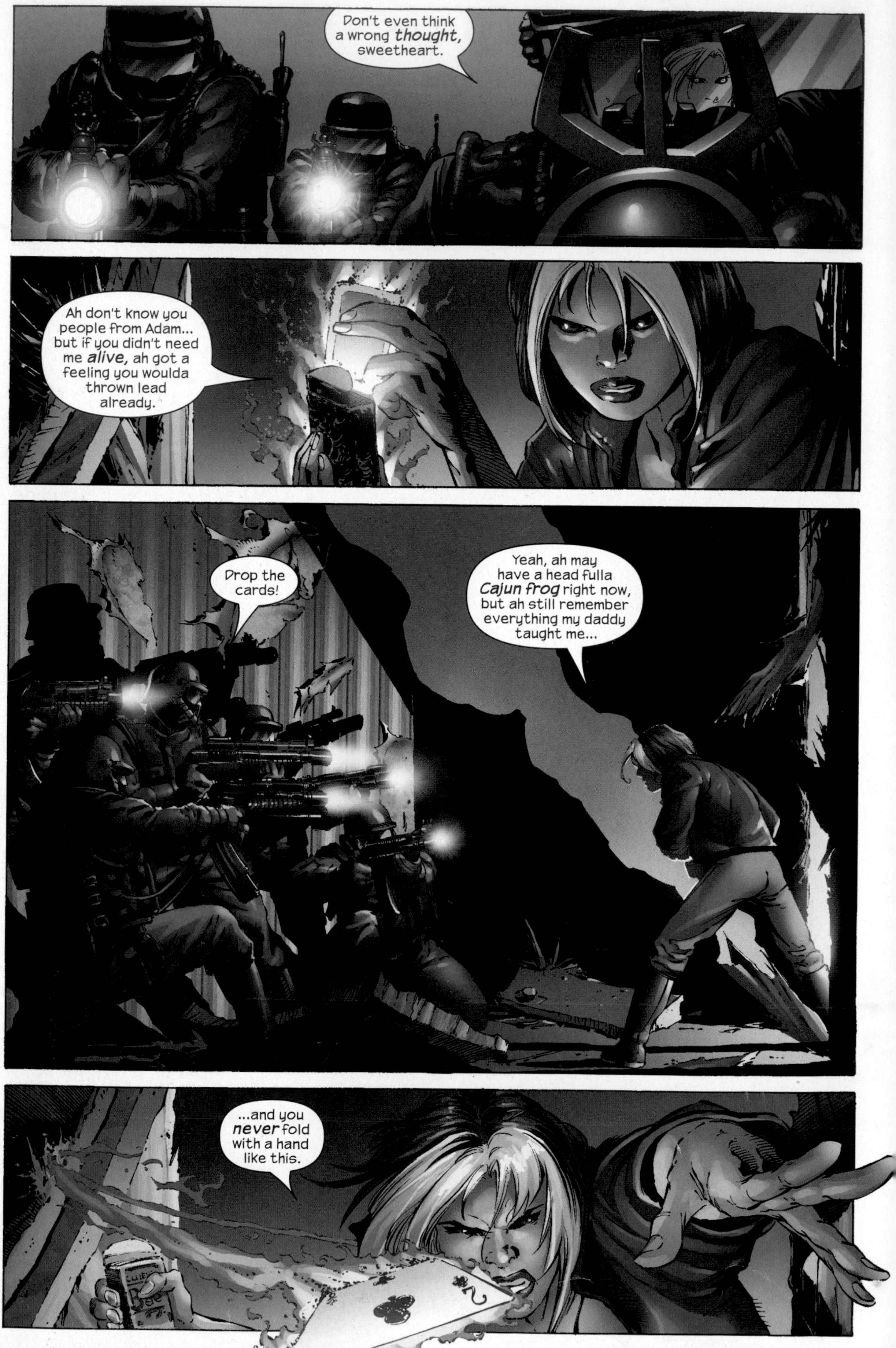
Don't even think a wrong thought, sweetheart.
Ah don't know you people from Adam... but if you didn't need me alive, ah got a feeling you woulda thrown lead already.
Drop the cards!
Yeah, ah may have a head fulla Cajun frog right now, but ah still remember everything my daddy taught me...
...and you never fold with a hand like this.

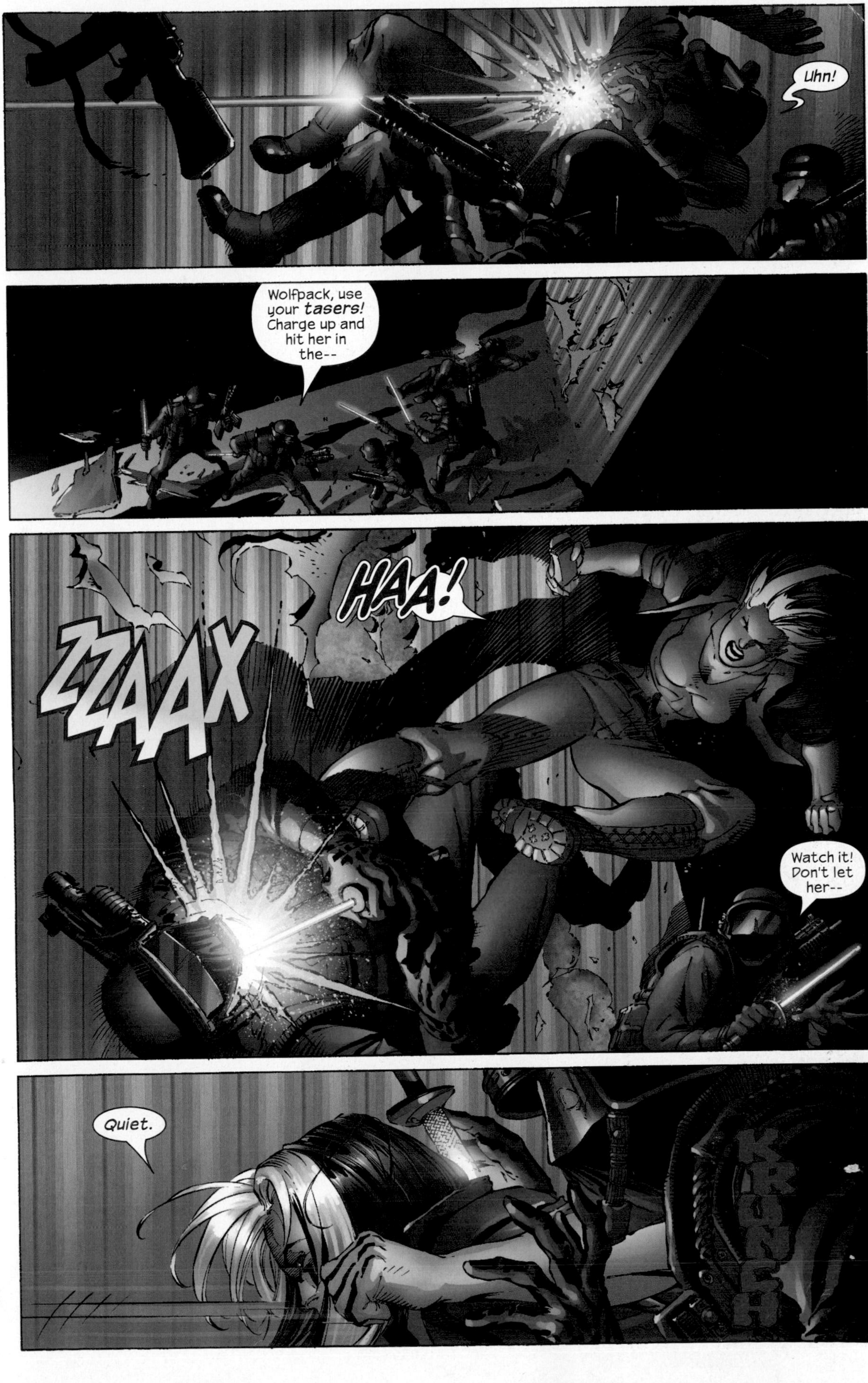
Uhn!
Wolfpack, use your *tasers!* Charge up and hit her in the--
ZZAAX
HAA!
Watch it! Don't let her--
Quiet.
KRUNCH

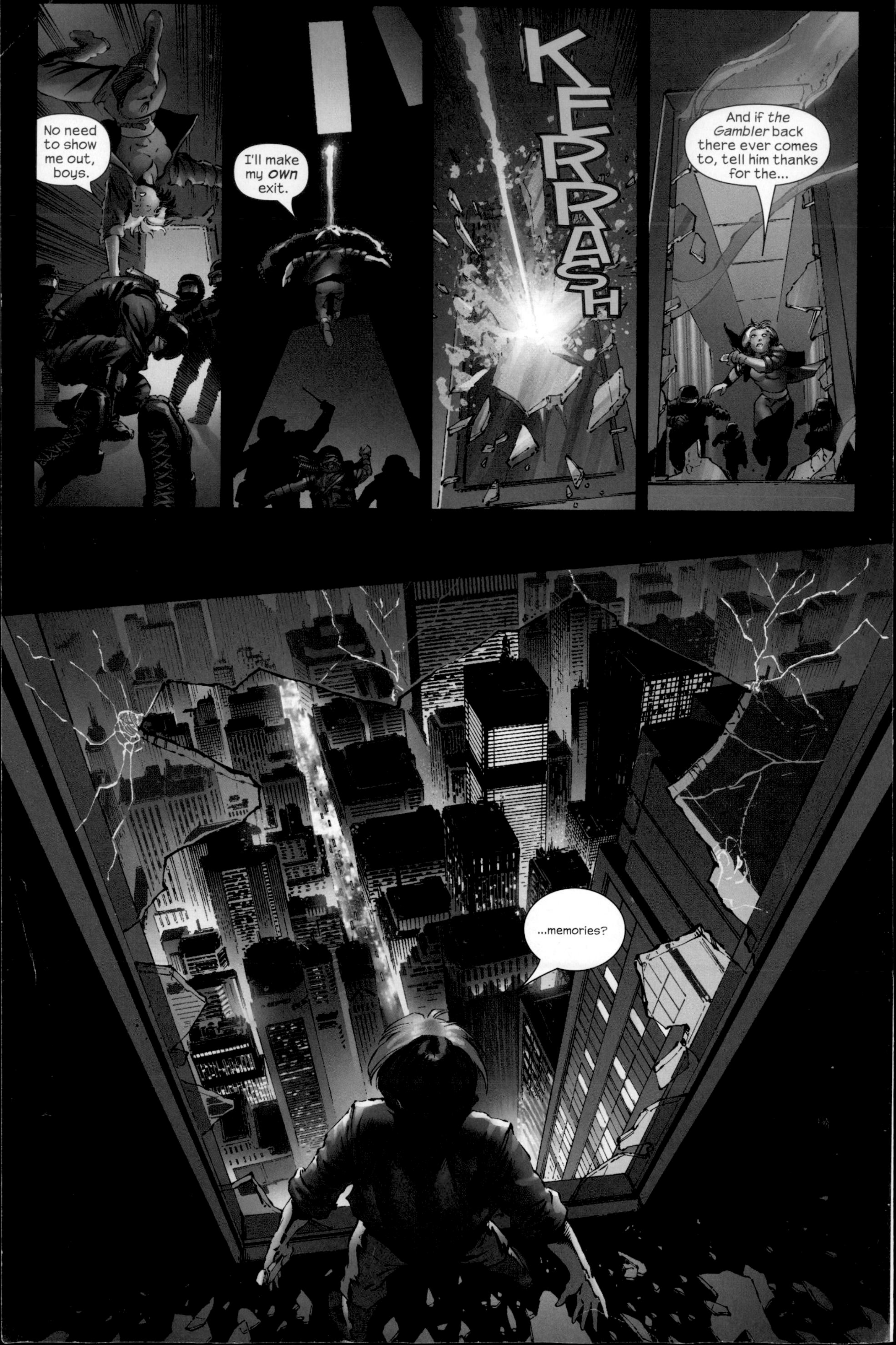
No need to show me out, boys.
I'll make my *own* exit.
KERRASH
And if *the Gambler* back there ever comes to, tell him thanks for the...
...memories?

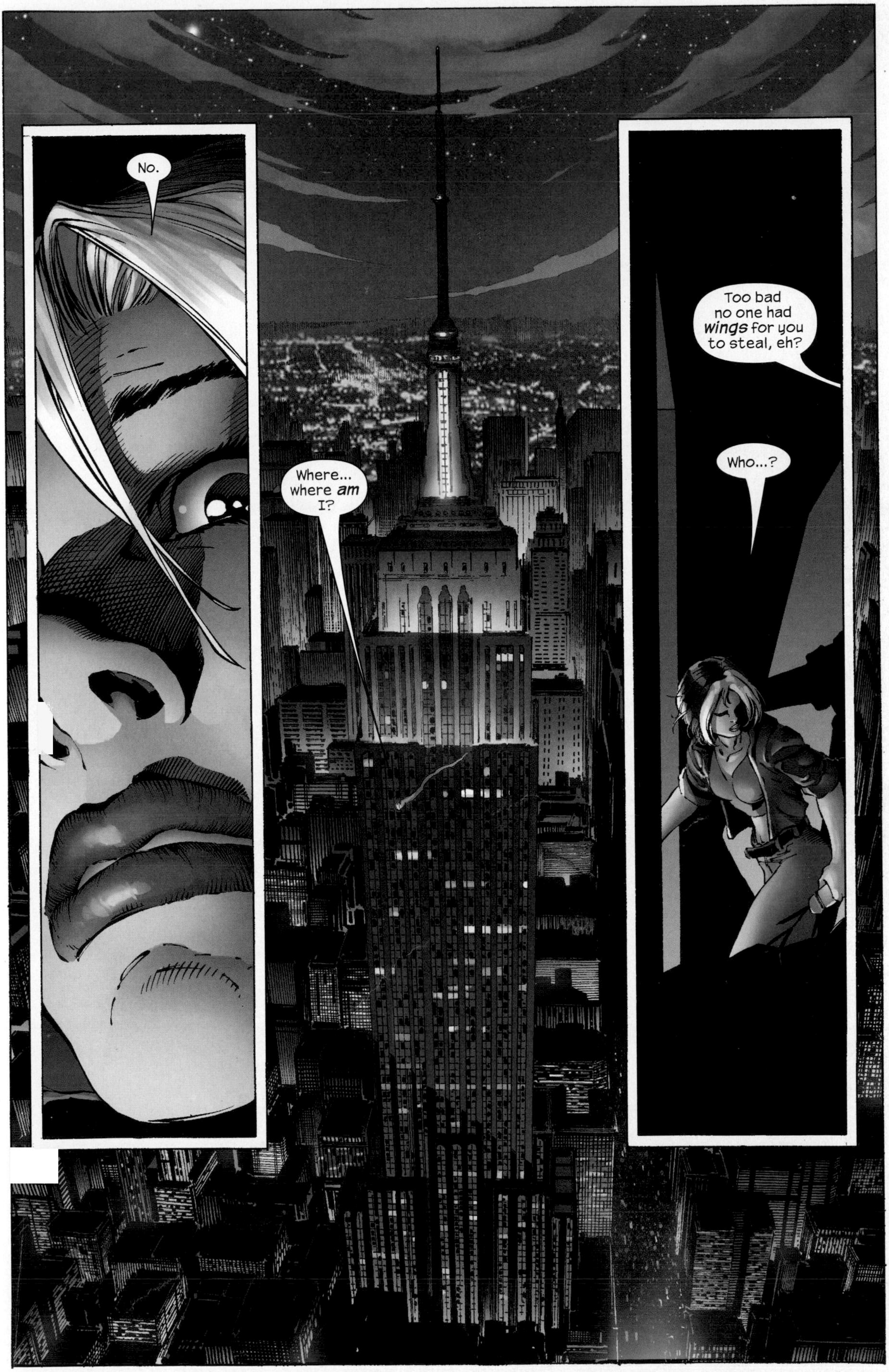

No.
Where... where *am* I?
Too bad no one had *wings* for you to steal, eh?
Who...?

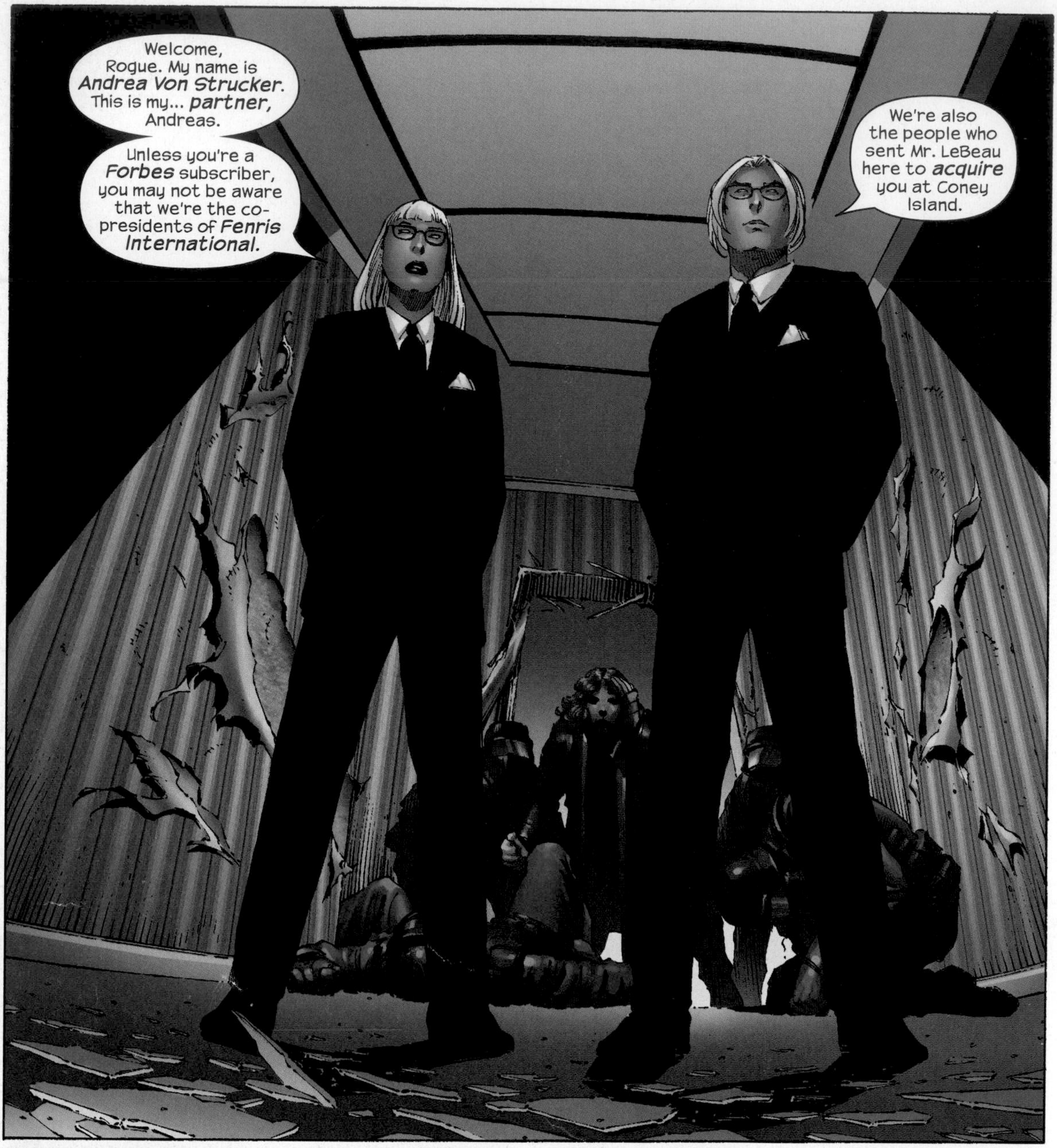
Welcome, Rogue. My name is Andrea Von Strucker. This is my... partner, Andreas.
Unless you're a Forbes subscriber, you may not be aware that we're the co-presidents of Fenris International.
We're also the people who sent Mr. LeBeau here to acquire you at Coney Island.

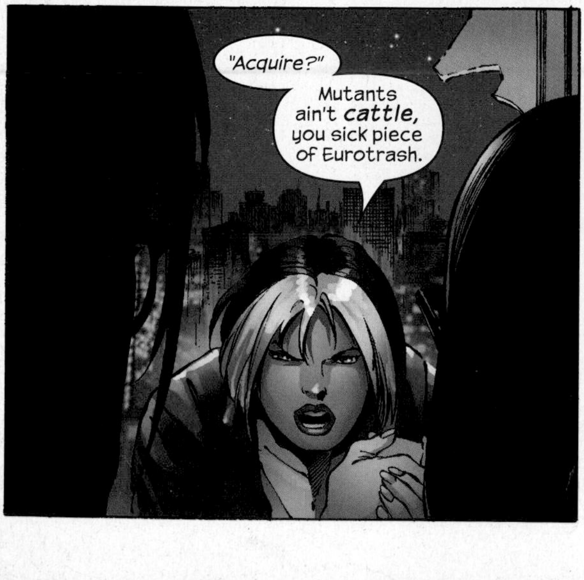
"Acquire?"
Mutants ain't cattle, you sick piece of Eurotrash.

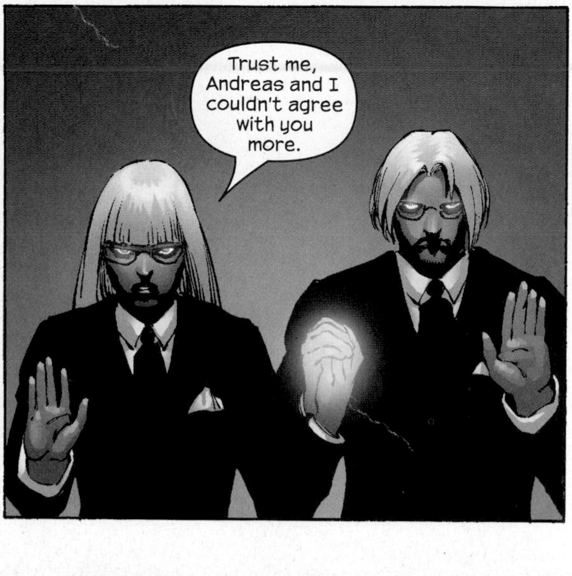
Trust me, Andreas and I couldn't agree with you more.

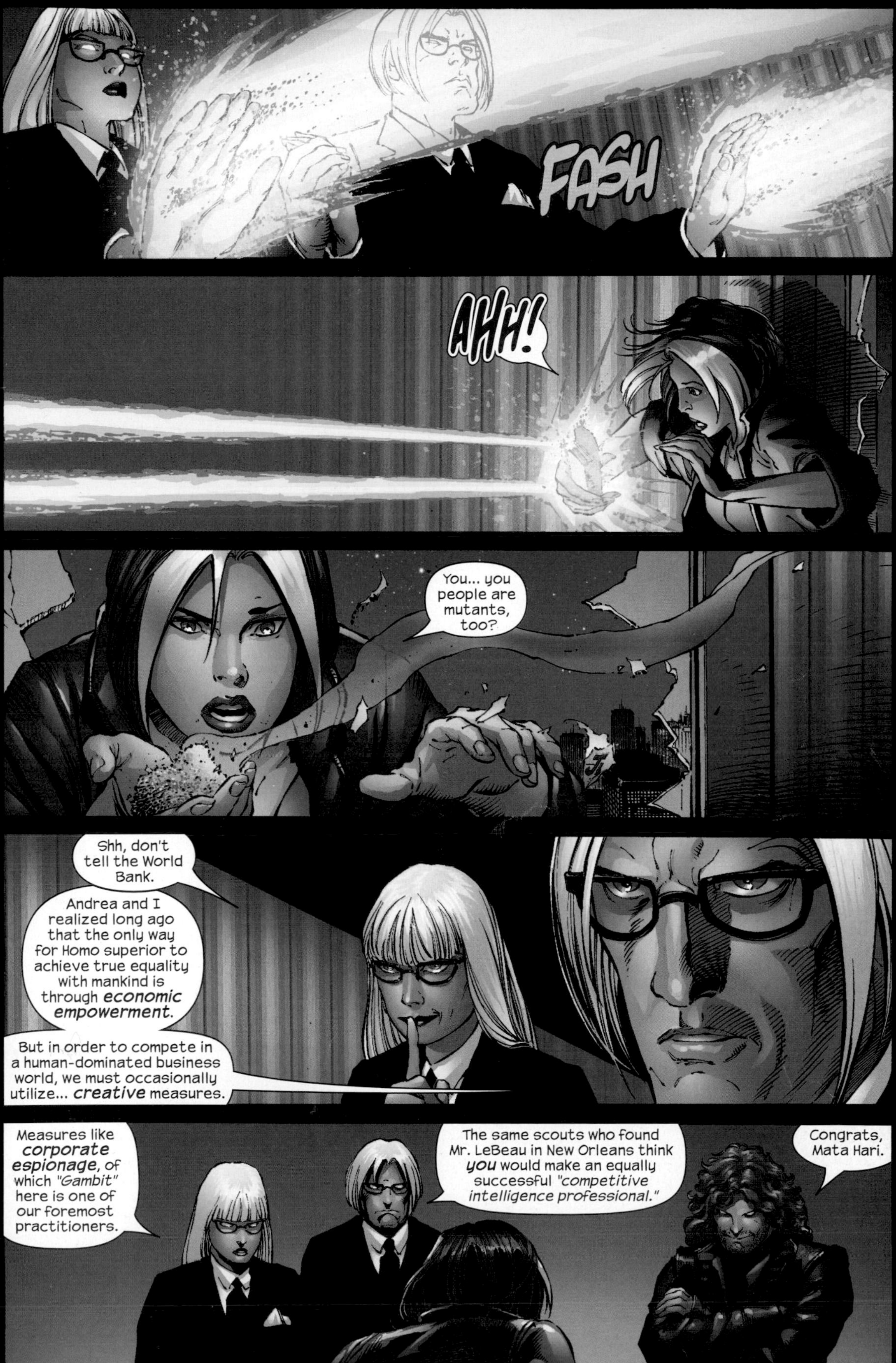
FASH
AHH!
You... you people are mutants, too?
Shh, don't tell the World Bank.
Andrea and I realized long ago that the only way for Homo superior to achieve true equality with mankind is through *economic empowerment*.
But in order to compete in a human-dominated business world, we must occasionally utilize... *creative* measures.
Measures like *corporate espionage*, of which *"Gambit"* here is one of our foremost practitioners.
The same scouts who found Mr. LeBeau in New Orleans think *you* would make an equally successful *"competitive intelligence professional."*
Congrats, Mata Hari.

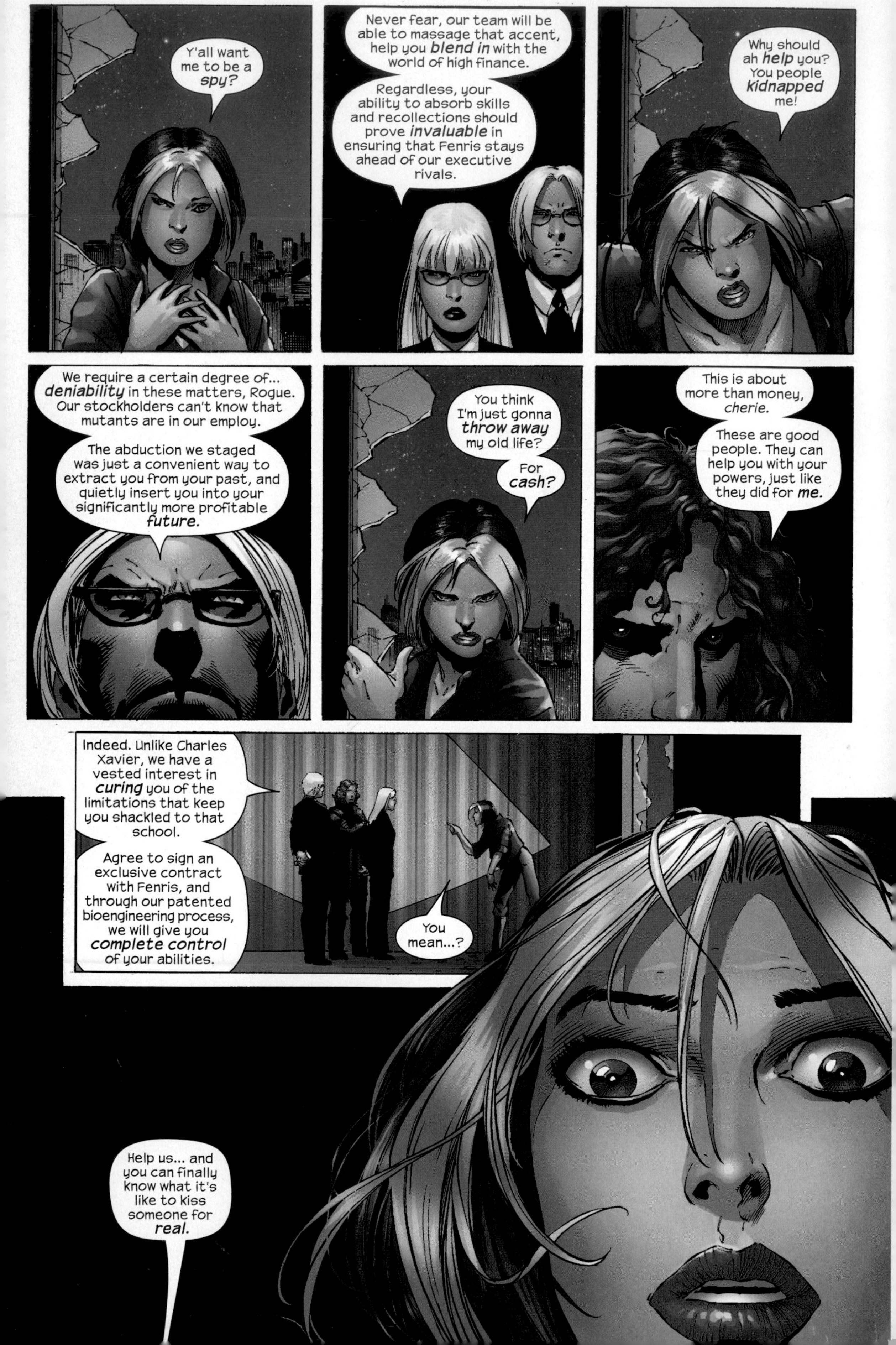

Y'all want me to be a *spy?*
Never fear, our team will be able to massage that accent, help you *blend in* with the world of high finance.
Regardless, your ability to absorb skills and recollections should prove *invaluable* in ensuring that Fenris stays ahead of our executive rivals.
Why should ah *help* you? You people *kidnapped* me!
We require a certain degree of... *deniability* in these matters, Rogue. Our stockholders can't know that mutants are in our employ.
The abduction we staged was just a convenient way to extract you from your past, and quietly insert you into your significantly more profitable *future.*
You think I'm just gonna *throw away* my old life?
For *cash?*
This is about more than money, *cherie.*
These are good people. They can help you with your powers, just like they did for *me.*
Indeed. Unlike Charles Xavier, we have a vested interest in *curing* you of the limitations that keep you shackled to that school.
Agree to sign an exclusive contract with Fenris, and through our patented bioengineering process, we will give you *complete control* of your abilities.
You mean...?
Help us... and you can finally know what it's like to kiss someone for *real.*

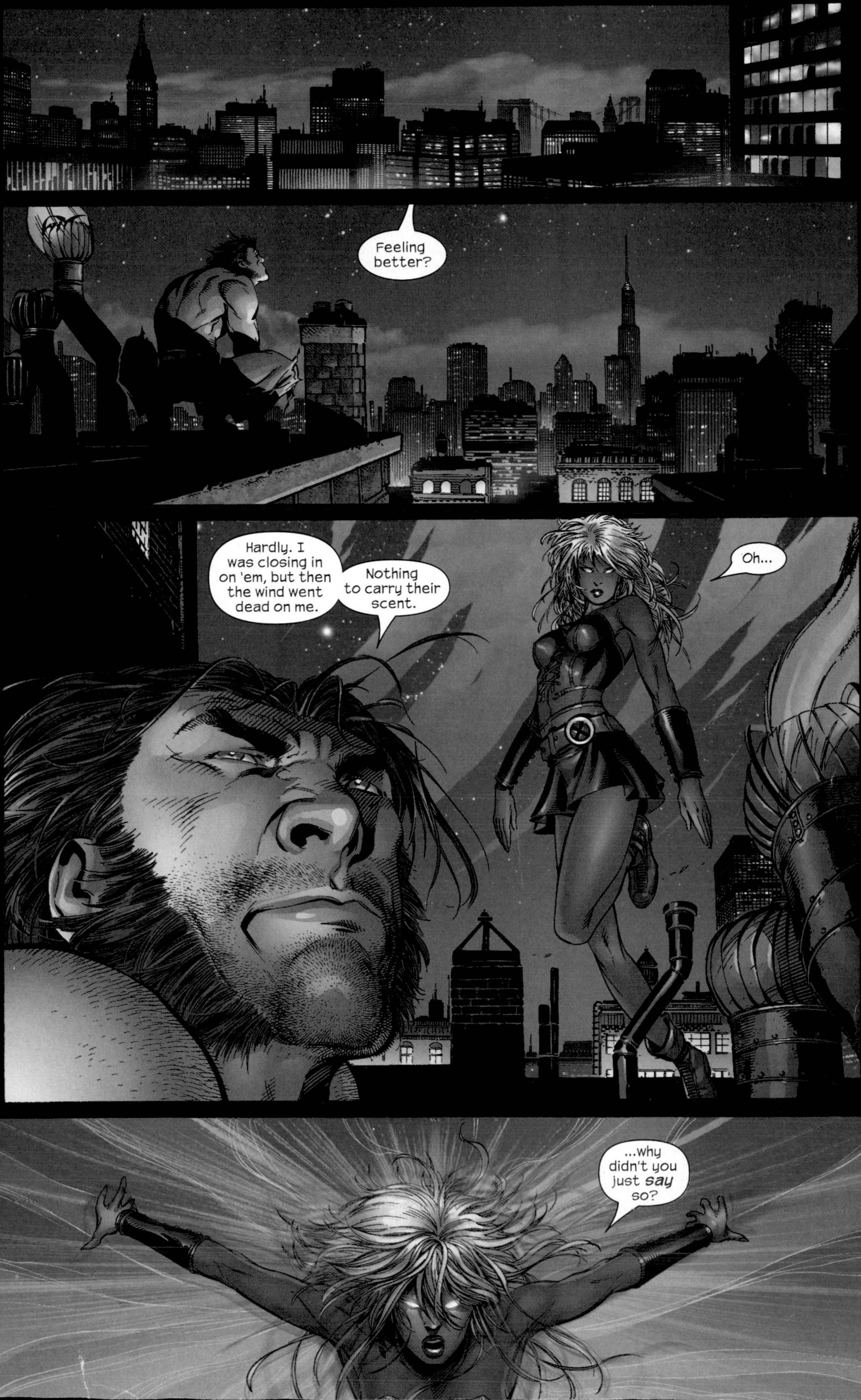
Feeling better?
Hardly. I was closing in on 'em, but then the wind went dead on me.
Nothing to carry their scent.
Oh...
...why didn't you just *say* so?

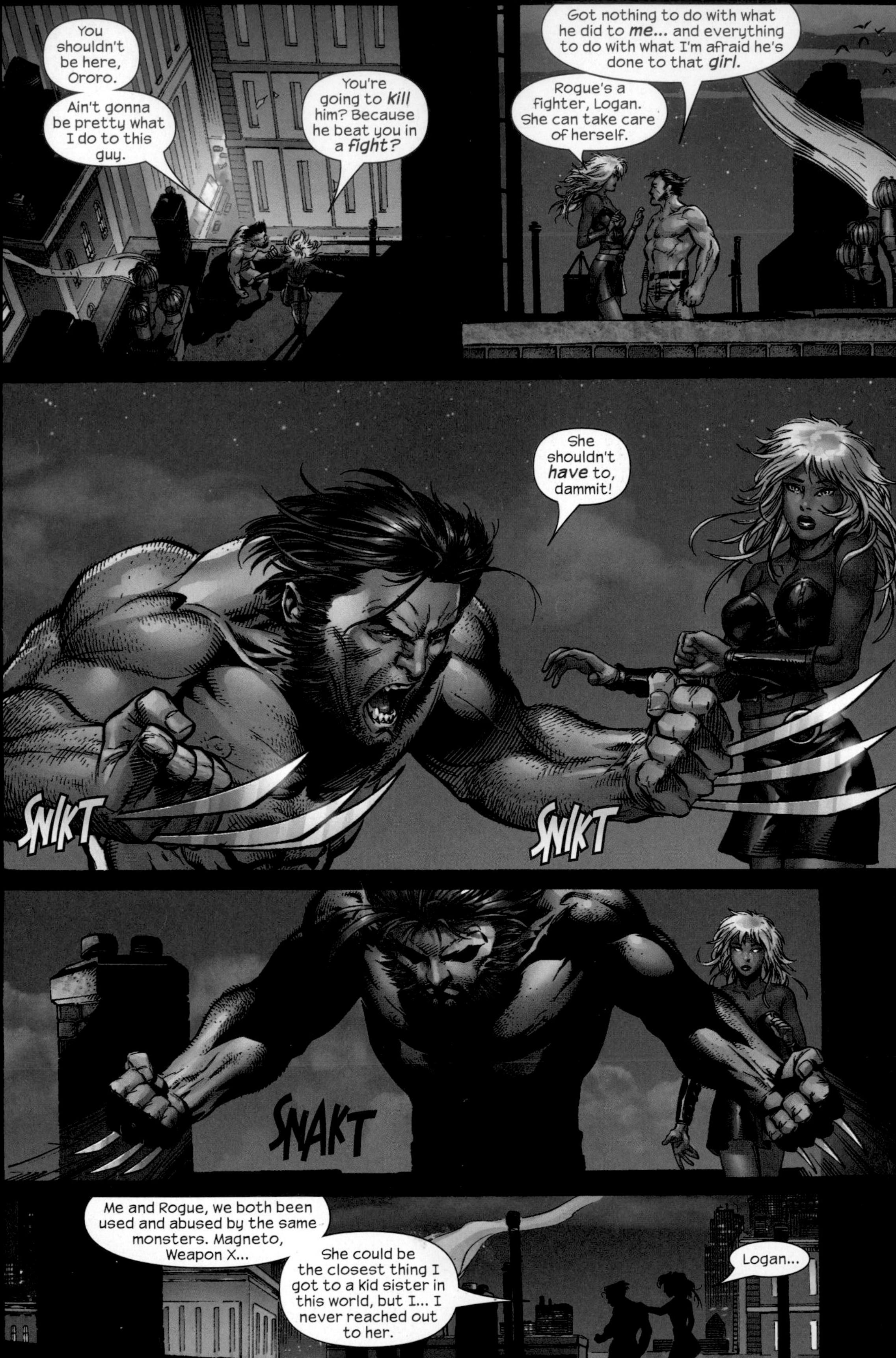
You shouldn't be here, Ororo.
Ain't gonna be pretty what I do to this guy.
You're going to kill him? Because he beat you in a fight?
Got nothing to do with what he did to me... and everything to do with what I'm afraid he's done to that girl.
Rogue's a fighter, Logan. She can take care of herself.
She shouldn't have to, dammit!
SNIKT
SNIKT
SNAKT
Me and Rogue, we both been used and abused by the same monsters. Magneto, Weapon X...
She could be the closest thing I got to a kid sister in this world, but I... I never reached out to her.
Logan...

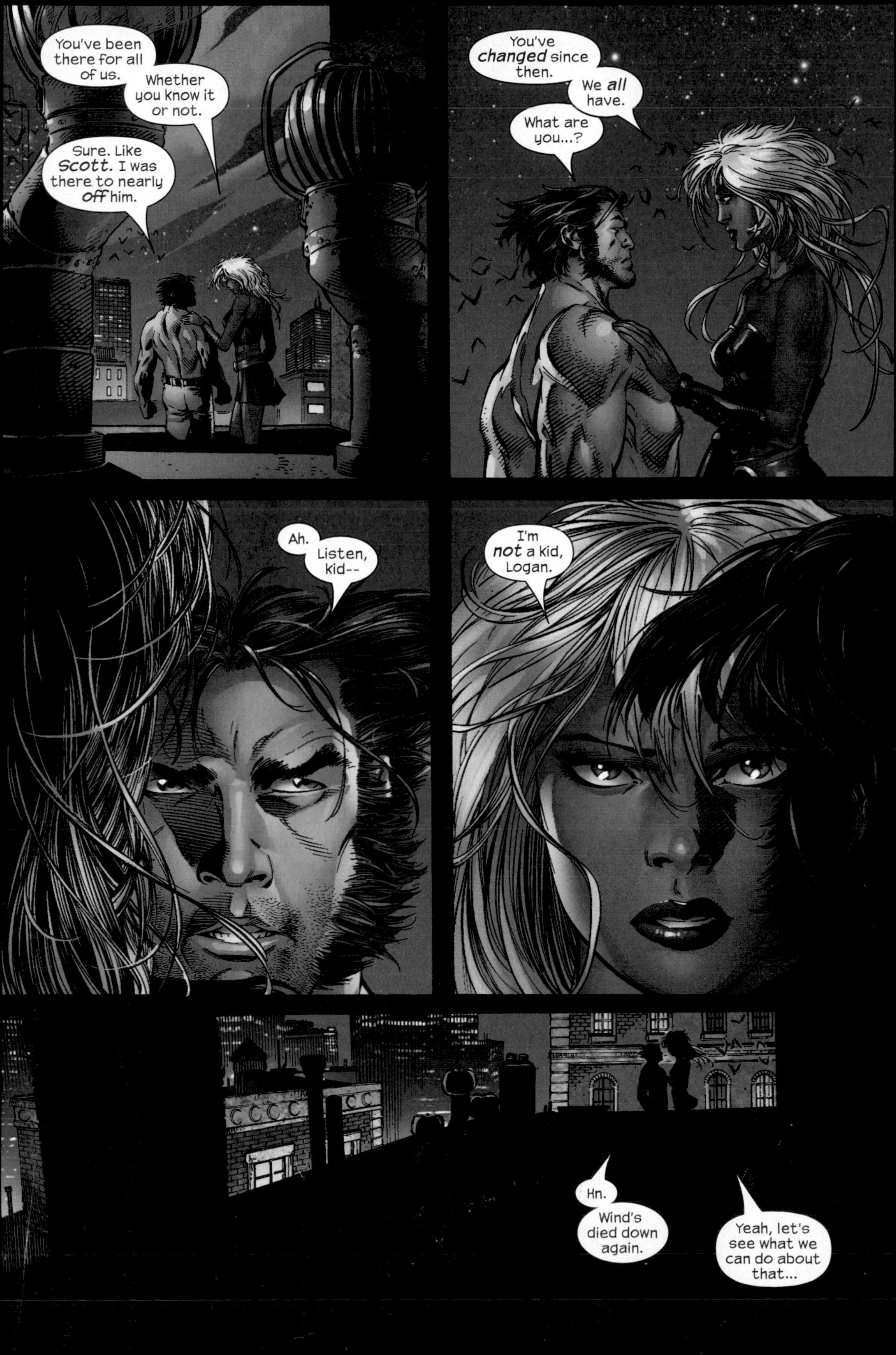
You've been there for all of us.
Whether you know it or not.
Sure. Like Scott. I was there to nearly off him.
You've changed since then.
We all have.
What are you...?
Ah. Listen, kid--
I'm not a kid, Logan.
Hn.
Wind's died down again.
Yeah, let's see what we can do about that...

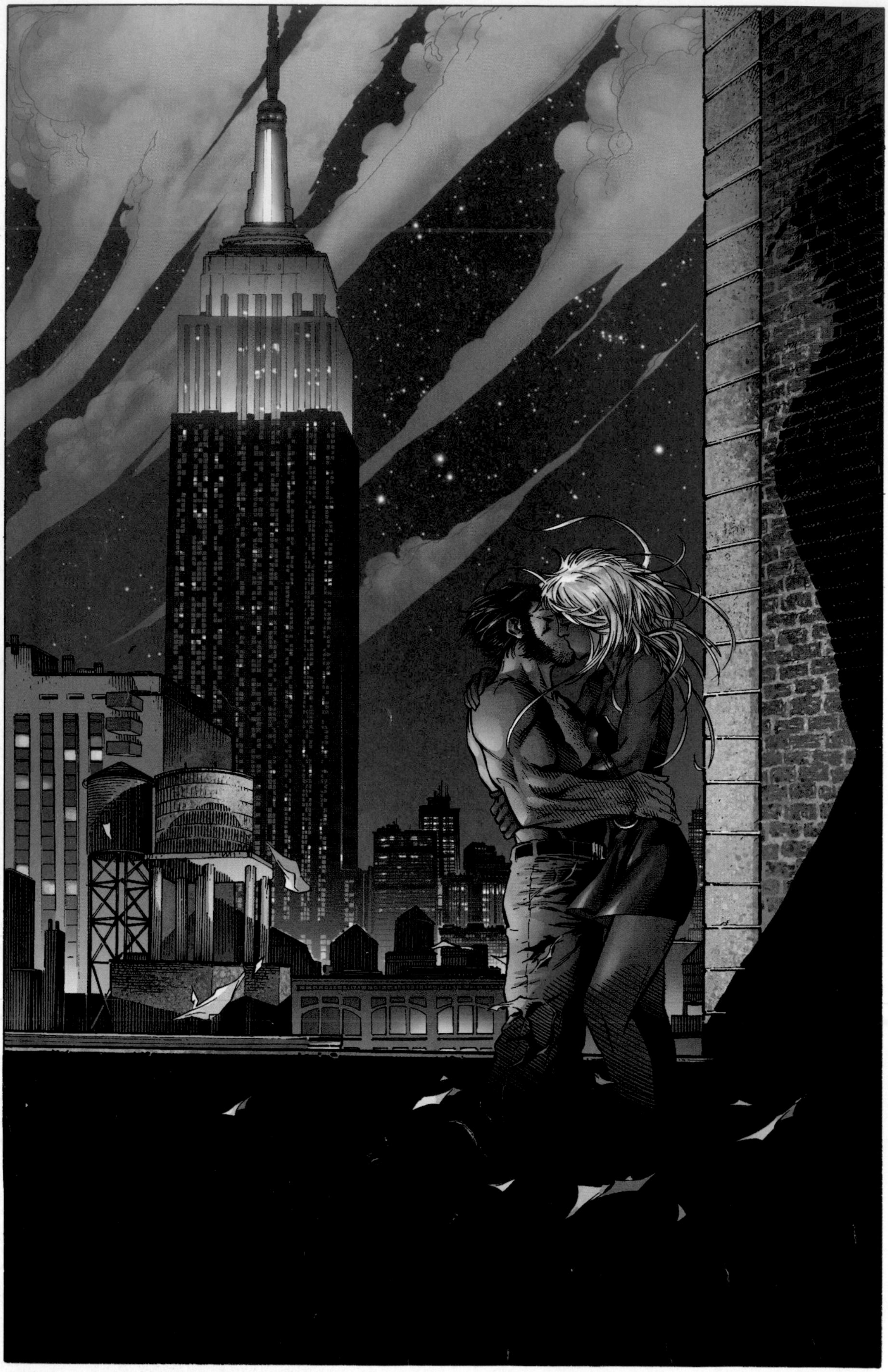

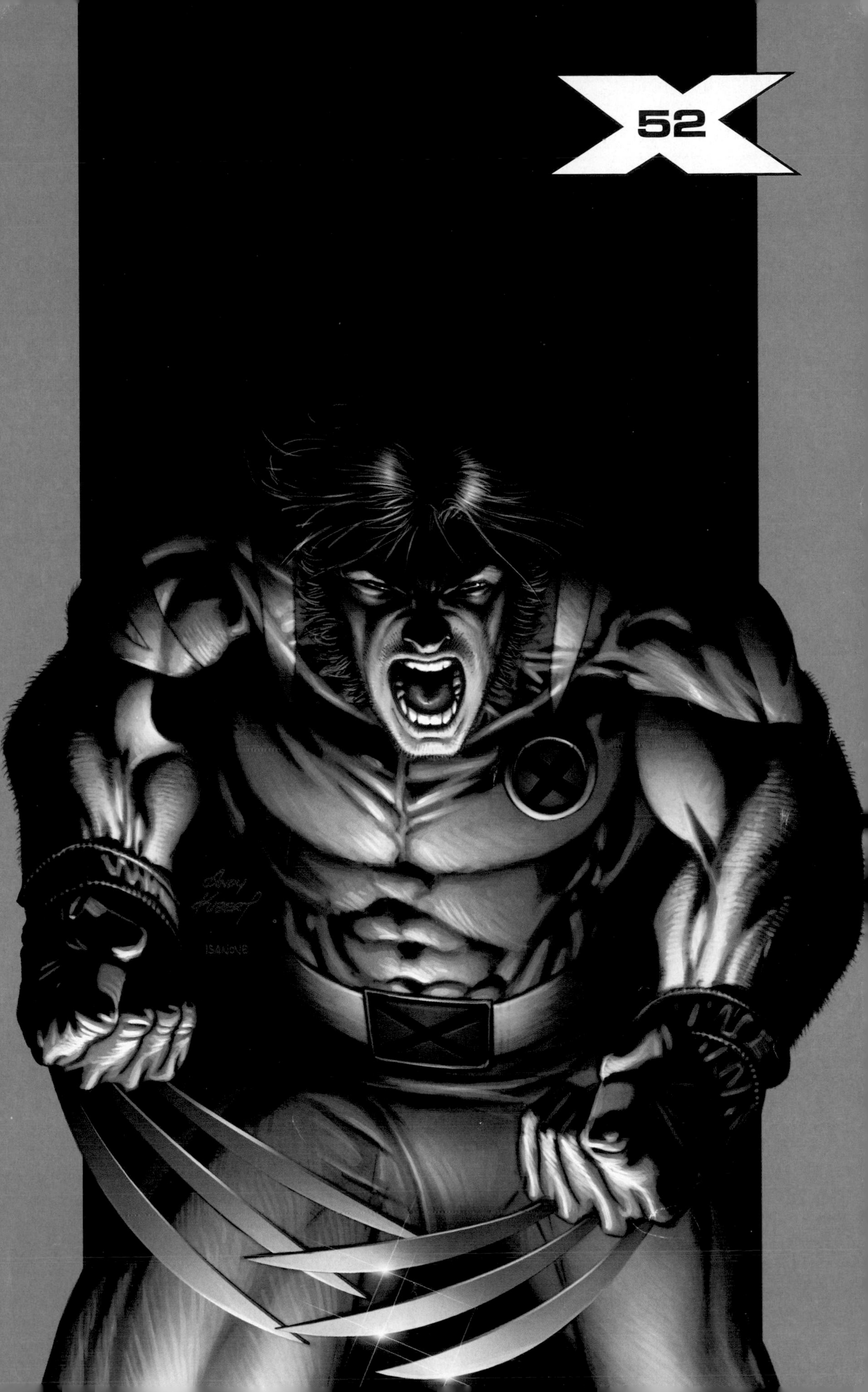
52

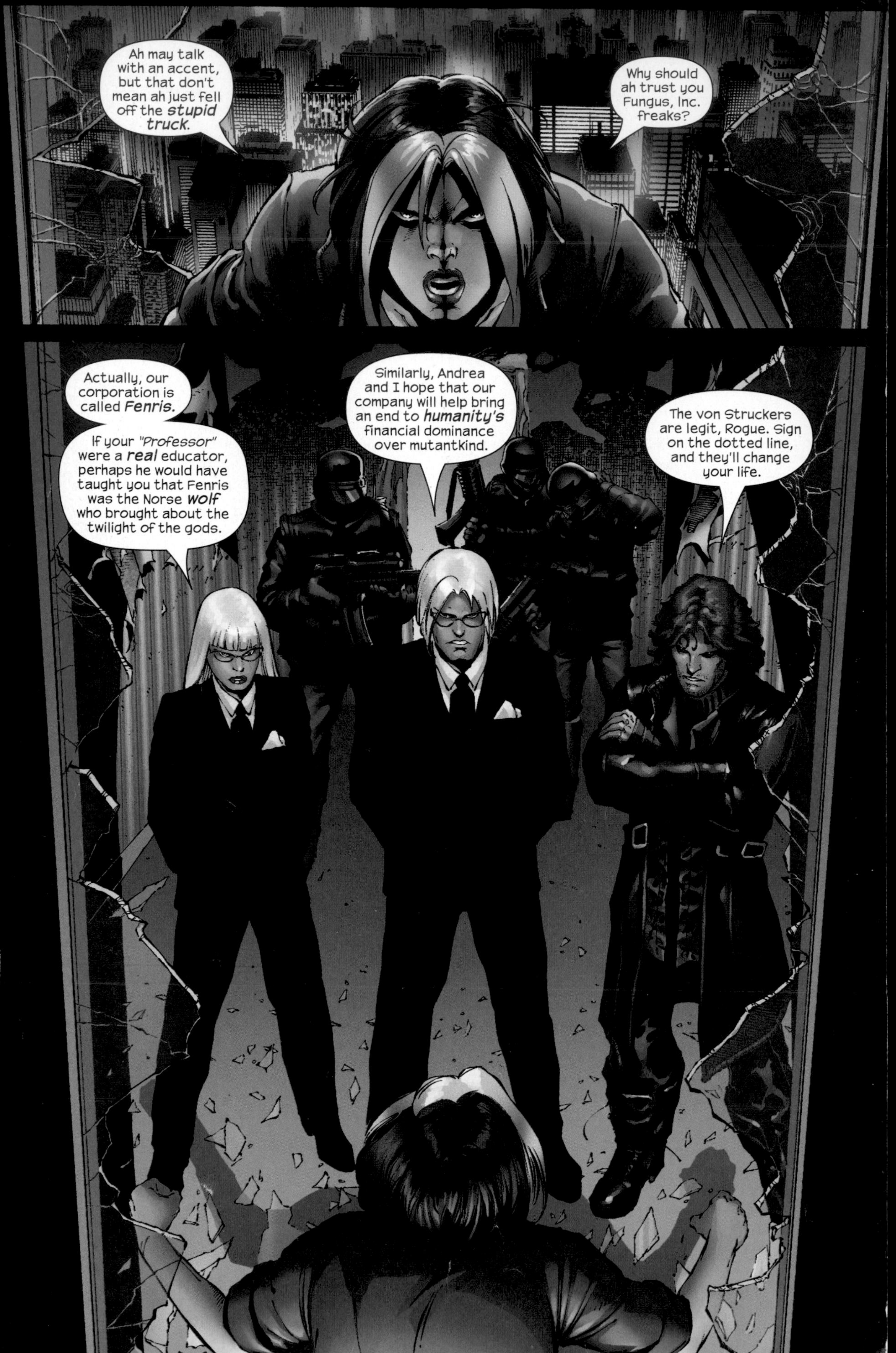
Ah may talk with an accent, but that don't mean ah just fell off the *stupid truck*.
Why should ah trust you Fungus, Inc. freaks?
Actually, our corporation is called *Fenris.*
If your *"Professor"* were a *real* educator, perhaps he would have taught you that Fenris was the Norse *wolf* who brought about the twilight of the gods.
Similarly, Andrea and I hope that our company will help bring an end to *humanity's* financial dominance over mutantkind.
The von Struckers are legit, Rogue. Sign on the dotted line, and they'll change your life.

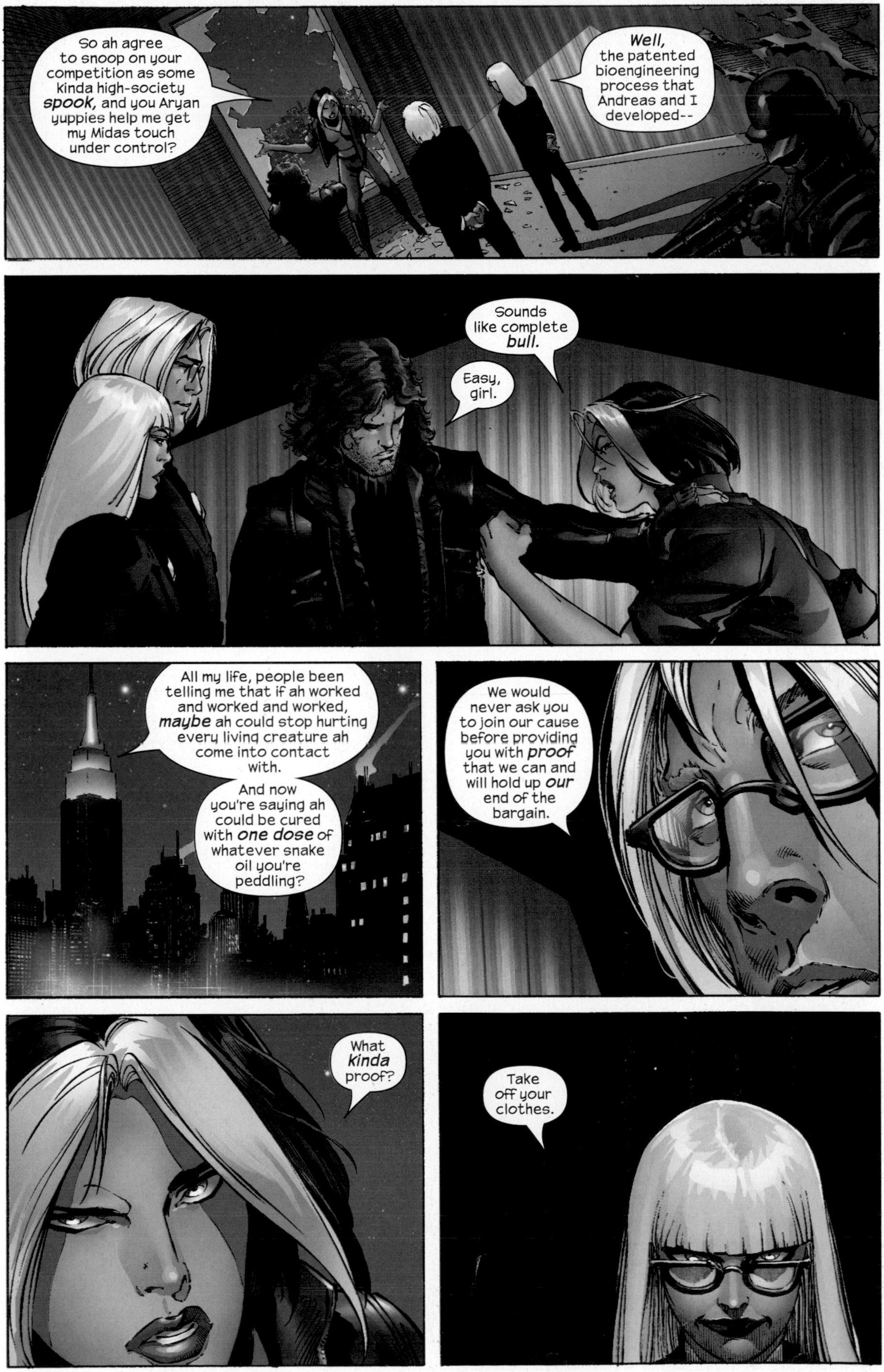
So ah agree to snoop on your competition as some kinda high-society *spook,* and you Aryan yuppies help me get my Midas touch under control?
Well, the patented bioengineering process that Andreas and I developed--
Sounds like complete *bull.*
Easy, girl.
All my life, people been telling me that if ah worked and worked and worked, *maybe* ah could stop hurting every living creature ah come into contact with.
And now you're saying ah could be cured with *one dose* of whatever snake oil you're peddling?
We would never ask you to join our cause before providing you with *proof* that we can and will hold up *our* end of the bargain.
What *kinda* proof?
Take off your clothes.

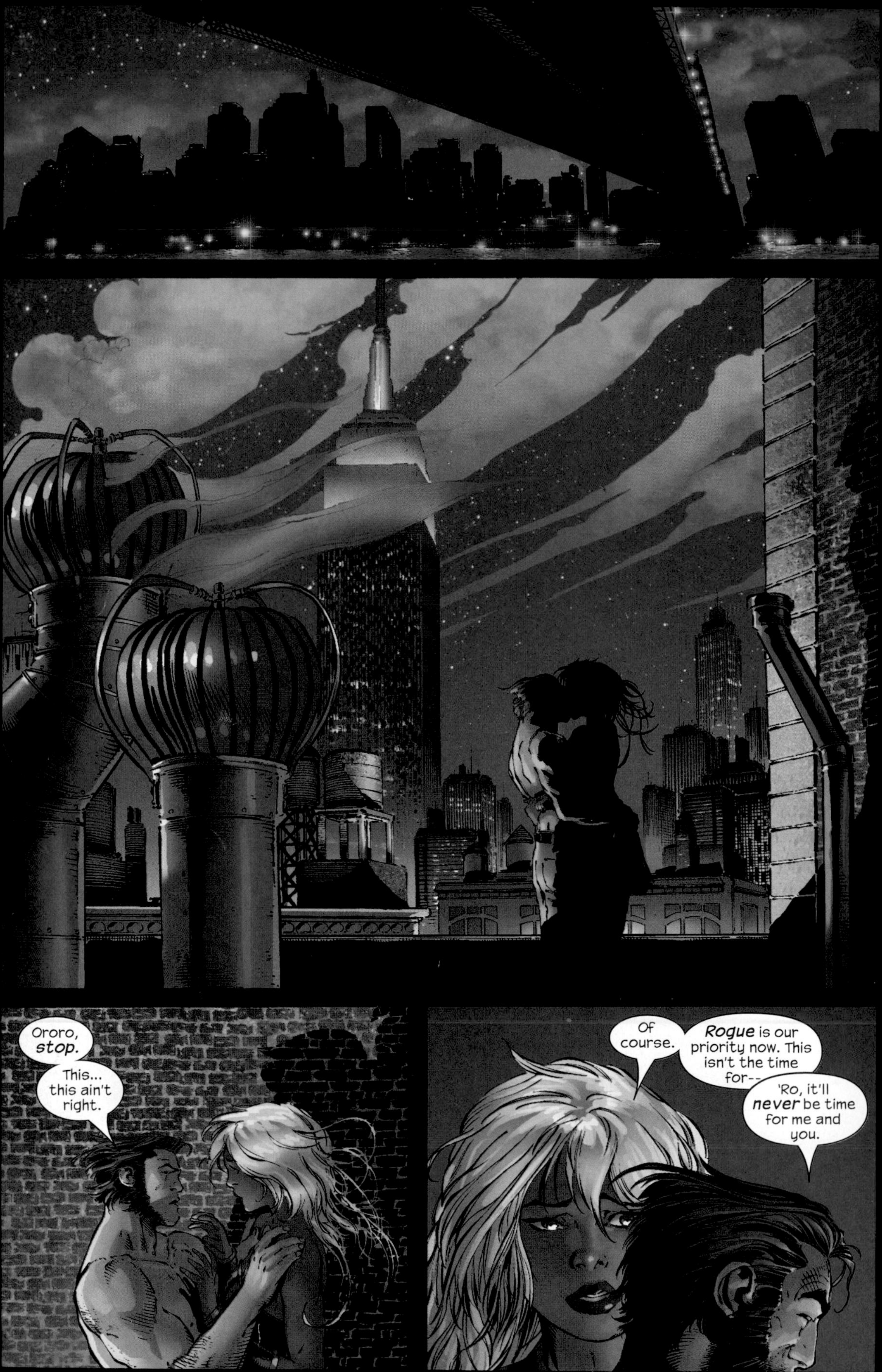
Ororo, **stop.**
This... this ain't right.
Of course.
Rogue is our priority now. This isn't the time for--
'Ro, it'll ***never*** be time for me and you.

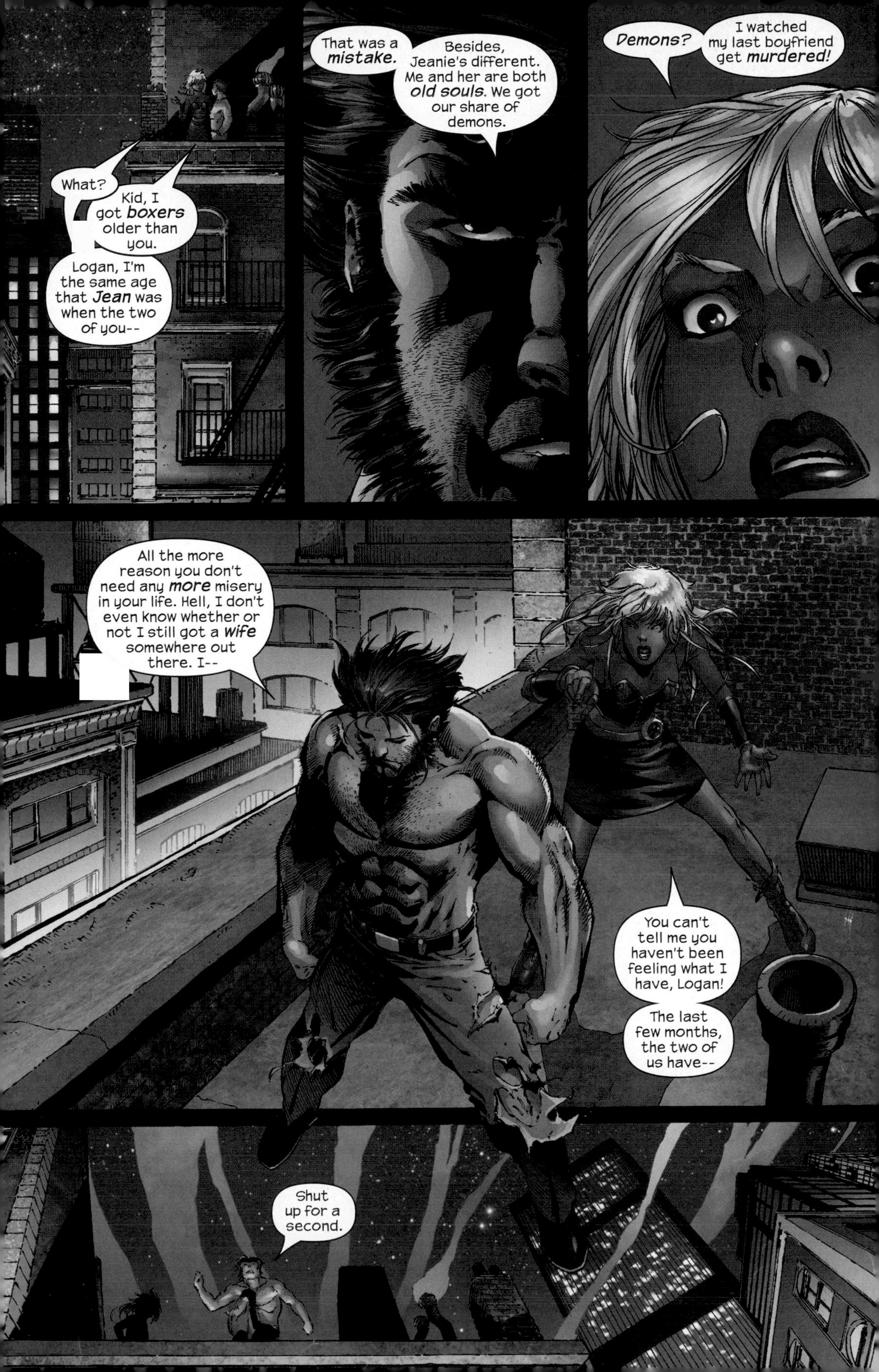
What?
Kid, I got boxers older than you.
Logan, I'm the same age that Jean was when the two of you--
That was a mistake.
Besides, Jeanie's different. Me and her are both old souls. We got our share of demons.
Demons?
I watched my last boyfriend get murdered!
All the more reason you don't need any more misery in your life. Hell, I don't even know whether or not I still got a wife somewhere out there. I--
You can't tell me you haven't been feeling what I have, Logan!
The last few months, the two of us have--
Shut up for a second.

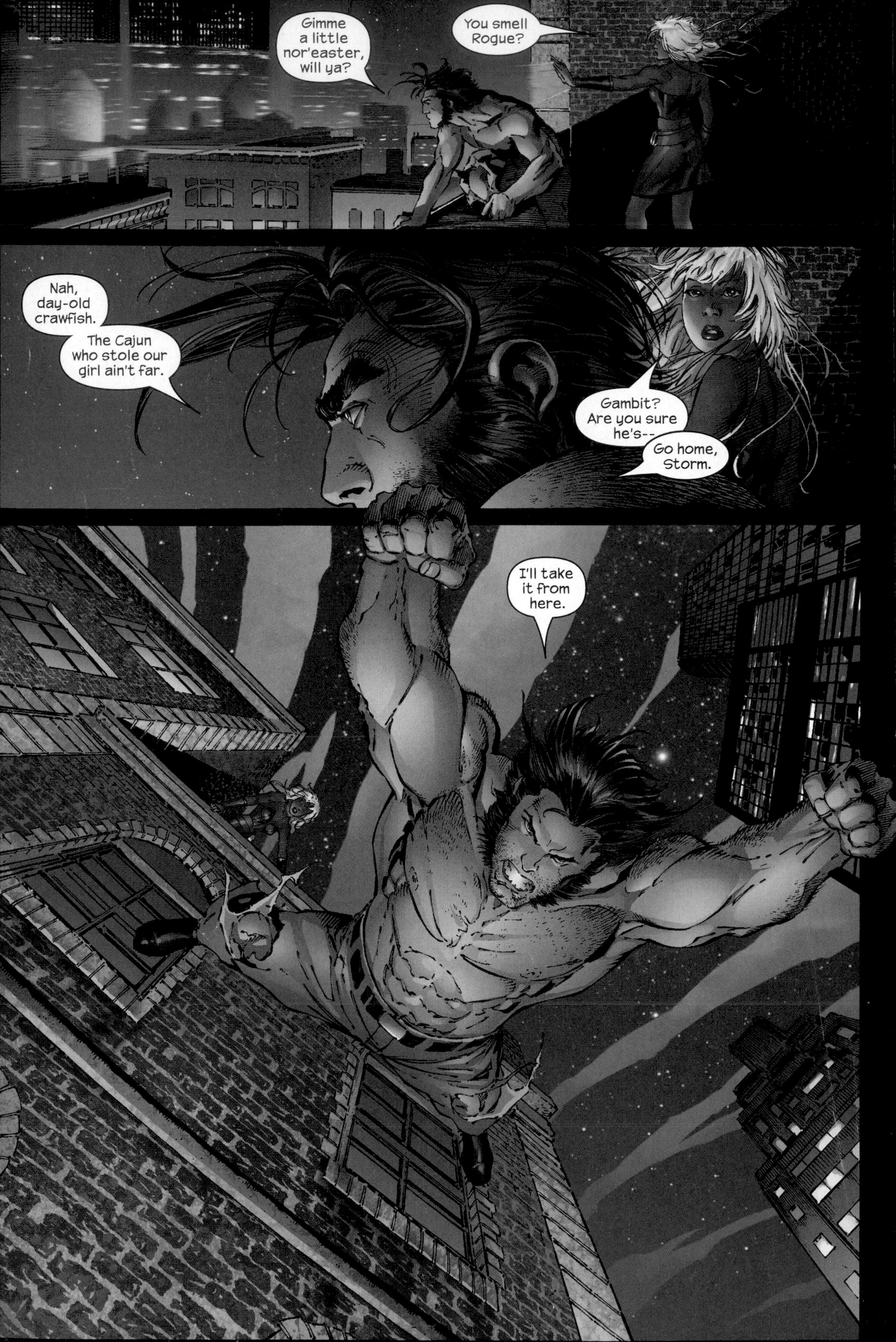
Gimme a little nor'easter, will ya?
You smell Rogue?
Nah, day-old crawfish.
The Cajun who stole our girl ain't far.
Gambit? Are you sure he's--
Go home, Storm.
I'll take it from here.

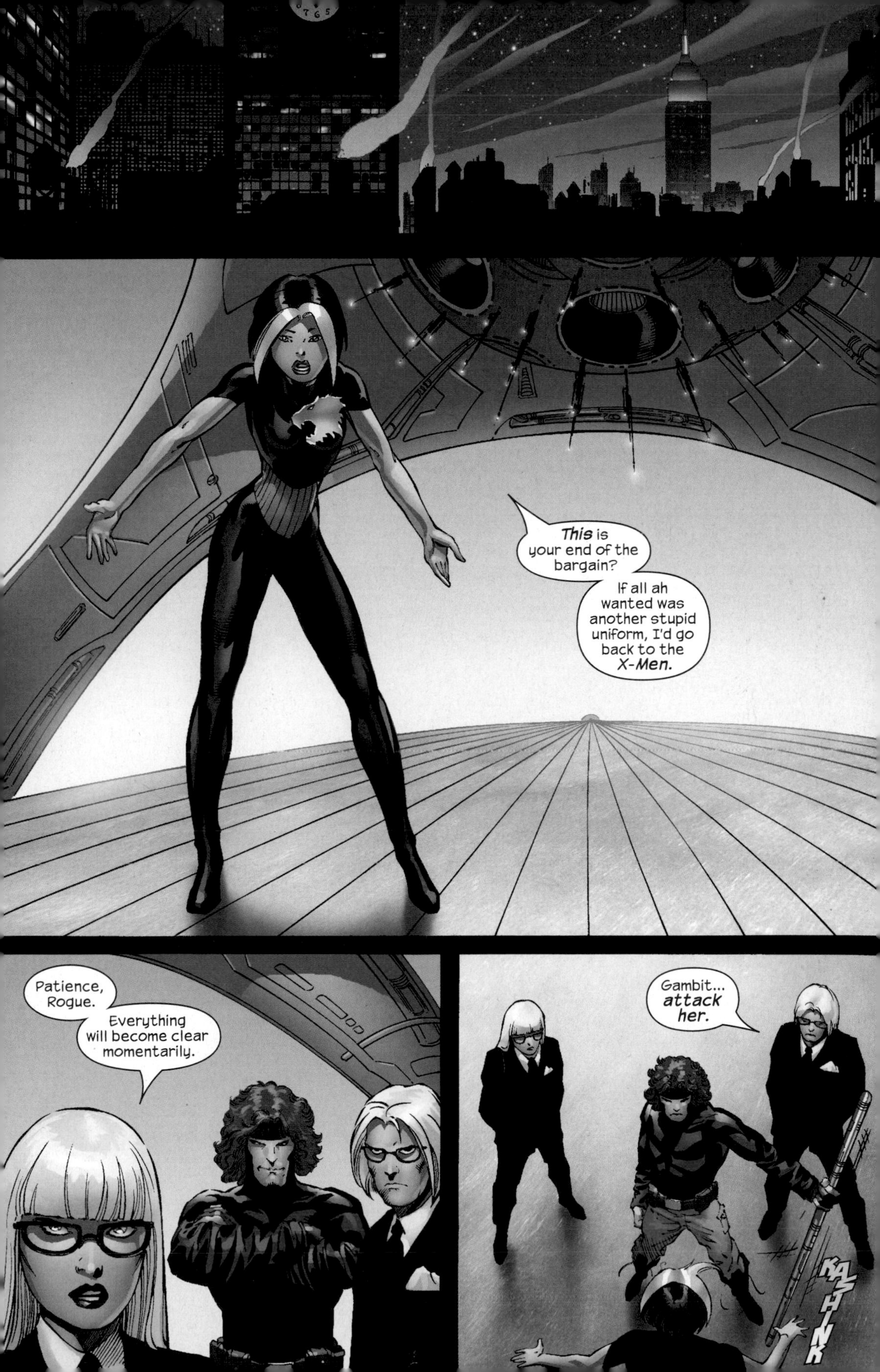
This is your end of the bargain?
If all ah wanted was another stupid uniform, I'd go back to the X-Men.
Patience, Rogue.
Everything will become clear momentarily.
Gambit... attack her.
KASHINK

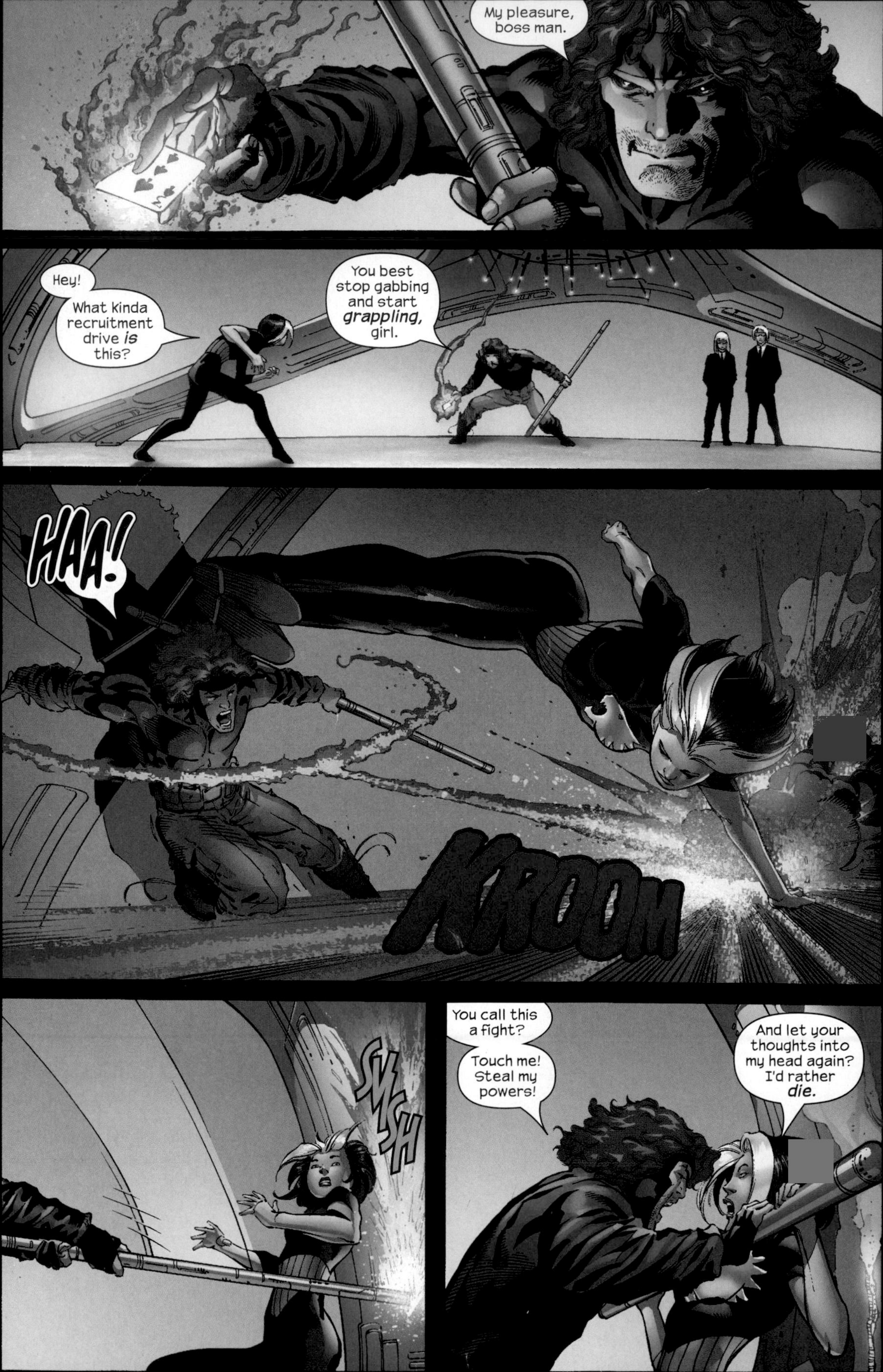

My pleasure, boss man.
Hey!
What kinda recruitment drive *is* this?
You best stop gabbing and start *grappling,* girl.
HAA!
KROOM
SNSH
You call this a fight?
Touch me! Steal my powers!
And let your thoughts into my head again? I'd rather *die.*

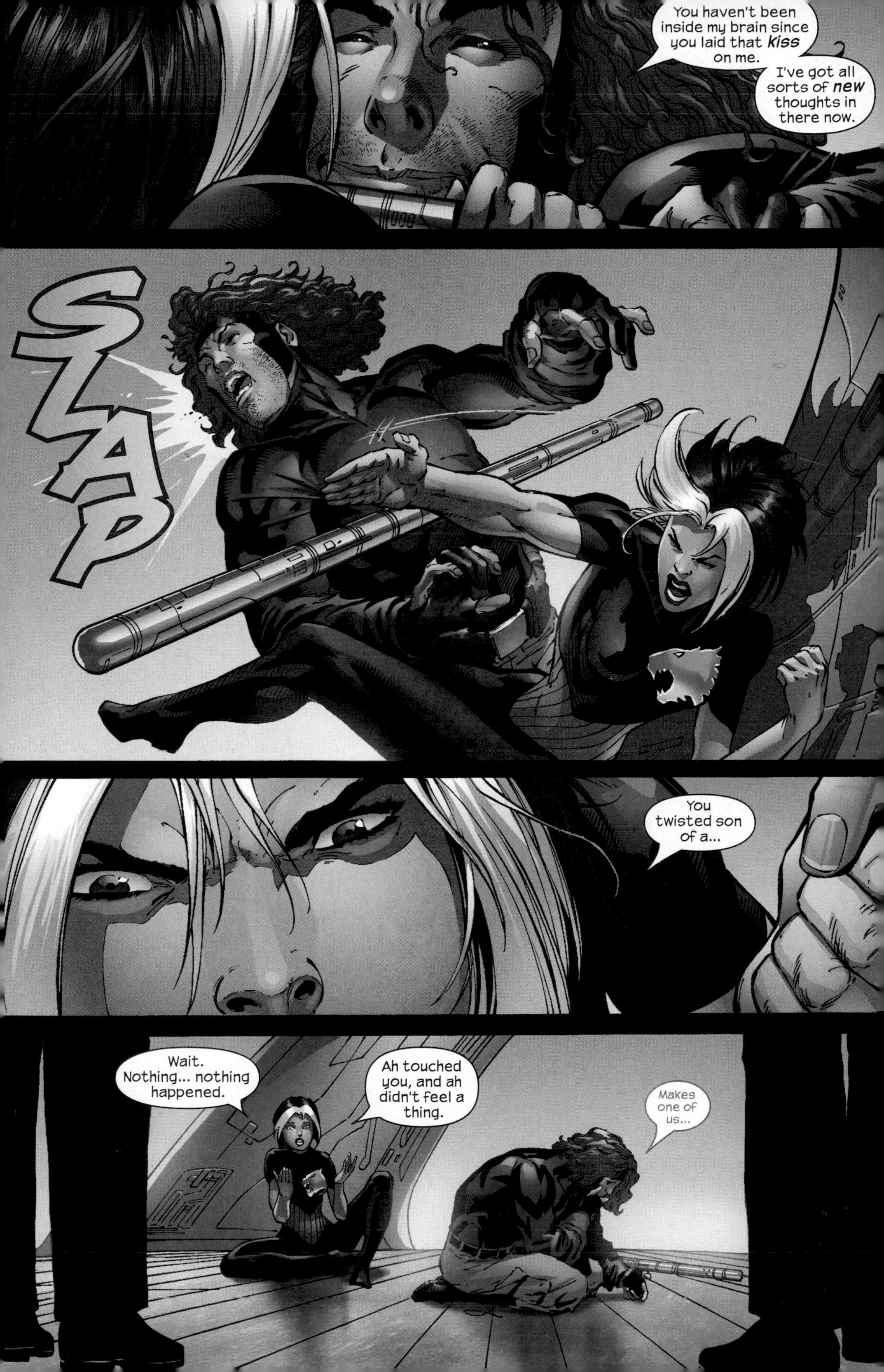
You haven't been inside my brain since you laid that *kiss* on me.
I've got all sorts of *new* thoughts in there now.
SLAP
You twisted son of a...
Wait. Nothing... nothing happened.
Ah touched you, and ah didn't feel a thing.
Makes one of us...

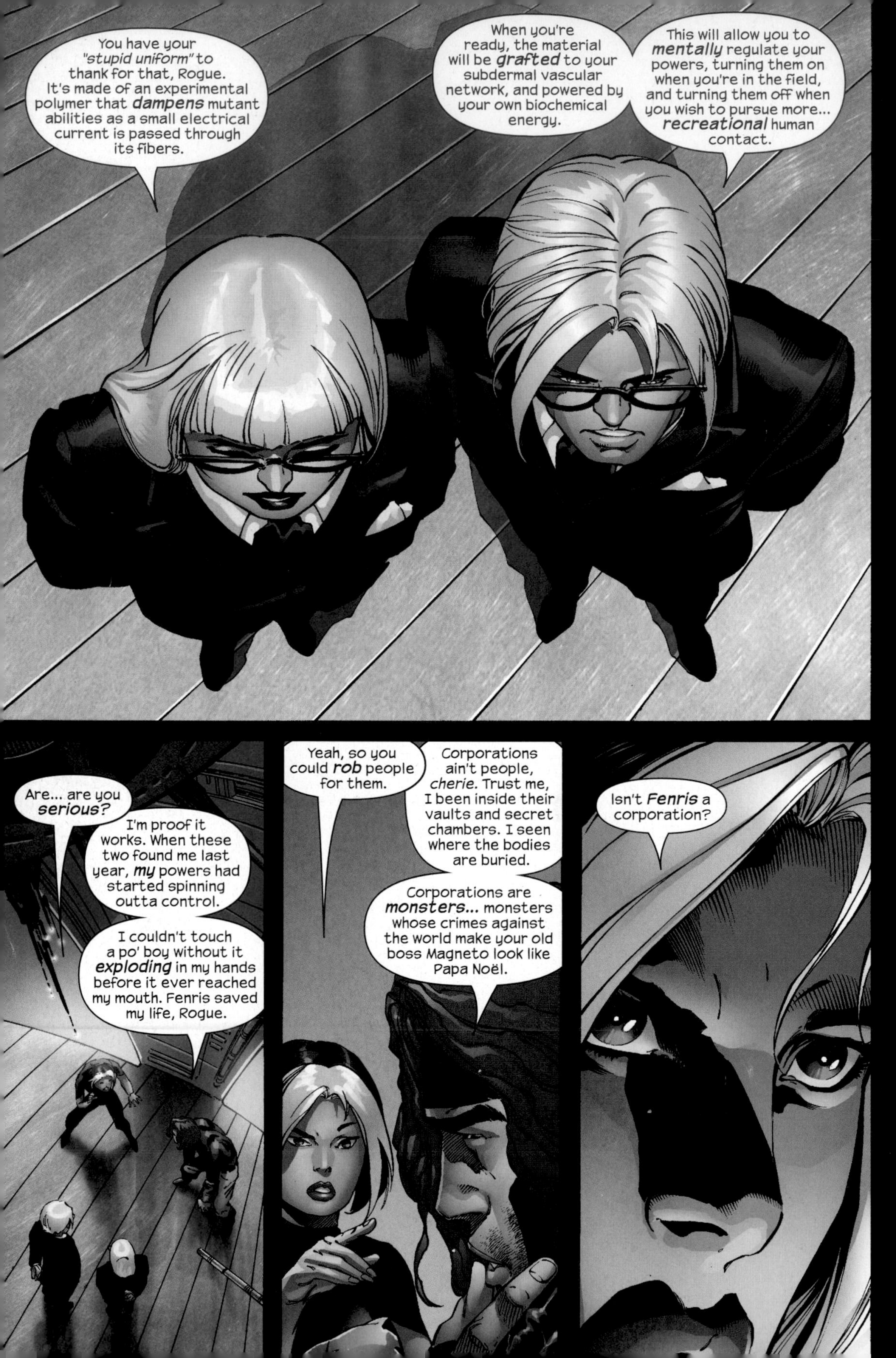
You have your "stupid uniform" to thank for that, Rogue. It's made of an experimental polymer that dampens mutant abilities as a small electrical current is passed through its fibers.
When you're ready, the material will be grafted to your subdermal vascular network, and powered by your own biochemical energy.
This will allow you to mentally regulate your powers, turning them on when you're in the field, and turning them off when you wish to pursue more... recreational human contact.
Are... are you serious?
I'm proof it works. When these two found me last year, my powers had started spinning outta control.
I couldn't touch a po' boy without it exploding in my hands before it ever reached my mouth. Fenris saved my life, Rogue.
Yeah, so you could rob people for them.
Corporations ain't people, cherie. Trust me, I been inside their vaults and secret chambers. I seen where the bodies are buried.
Corporations are monsters... monsters whose crimes against the world make your old boss Magneto look like Papa Noël.
Isn't Fenris a corporation?

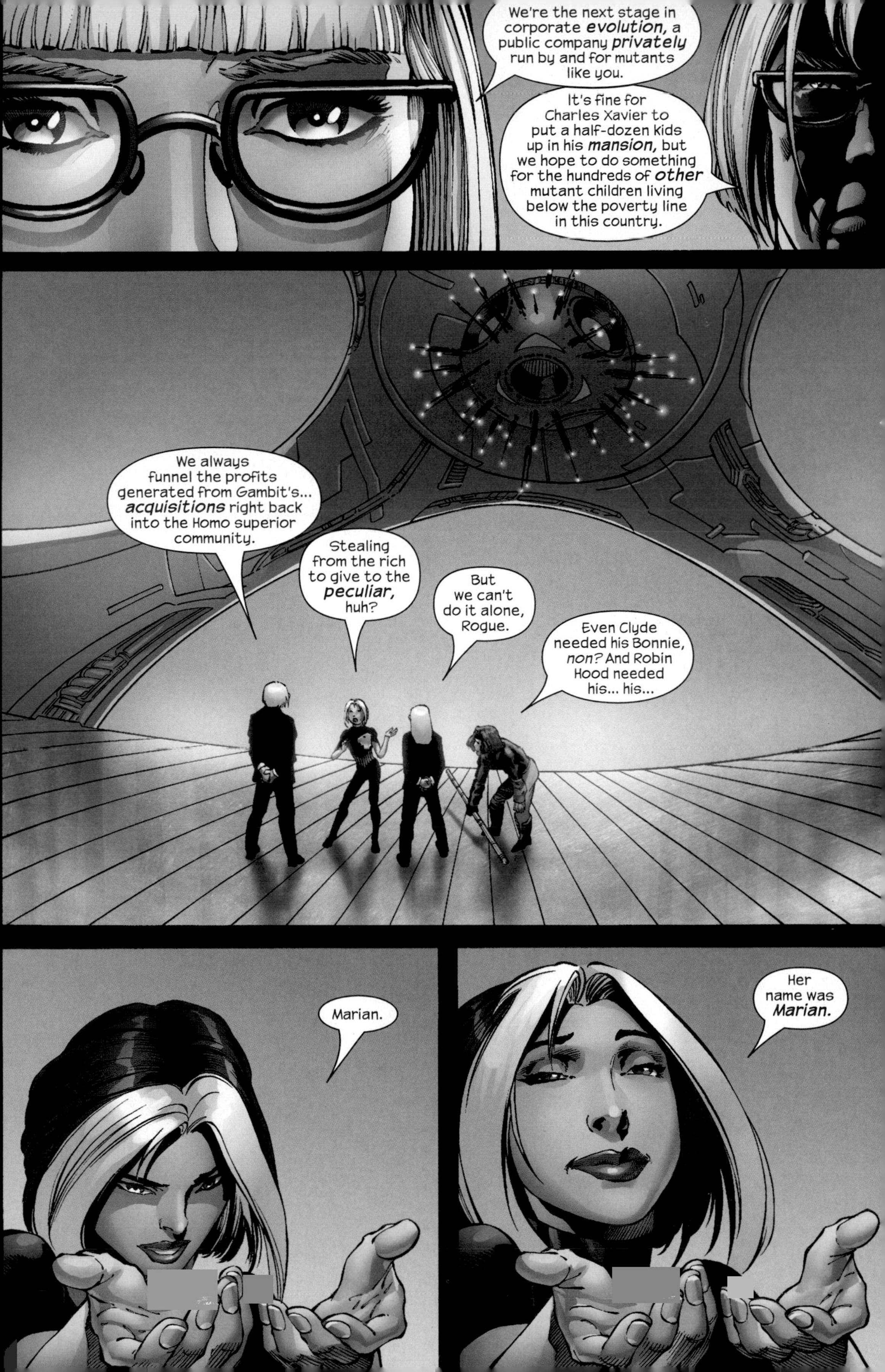
We're the next stage in corporate *evolution,* a public company *privately* run by and for mutants like you.
It's fine for Charles Xavier to put a half-dozen kids up in his *mansion,* but we hope to do something for the hundreds of *other* mutant children living below the poverty line in this country.
We always funnel the profits generated from Gambit's... *acquisitions* right back into the Homo superior community.
Stealing from the rich to give to the *peculiar,* huh?
But we can't do it alone, Rogue.
Even Clyde needed his Bonnie, *non?* And Robin Hood needed his... his...
Marian.
Her name was *Marian.*

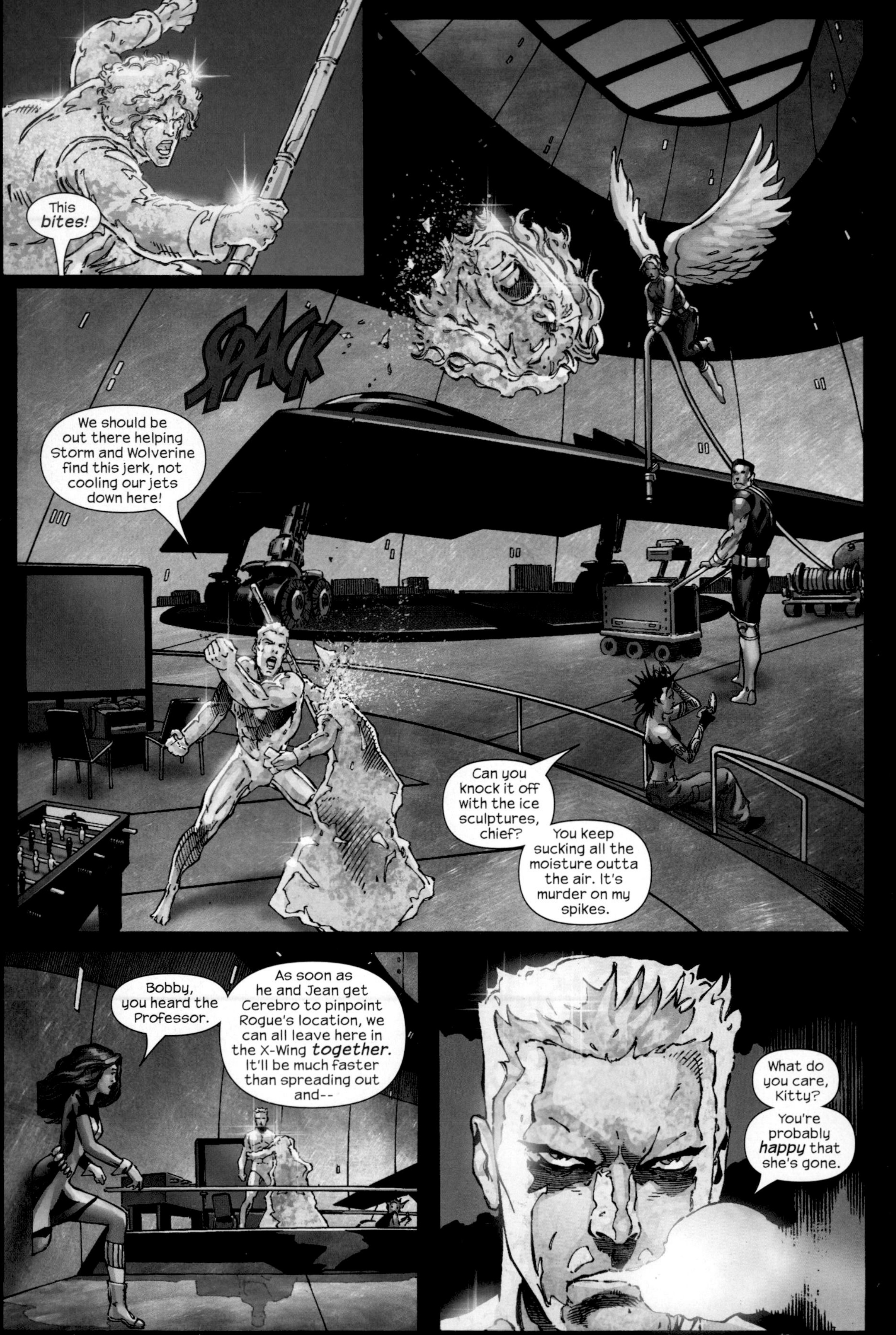

This bites!
SPACK
We should be out there helping Storm and Wolverine find this jerk, not cooling our jets down here!
Can you knock it off with the ice sculptures, chief?
You keep sucking all the moisture outta the air. It's murder on my spikes.
Bobby, you heard the Professor.
As soon as he and Jean get Cerebro to pinpoint Rogue's location, we can all leave here in the X-Wing together. It'll be much faster than spreading out and--
What do you care, Kitty?
You're probably happy that she's gone.

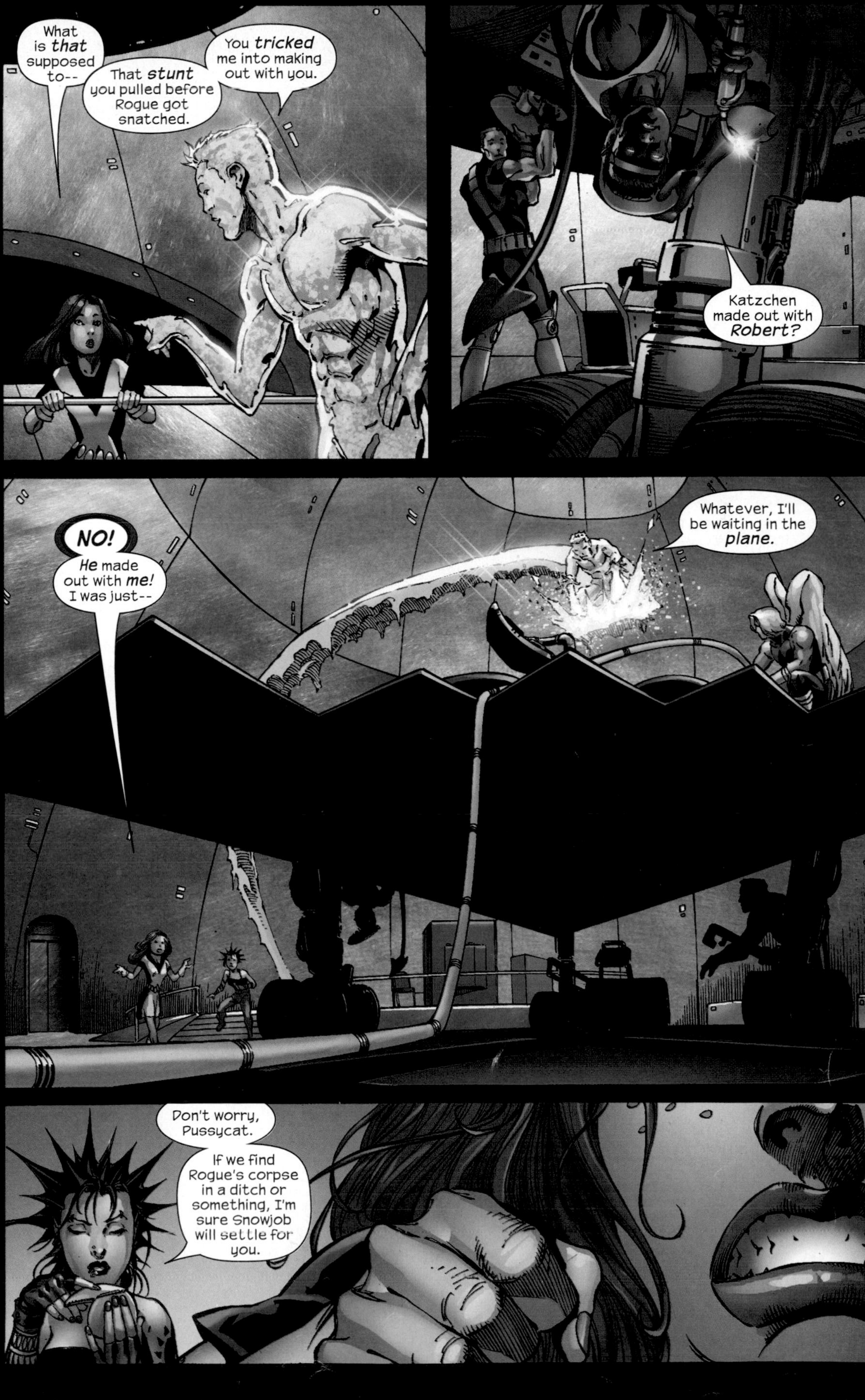
What is that supposed to--
That stunt you pulled before Rogue got snatched.
You tricked me into making out with you.
Katzchen made out with Robert?
NO!
He made out with me! I was just--
Whatever, I'll be waiting in the plane.
Don't worry, Pussycat.
If we find Rogue's corpse in a ditch or something, I'm sure Snowjob will settle for you.

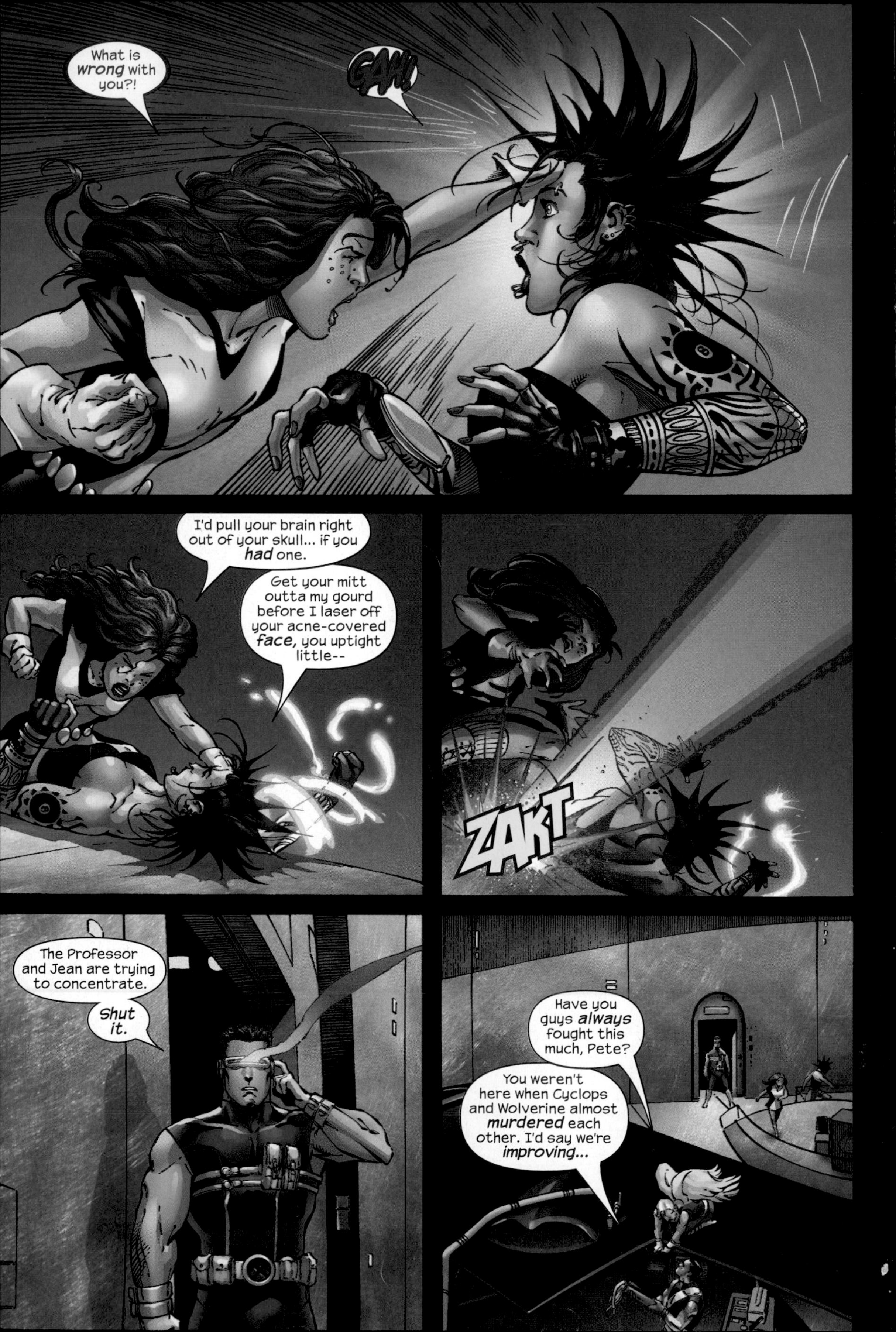
What is *wrong* with you?!
GAH!
I'd pull your brain right out of your skull... if you *had* one.
Get your mitt outta my gourd before I laser off your acne-covered *face*, you uptight little--
ZAKT
The Professor and Jean are trying to concentrate.
Shut it.
Have you guys *always* fought this much, Pete?
You weren't here when Cyclops and Wolverine almost *murdered* each other. I'd say we're *improving...*

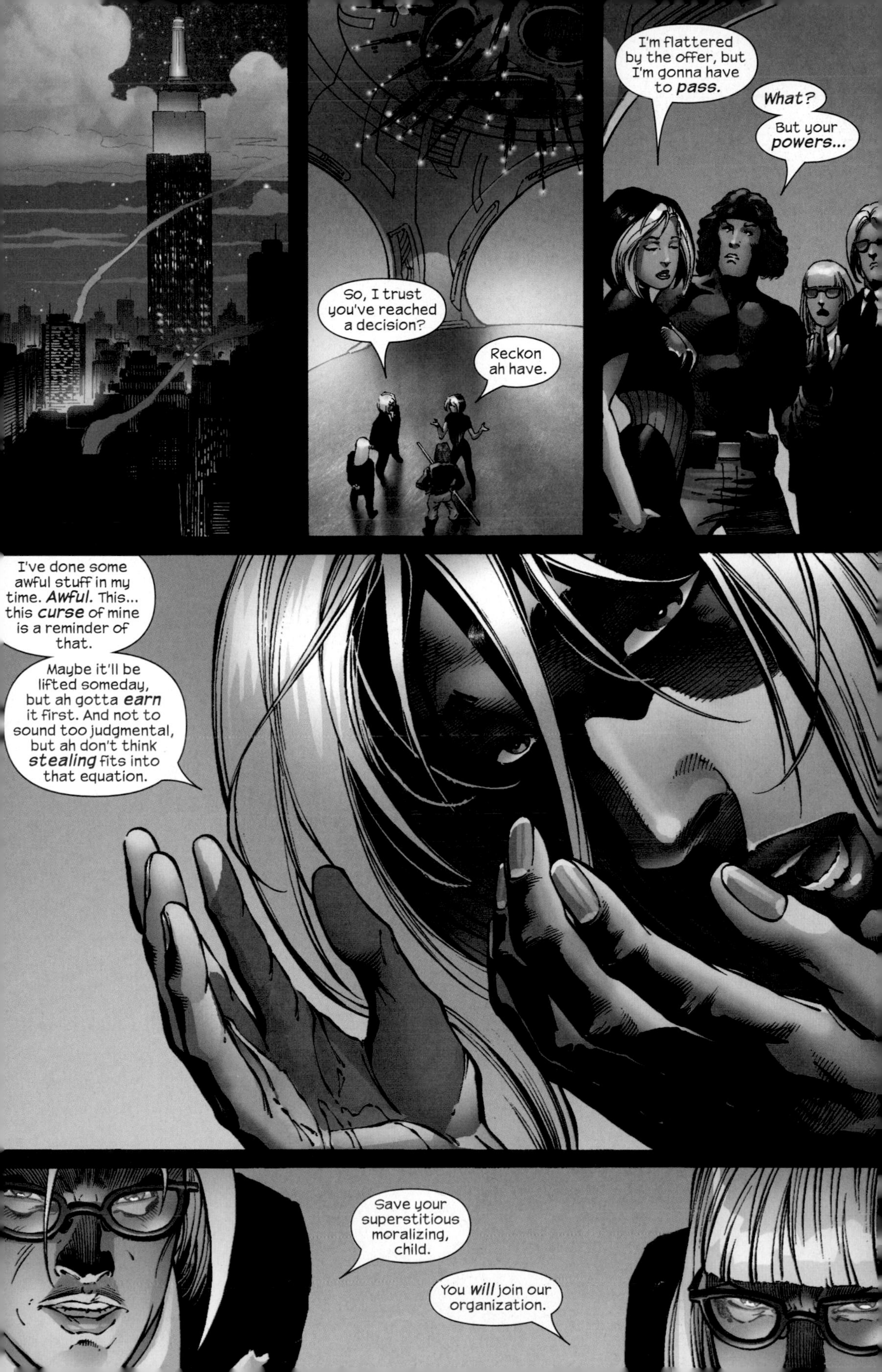

So, I trust you've reached a decision?
Reckon ah have.
I'm flattered by the offer, but I'm gonna have to pass.
What?
But your powers...
I've done some awful stuff in my time. Awful. This... this curse of mine is a reminder of that.
Maybe it'll be lifted someday, but ah gotta earn it first. And not to sound too judgmental, but ah don't think stealing fits into that equation.
Save your superstitious moralizing, child.
You will join our organization.

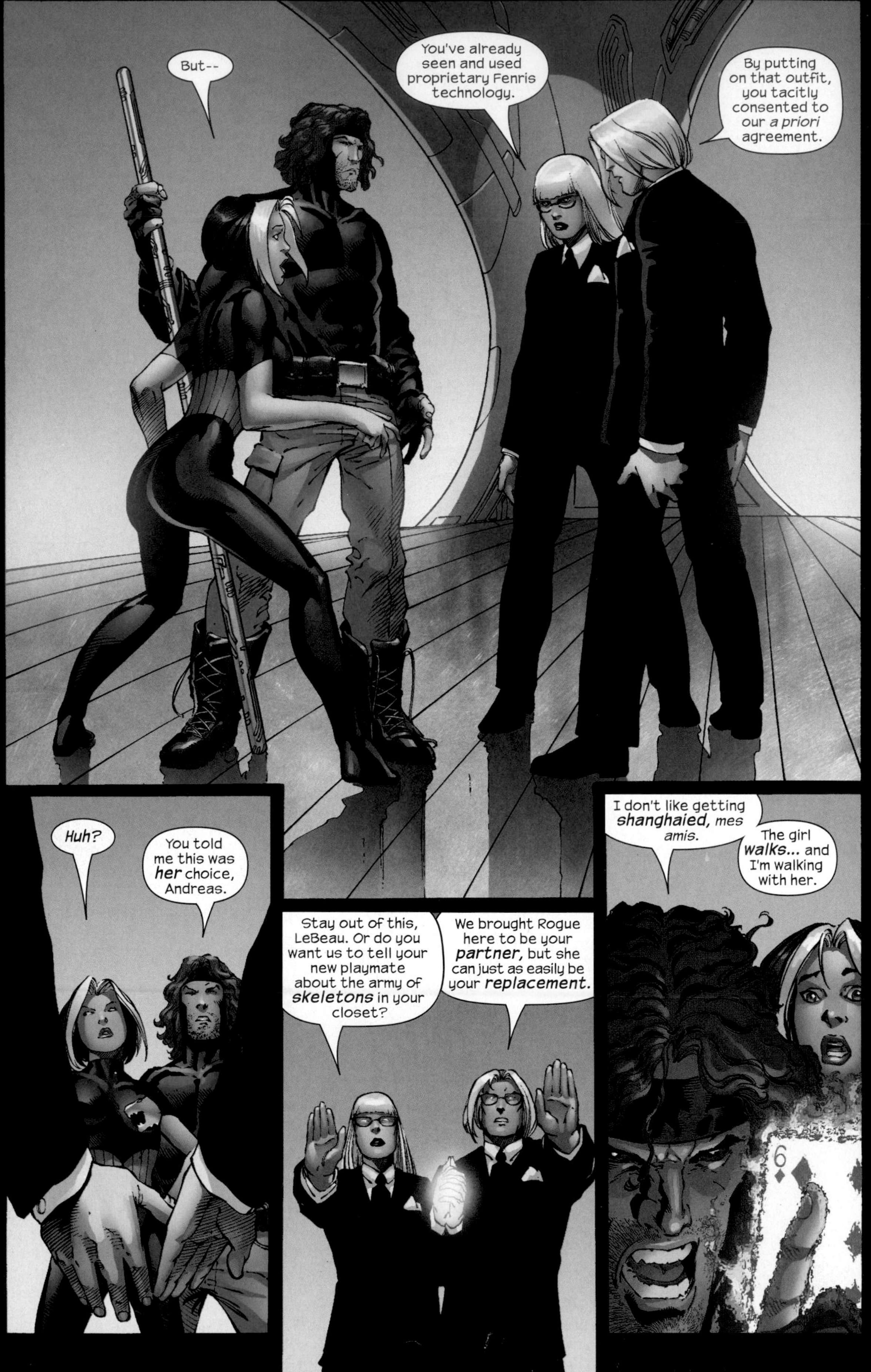
But--
You've already seen and used proprietary Fenris technology.
By putting on that outfit, you tacitly consented to our *a priori* agreement.
Huh?
You told me this was **her** choice, Andreas.
Stay out of this, LeBeau. Or do you want us to tell your new playmate about the army of **skeletons** in your closet?
We brought Rogue here to be your **partner,** but she can just as easily be your **replacement.**
I don't like getting **shanghaied,** *mes amis.*
The girl **walks...** and I'm walking with her.

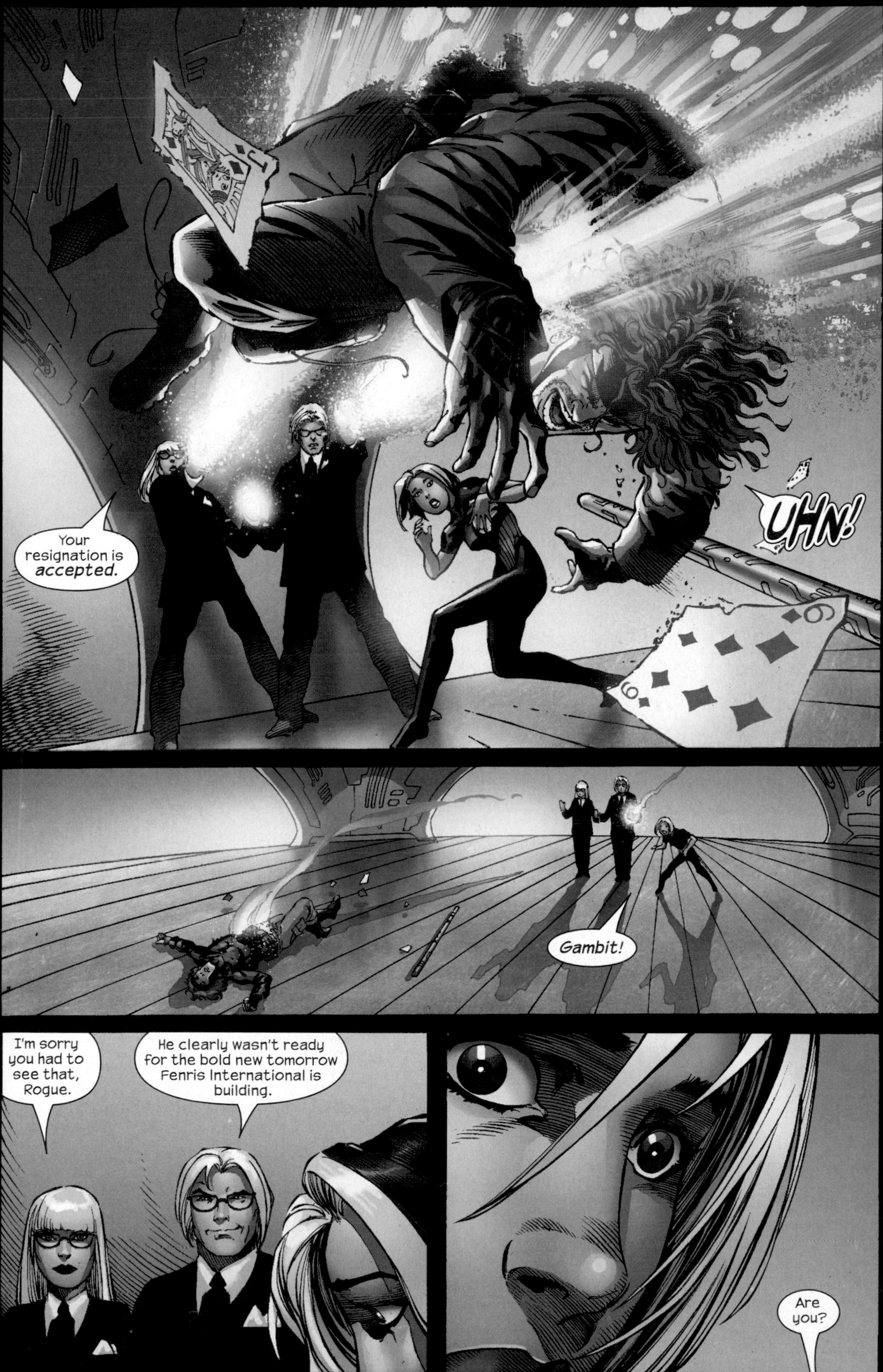
UHN!
Your resignation is *accepted.*
Gambit!
I'm sorry you had to see that, Rogue.
He clearly wasn't ready for the bold new tomorrow Fenris International is building.
Are you?

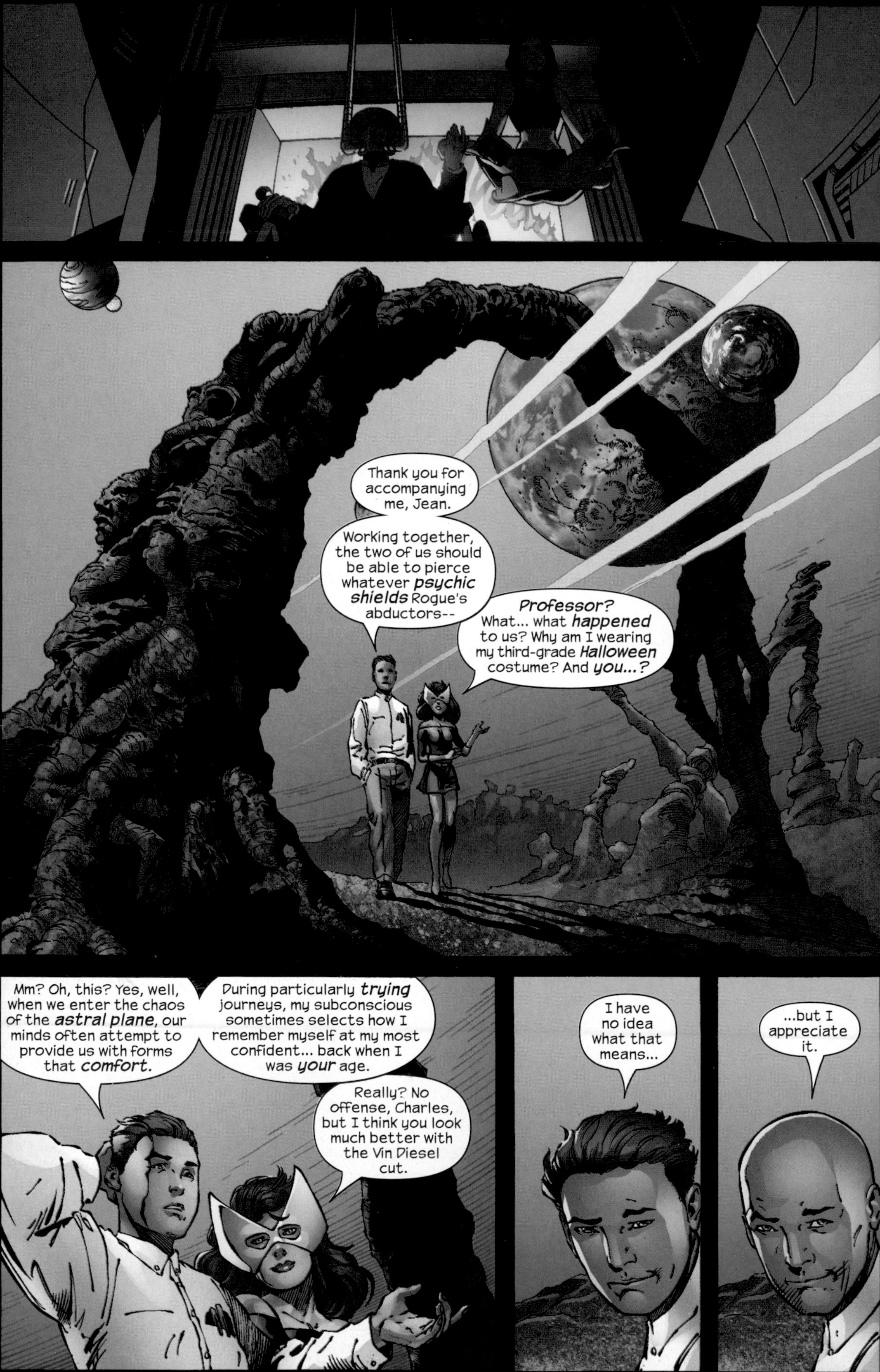
Thank you for accompanying me, Jean.
Working together, the two of us should be able to pierce whatever psychic shields Rogue's abductors--
Professor? What... what happened to us? Why am I wearing my third-grade Halloween costume? And you...?
Mm? Oh, this? Yes, well, when we enter the chaos of the astral plane, our minds often attempt to provide us with forms that comfort.
During particularly trying journeys, my subconscious sometimes selects how I remember myself at my most confident... back when I was your age.
Really? No offense, Charles, but I think you look much better with the Vin Diesel cut.
I have no idea what that means...
...but I appreciate it.

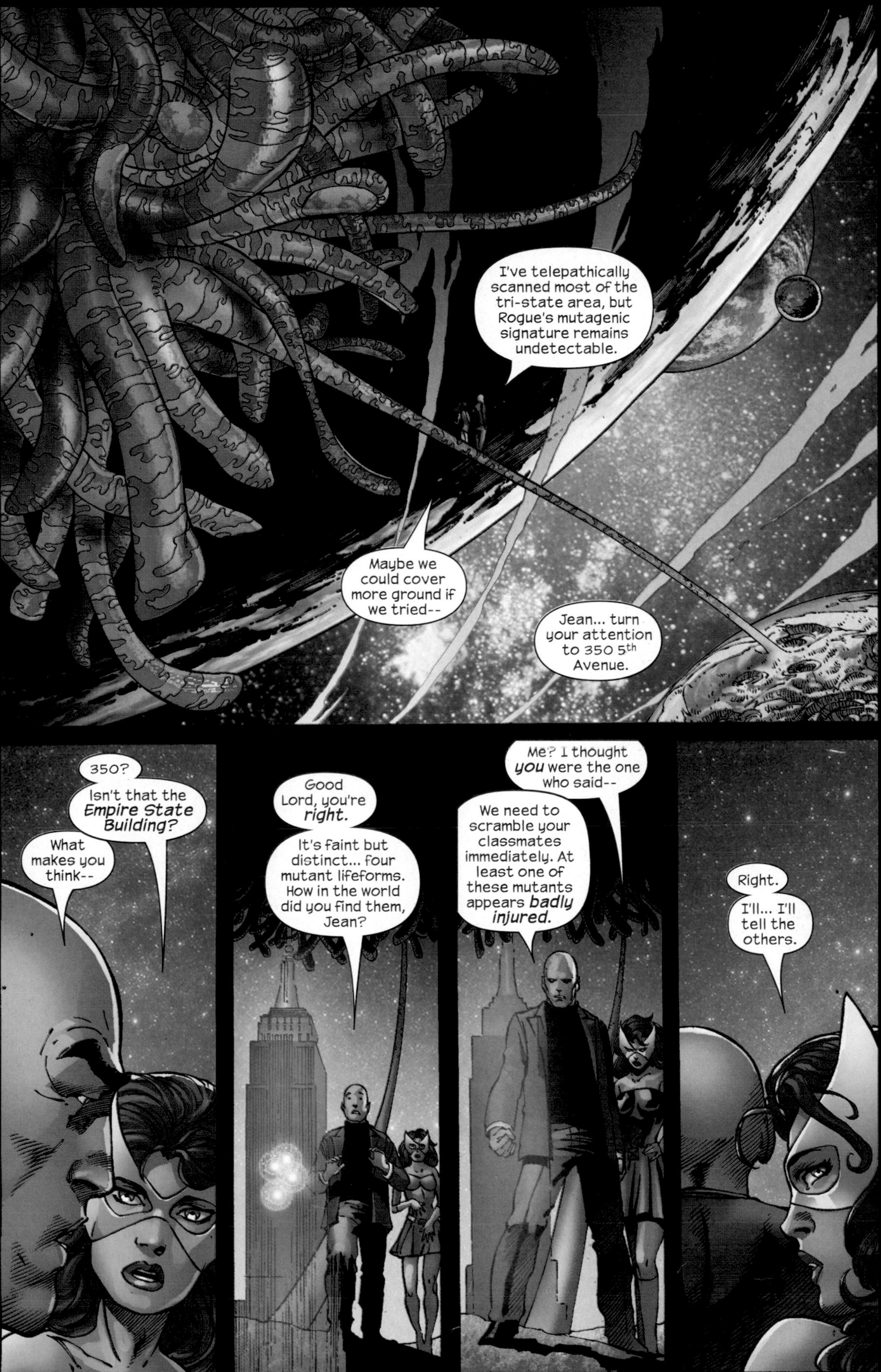
I've telepathically scanned most of the tri-state area, but Rogue's mutagenic signature remains undetectable.
Maybe we could cover more ground if we tried--
Jean... turn your attention to 350 5th Avenue.
350?
Isn't that the Empire State Building?
What makes you think--
Good Lord, you're right.
It's faint but distinct... four mutant lifeforms. How in the world did you find them, Jean?
Me? I thought you were the one who said--
We need to scramble your classmates immediately. At least one of these mutants appears badly injured.
Right.
I'll... I'll tell the others.

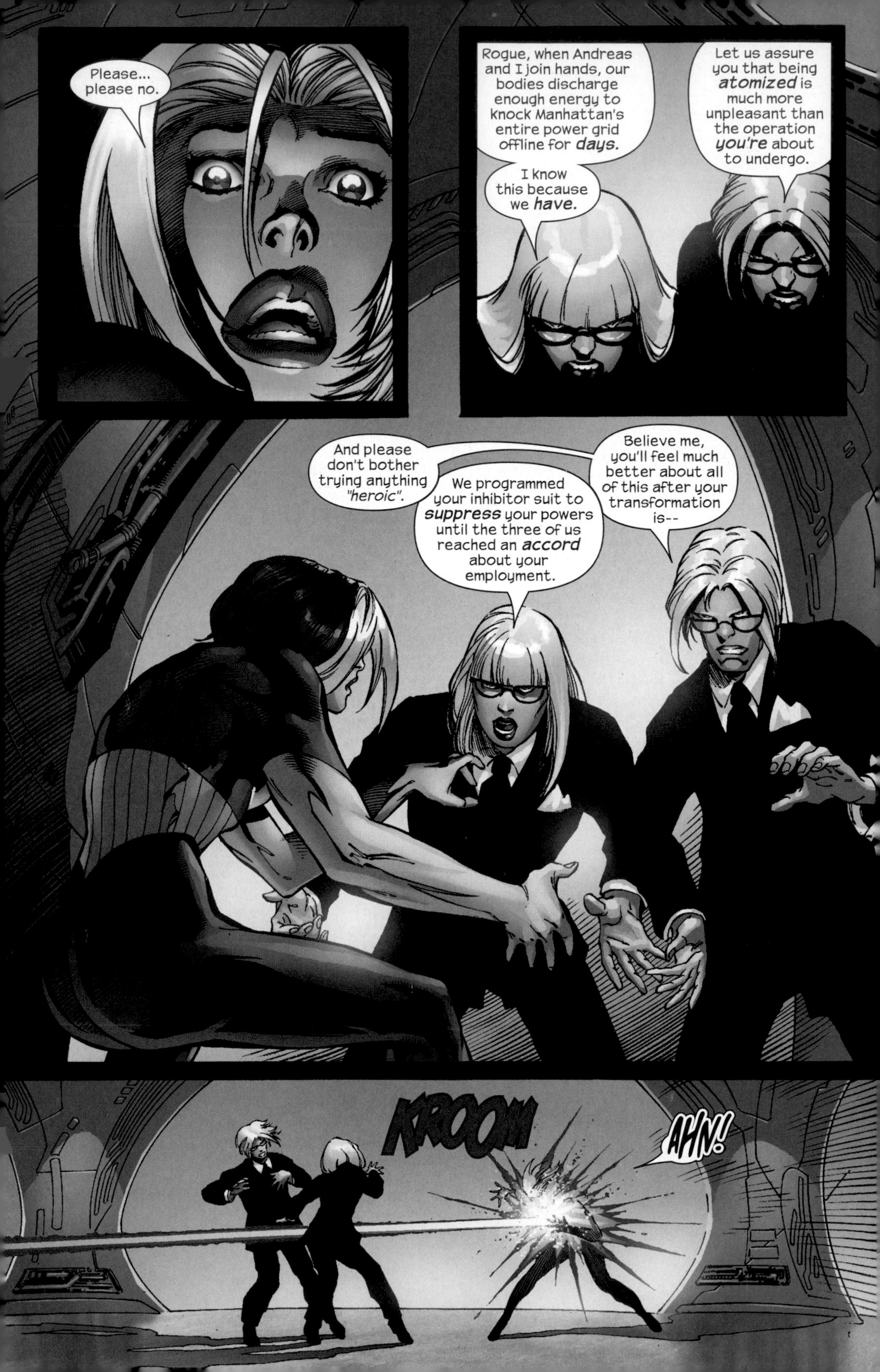
Please... please no.
Rogue, when Andreas and I join hands, our bodies discharge enough energy to knock Manhattan's entire power grid offline for *days.*
I know this because we *have.*
Let us assure you that being *atomized* is much more unpleasant than the operation *you're* about to undergo.
And please don't bother trying anything "*heroic*".
We programmed your inhibitor suit to *suppress* your powers until the three of us reached an *accord* about your employment.
Believe me, you'll feel much better about all of this after your transformation is--
KROOM
AHN!

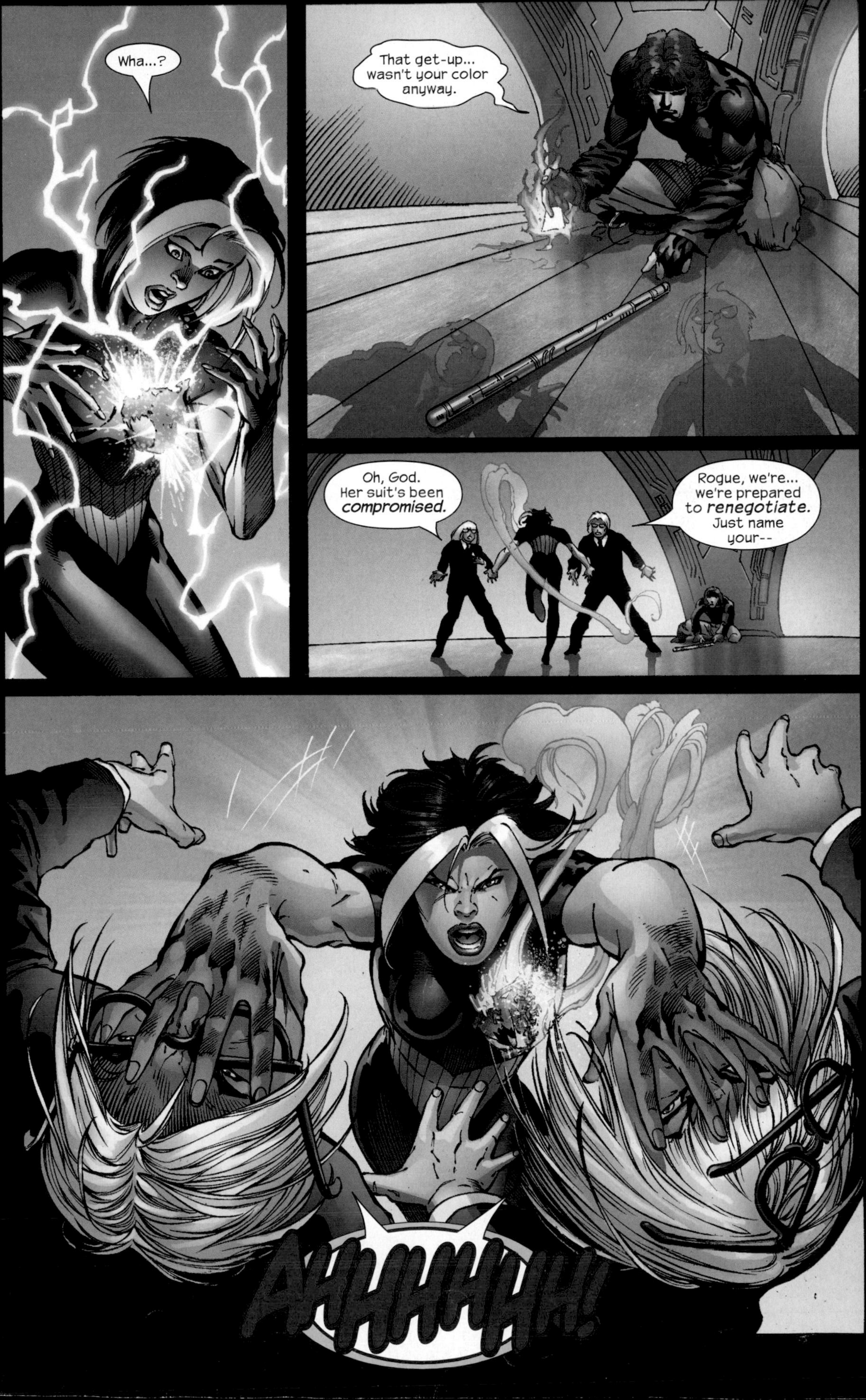
Wha...?
That get-up... wasn't your color anyway.
Oh, God. Her suit's been compromised.
Rogue, we're... we're prepared to renegotiate. Just name your--
AHHHHHH!

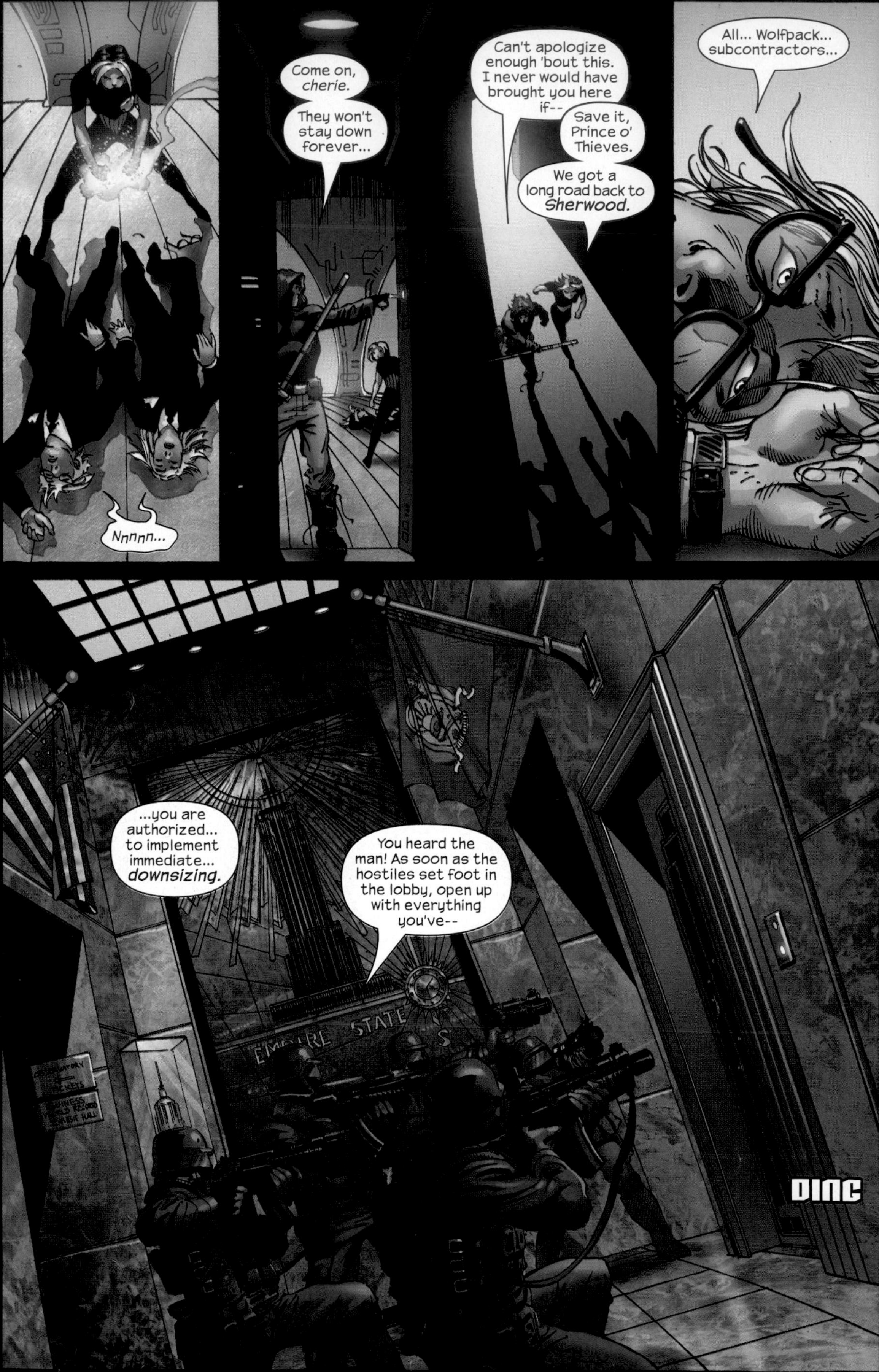

Nnnnn...
Come on, cherie.
They won't stay down forever...
Can't apologize enough 'bout this. I never would have brought you here if--
Save it, Prince o' Thieves.
We got a long road back to Sherwood.
All... Wolfpack... subcontractors...
...you are authorized... to implement immediate... downsizing.
You heard the man! As soon as the hostiles set foot in the lobby, open up with everything you've--
EMPIRE STATE
DING

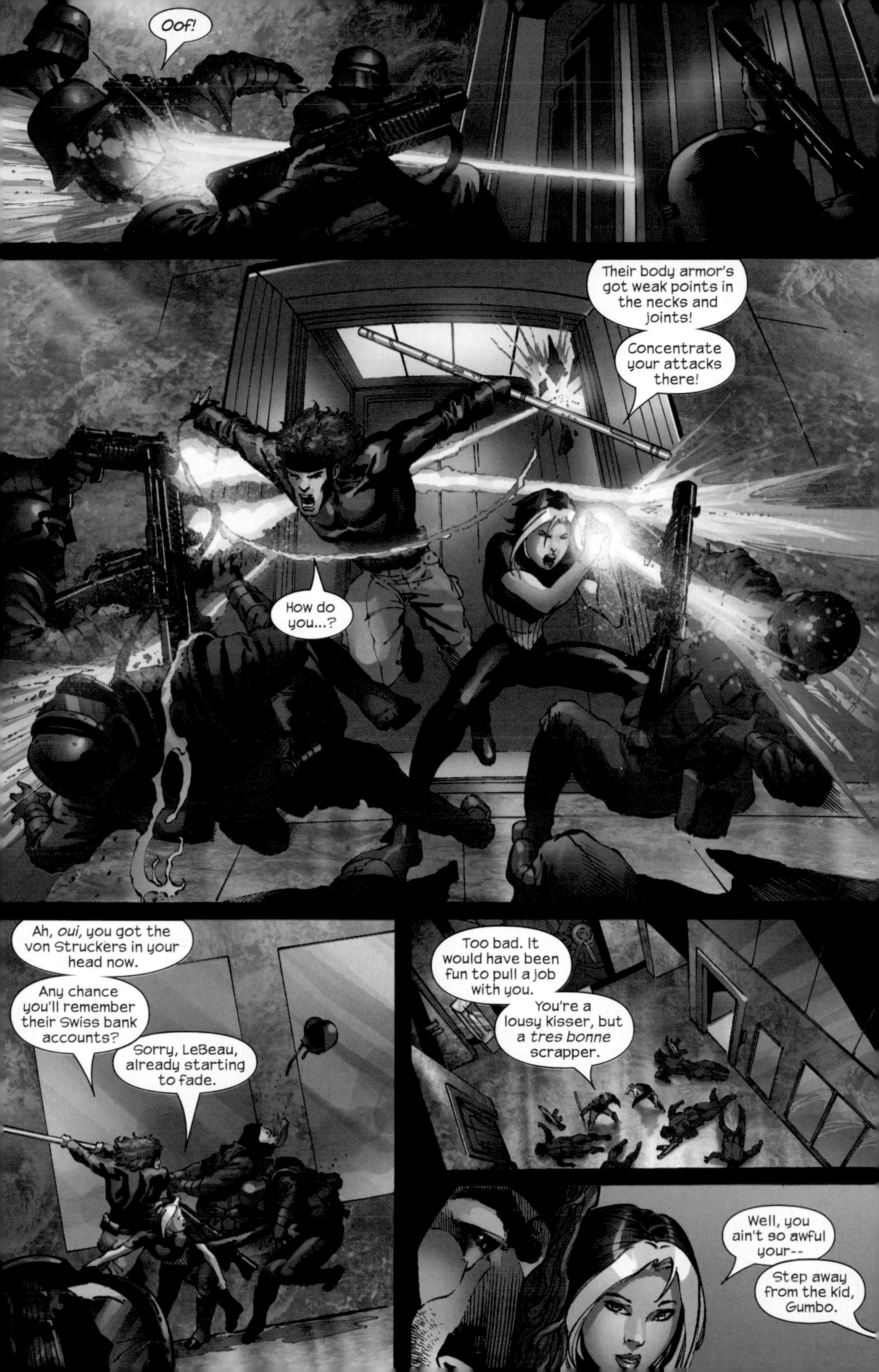
Oof!
Their body armor's got weak points in the necks and joints!
Concentrate your attacks there!
How do you...?
Ah, *oui,* you got the von Struckers in your head now.
Any chance you'll remember their Swiss bank accounts?
Sorry, LeBeau, already starting to fade.
Too bad. It would have been fun to pull a job with you.
You're a lousy kisser, but a *tres bonne* scrapper.
Well, you ain't so awful your--
Step away from the kid, Gumbo.

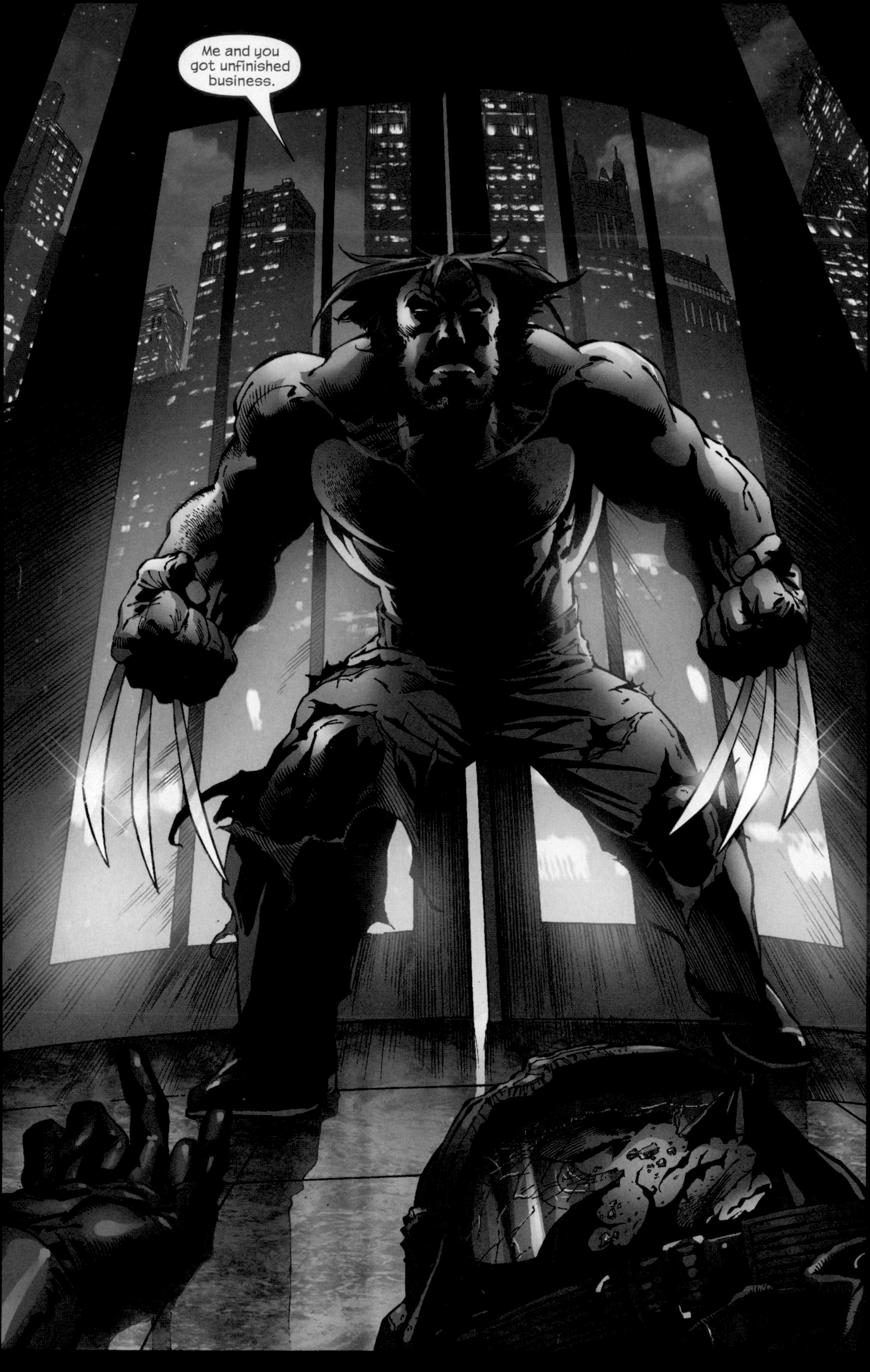
Me and you got unfinished business.

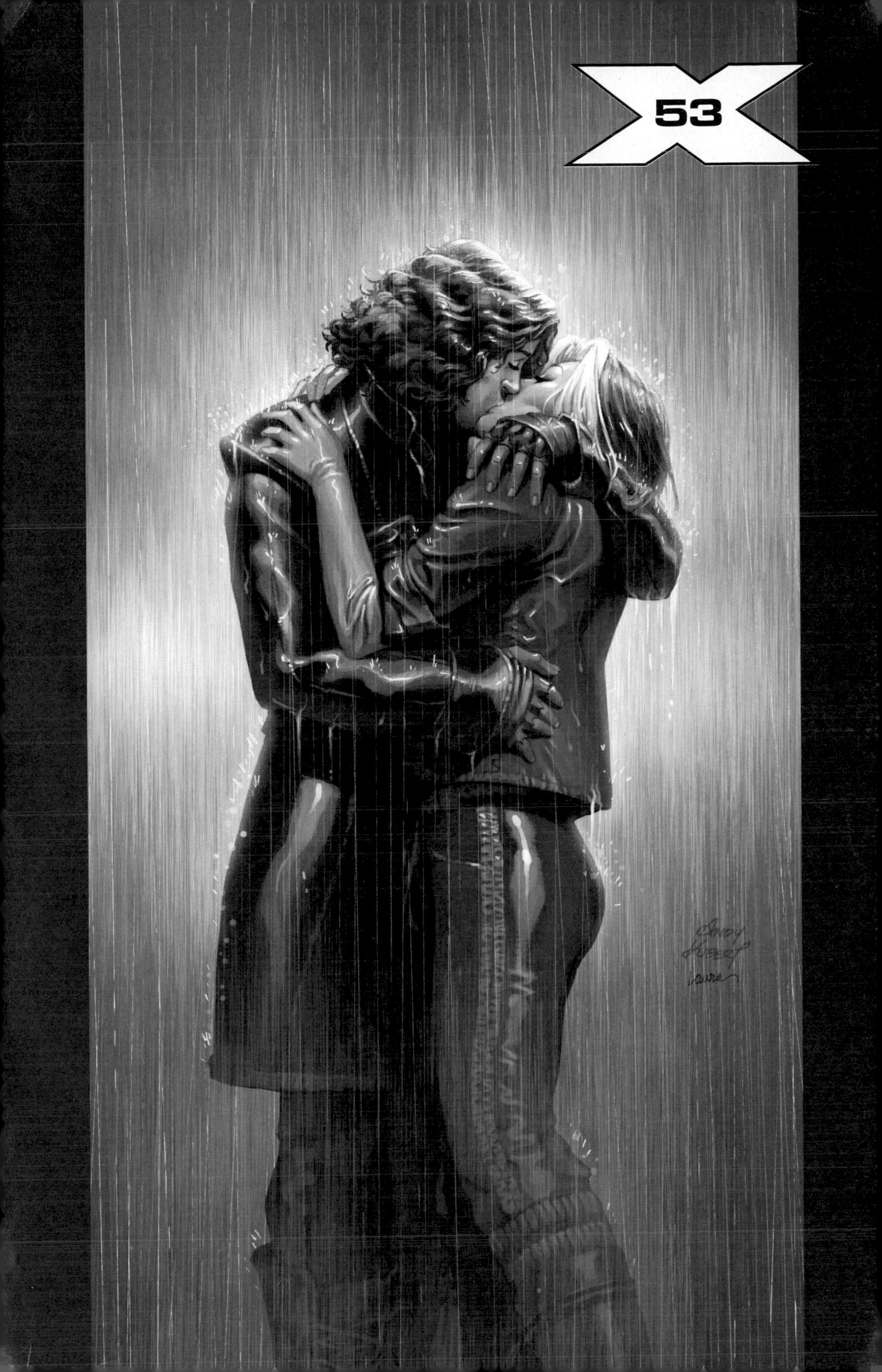
53

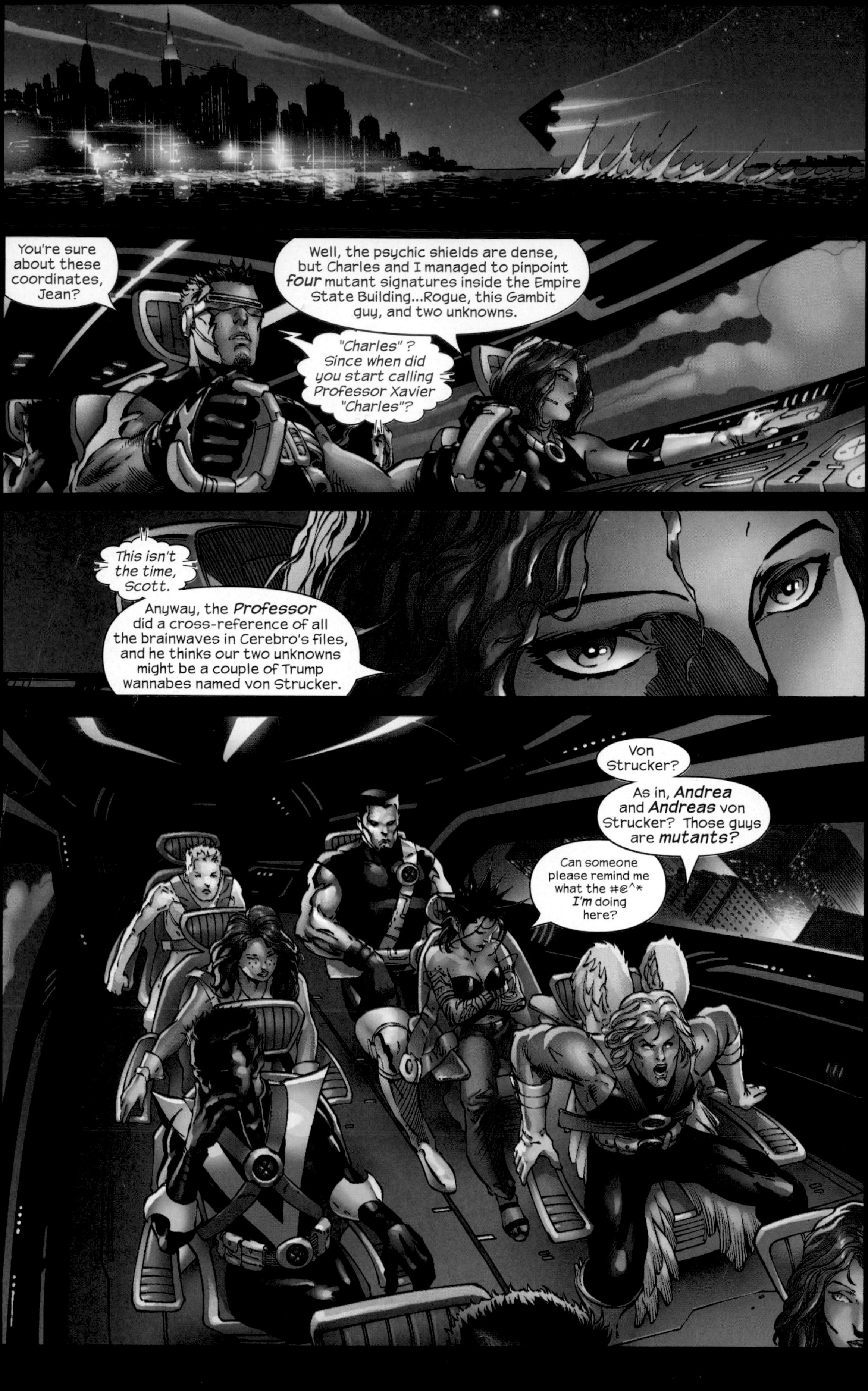
You're sure about these coordinates, Jean?
Well, the psychic shields are dense, but Charles and I managed to pinpoint *four* mutant signatures inside the Empire State Building...Rogue, this Gambit guy, and two unknowns.
"Charles"? Since when did you start calling Professor Xavier "Charles"?
This isn't the time, Scott.
Anyway, the *Professor* did a cross-reference of all the brainwaves in Cerebro's files, and he thinks our two unknowns might be a couple of Trump wannabes named von Strucker.
Von Strucker?
As in, *Andrea* and *Andreas* von Strucker? Those guys are *mutants?*
Can someone please remind me what the #@^* *I'm* doing here?

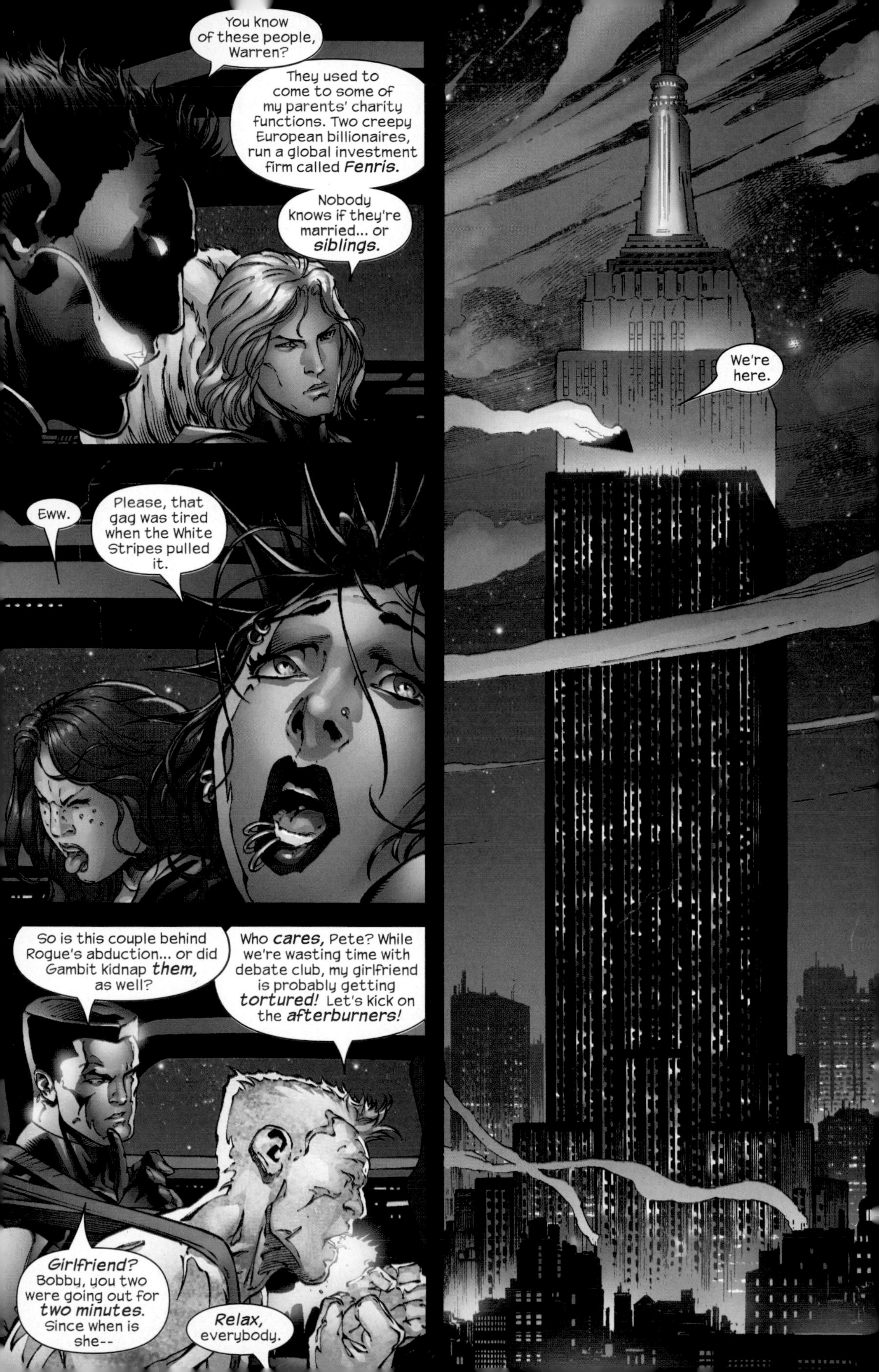
You know of these people, Warren?
They used to come to some of my parents' charity functions. Two creepy European billionaires, run a global investment firm called Fenris.
Nobody knows if they're married... or siblings.
We're here.
Eww.
Please, that gag was tired when the White Stripes pulled it.
So is this couple behind Rogue's abduction... or did Gambit kidnap them, as well?
Who cares, Pete? While we're wasting time with debate club, my girlfriend is probably getting tortured! Let's kick on the afterburners!
Girlfriend? Bobby, you two were going out for two minutes. Since when is she--
Relax, everybody.

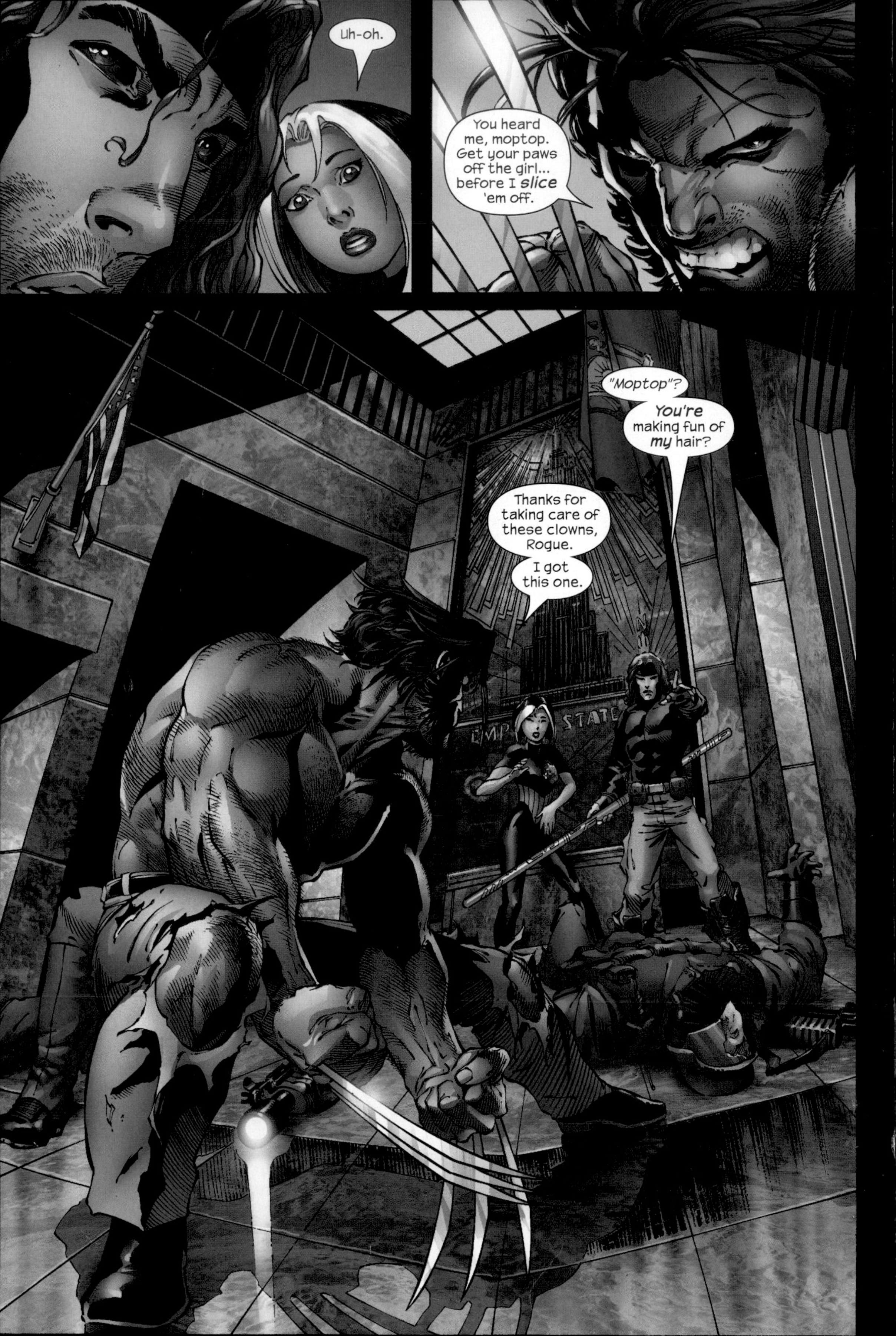
Uh-oh.
You heard me, moptop. Get your paws off the girl... before I *slice* 'em off.
Thanks for taking care of these clowns, Rogue.
I got this one.
"Moptop"?
You're making fun of *my* hair?

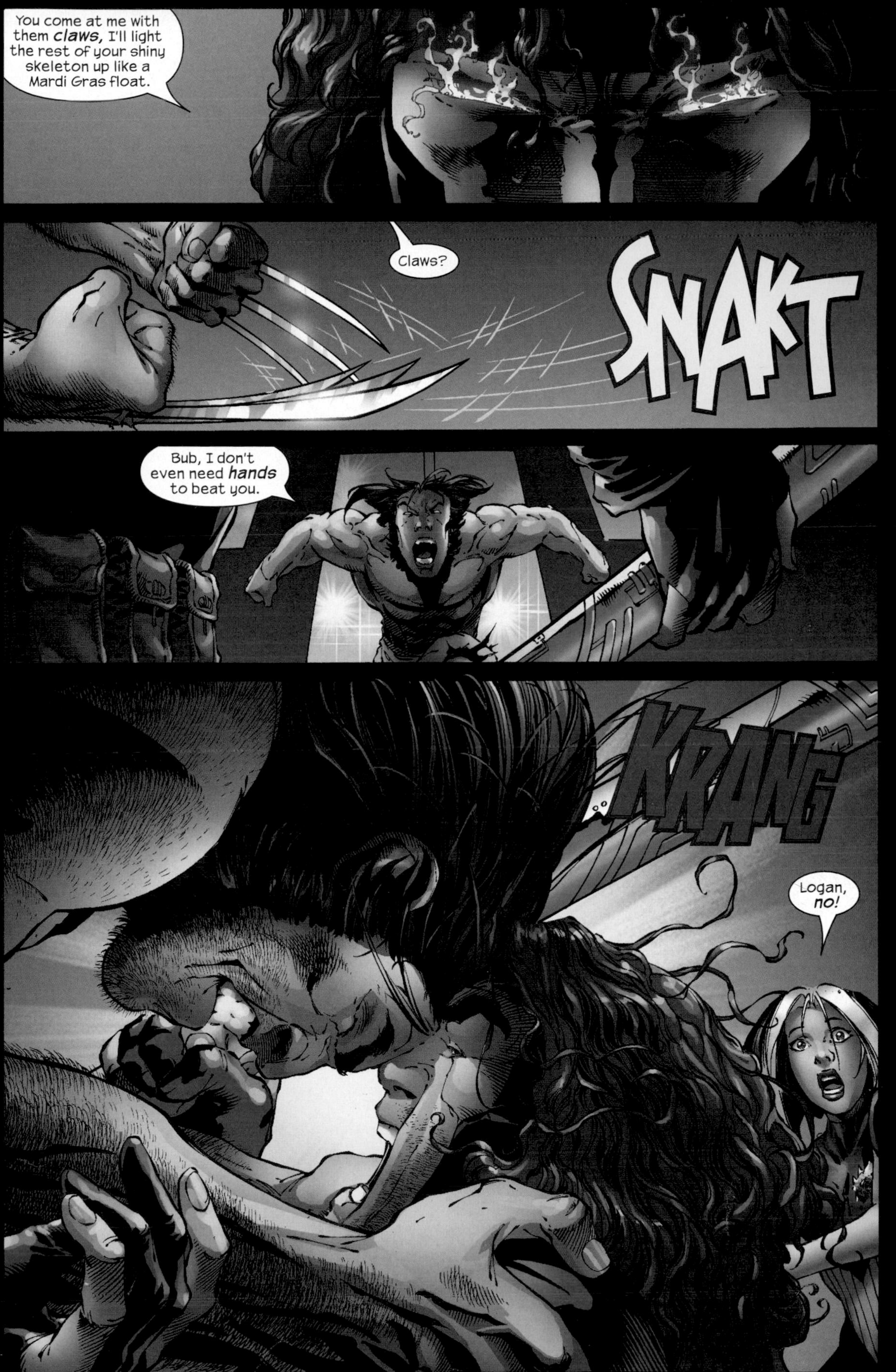
You come at me with them *claws,* I'll light the rest of your shiny skeleton up like a Mardi Gras float.
Claws?
SNAKT
Bub, I don't even need ***hands*** to beat you.
KRANG
Logan, ***no!***

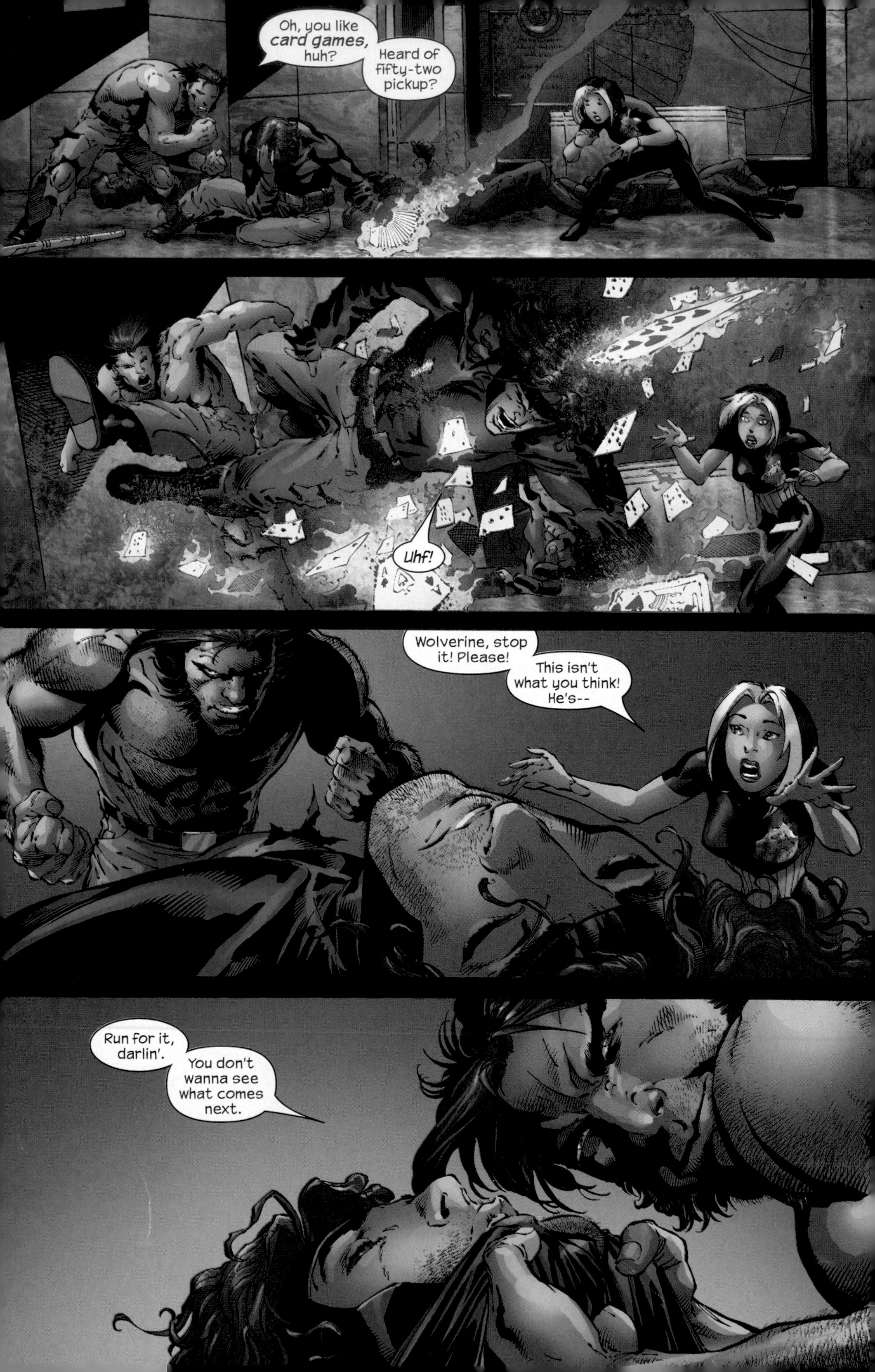
Oh, you like card games, huh?
Heard of fifty-two pickup?
Uhf!
Wolverine, stop it! Please!
This isn't what you think! He's--
Run for it, darlin'.
You don't wanna see what comes next.

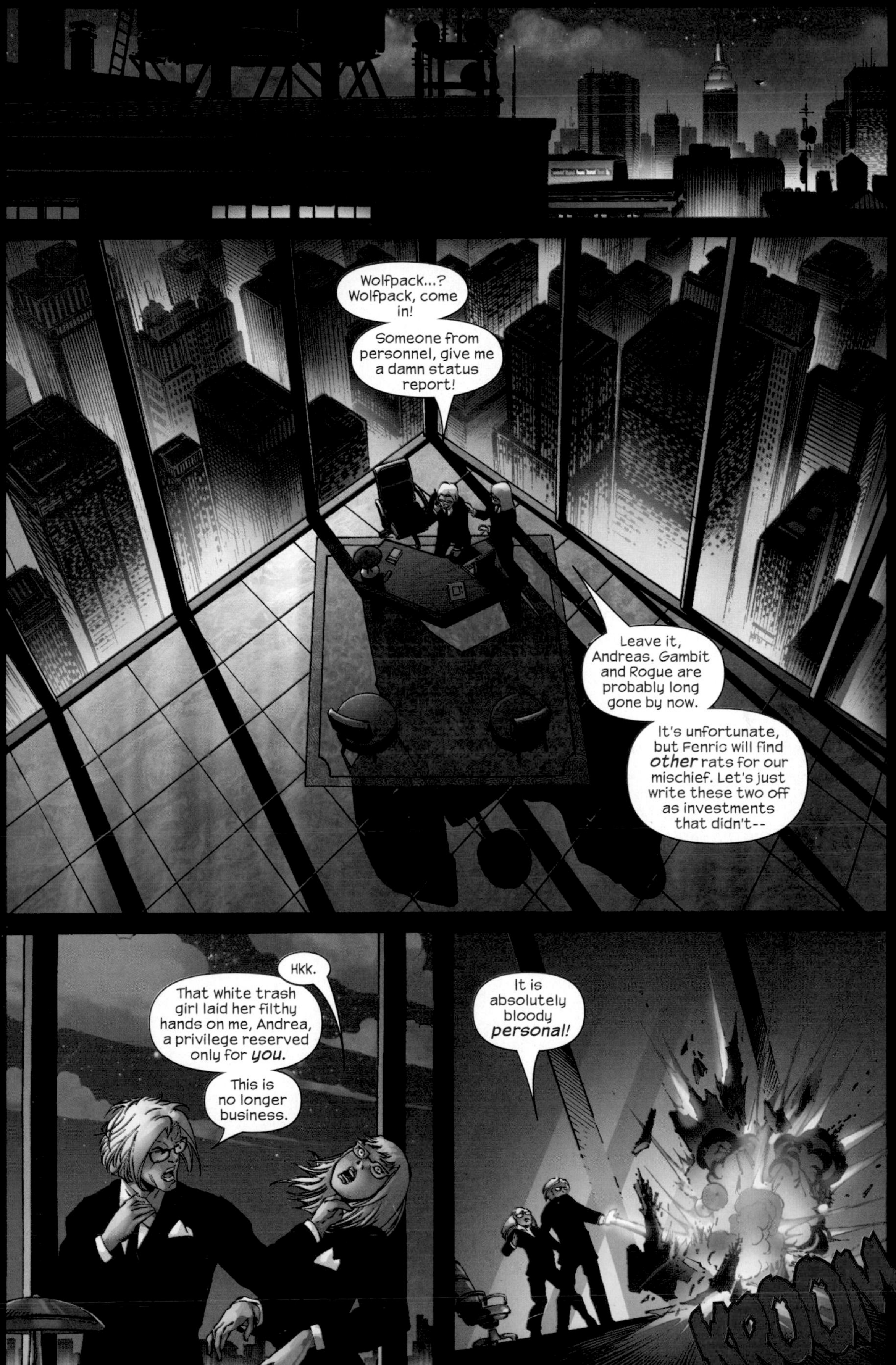
Wolfpack...? Wolfpack, come in!
Someone from personnel, give me a damn status report!
Leave it, Andreas. Gambit and Rogue are probably long gone by now.
It's unfortunate, but Fenris will find *other* rats for our mischief. Let's just write these two off as investments that didn't--
Hkk.
That white trash girl laid her filthy hands on me, Andrea, a privilege reserved only for *you.*
This is no longer business.
It is absolutely bloody *personal!*
KROOM

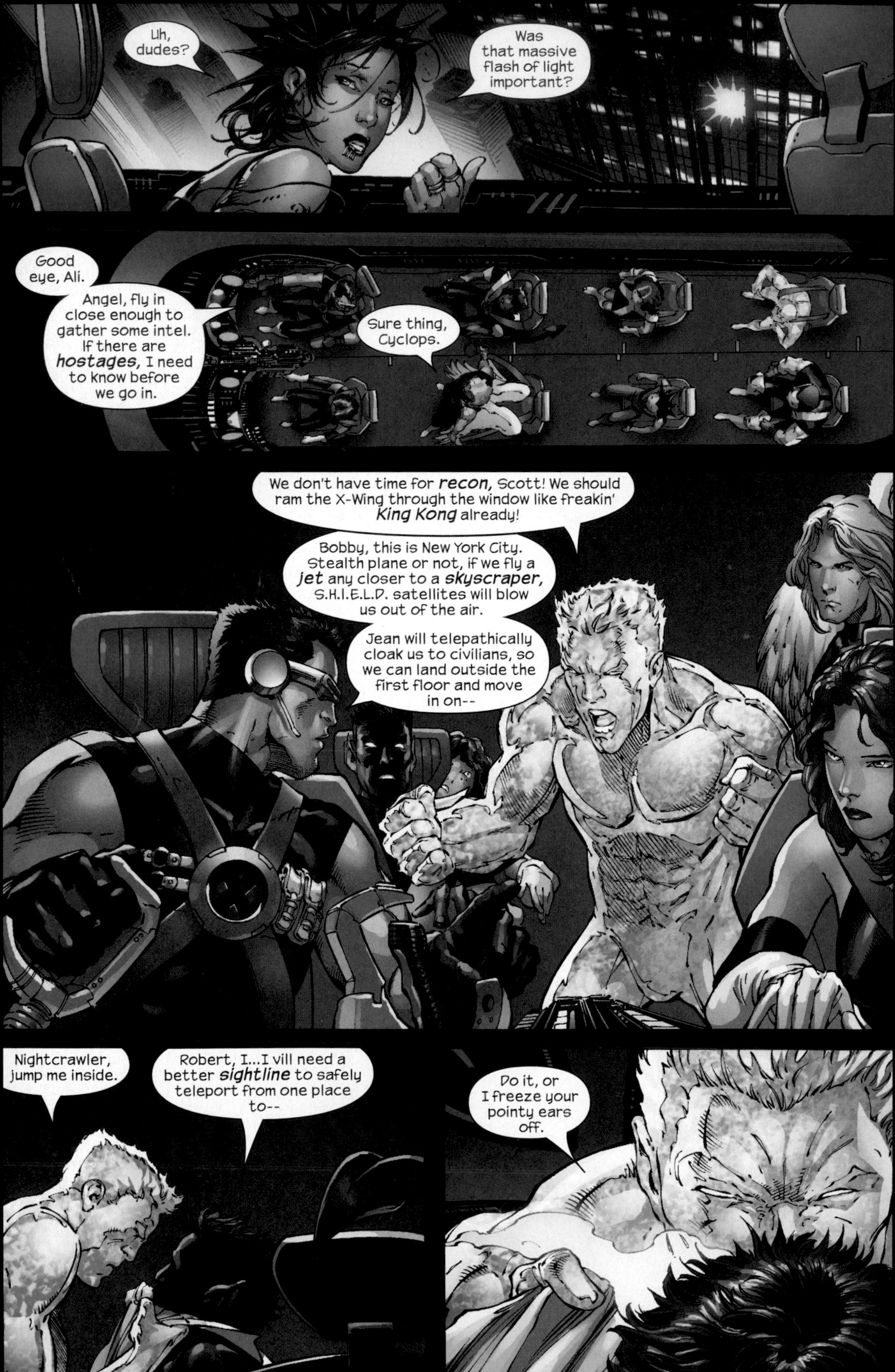
Uh, dudes?
Was that massive flash of light important?
Good eye, Ali.
Angel, fly in close enough to gather some intel. If there are *hostages,* I need to know before we go in.
Sure thing, Cyclops.
We don't have time for *recon,* Scott! We should ram the X-Wing through the window like freakin' *King Kong* already!
Bobby, this is New York City. Stealth plane or not, if we fly a *jet* any closer to a *skyscraper,* S.H.I.E.L.D. satellites will blow us out of the air.
Jean will telepathically cloak us to civilians, so we can land outside the first floor and move in on--
Nightcrawler, jump me inside.
Robert, I...I vill need a better *sightline* to safely teleport from one place to--
Do it, or I freeze your pointy ears off.

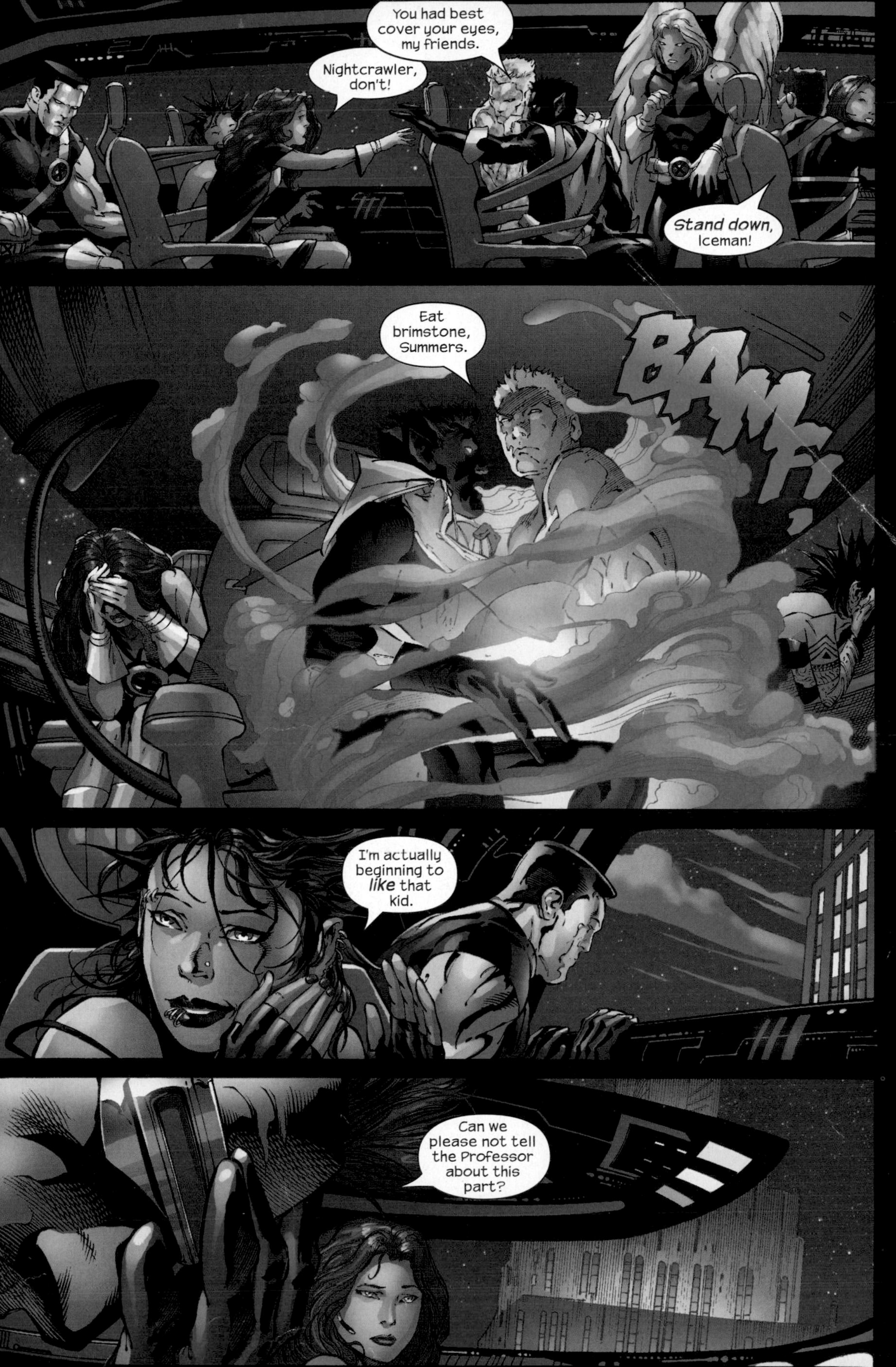
You had best cover your eyes, my friends.
Nightcrawler, don't!
Stand down, Iceman!
Eat brimstone, Summers.
BAMF!
I'm actually beginning to *like* that kid.
Can we please not tell the Professor about this part?

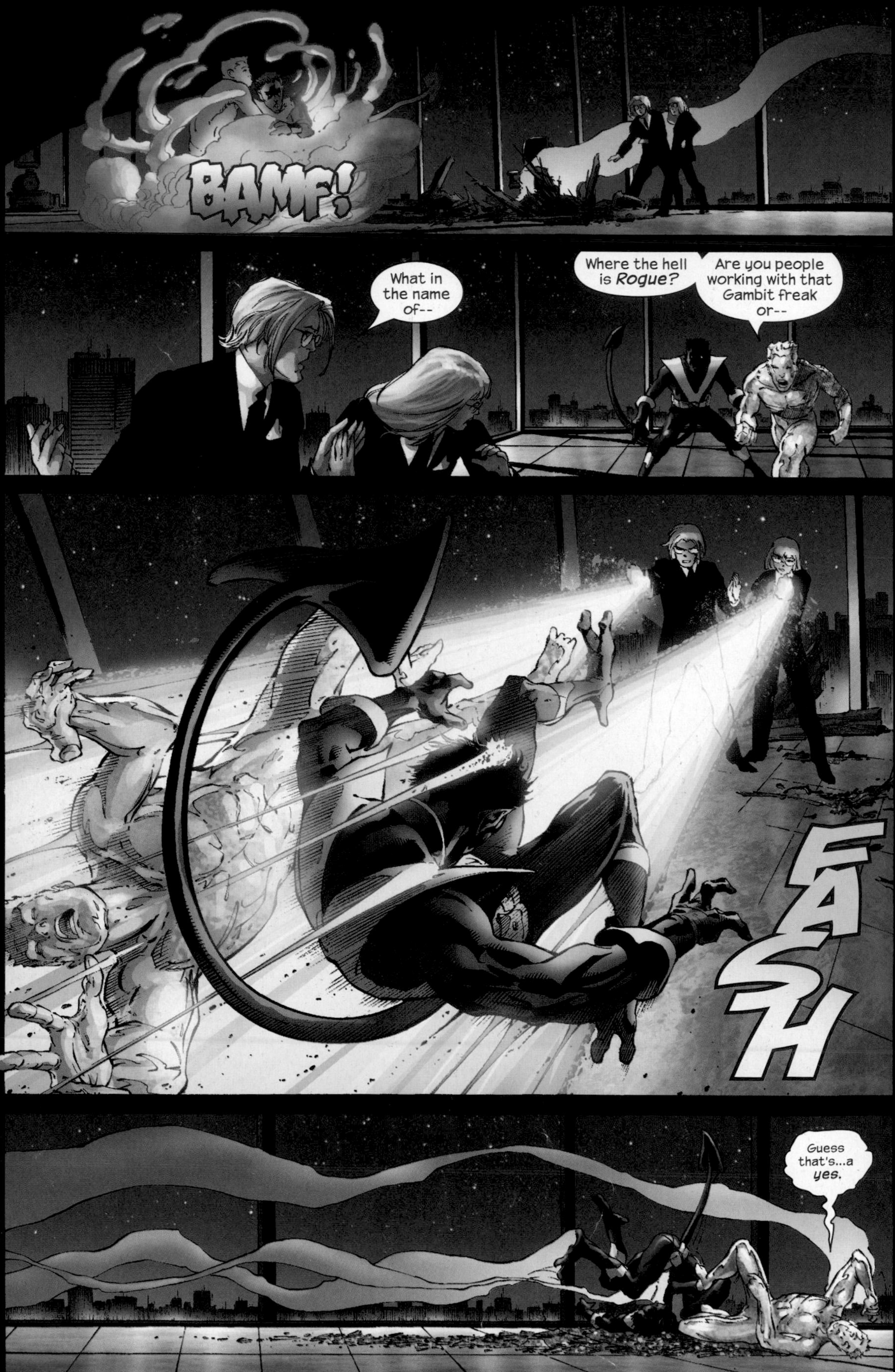
BAMF!
What in the name of--
Where the hell is *Rogue*?
Are you people working with that Gambit freak or--
FASH
Guess that's...a *yes*.

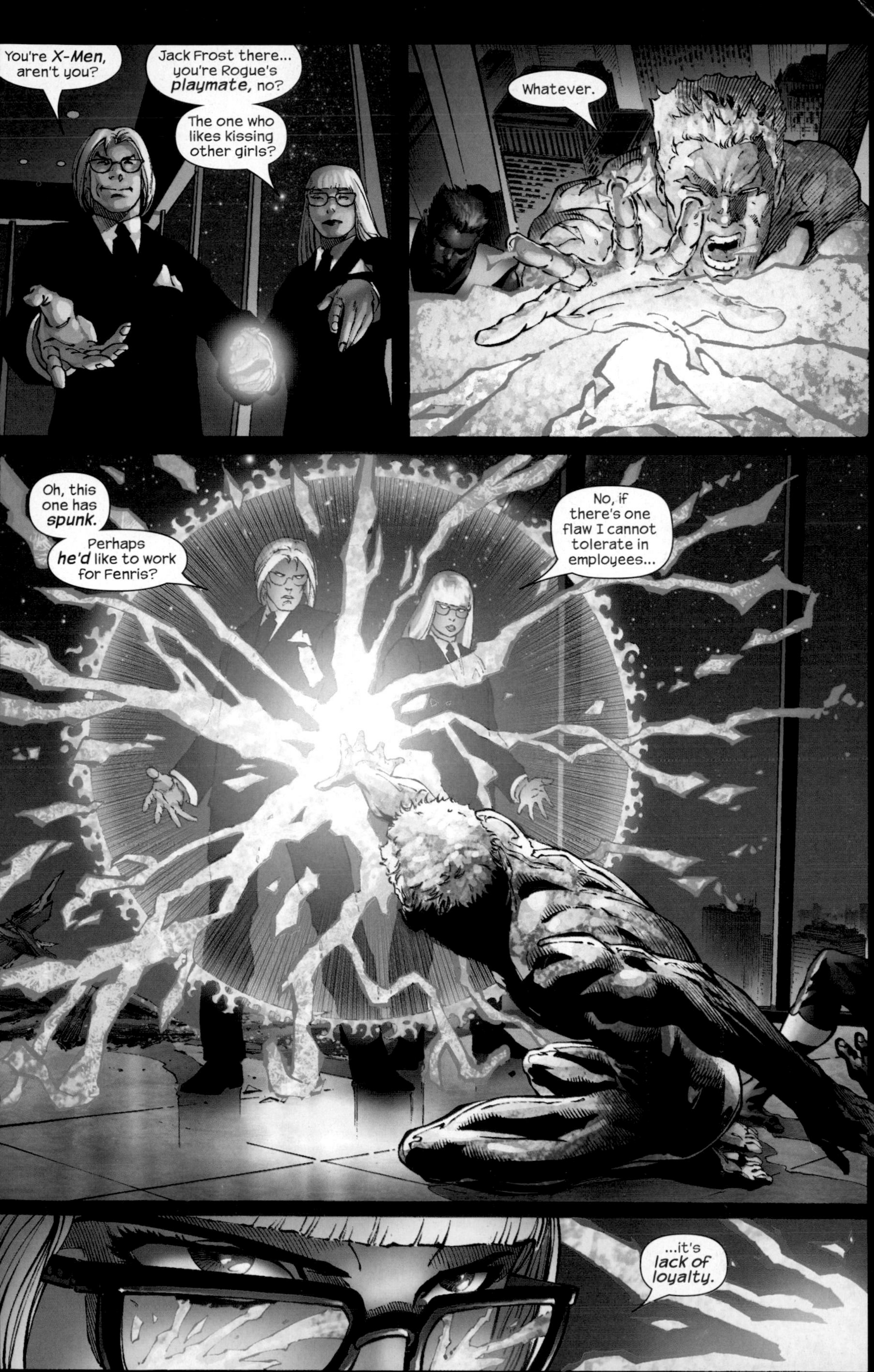

You're X-Men, aren't you?
Jack Frost there... you're Rogue's playmate, no?
The one who likes kissing other girls?
Whatever.
Oh, this one has spunk.
Perhaps he'd like to work for Fenris?
No, if there's one flaw I cannot tolerate in employees...
...it's lack of loyalty.

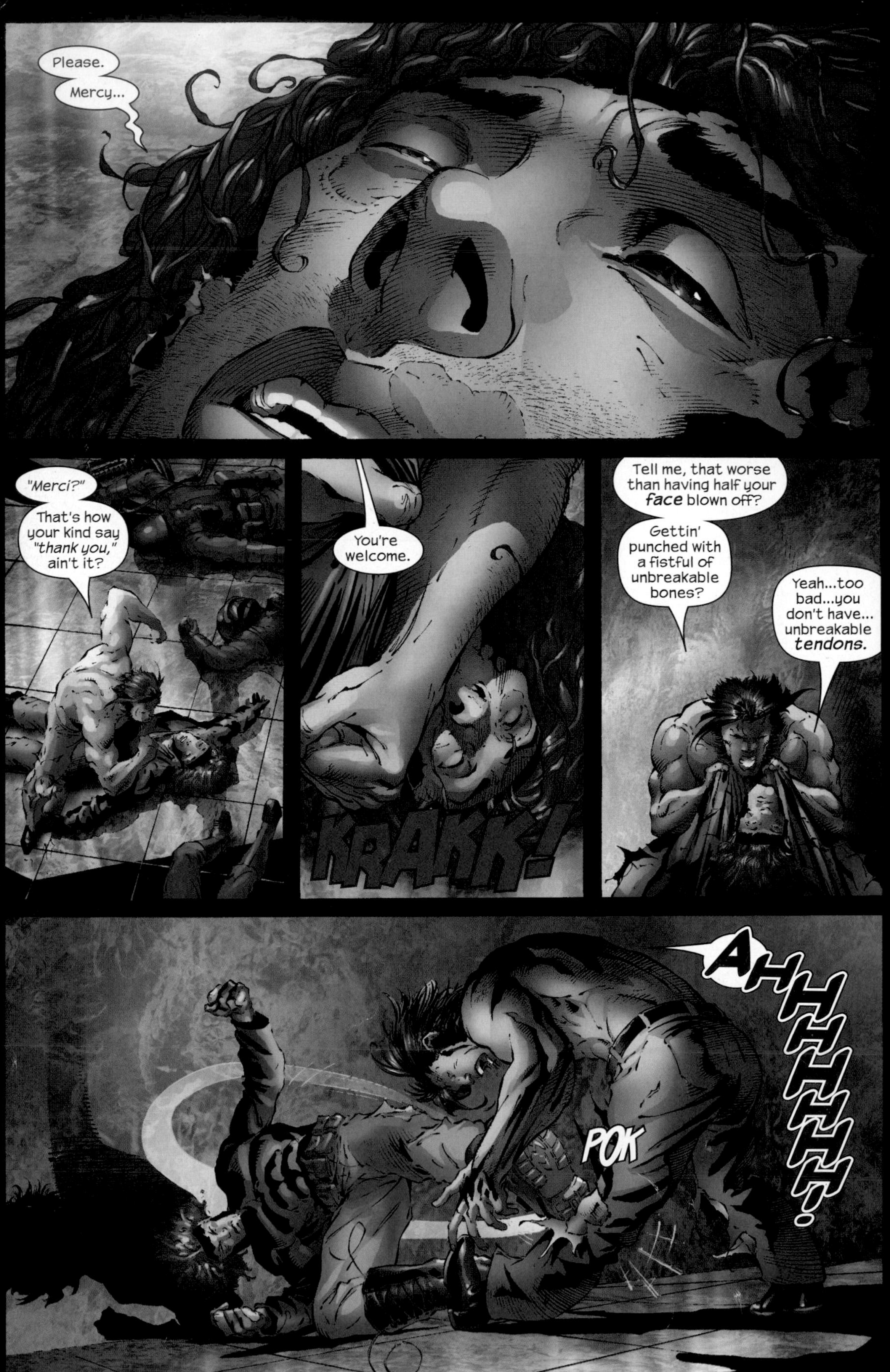

Please.
Mercy...
"Merci?"
That's how your kind say "thank you," ain't it?
You're welcome.
KRAKK!
Tell me, that worse than having half your face blown off?
Gettin' punched with a fistful of unbreakable bones?
Yeah...too bad...you don't have... unbreakable tendons.
AHHHHHHHH!
POK

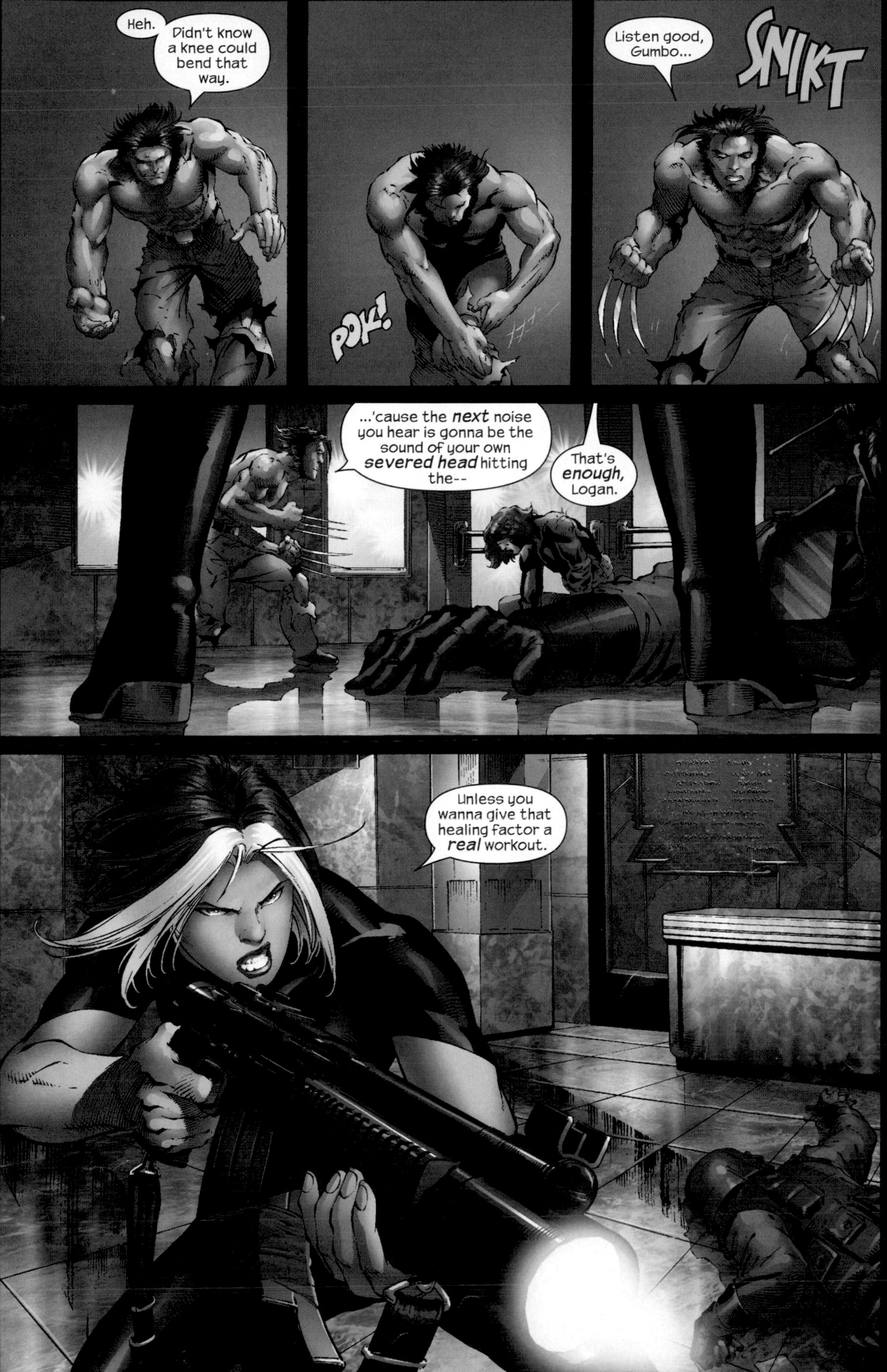
Heh.
Didn't know a knee could bend that way.
POK!
Listen good, Gumbo...
SNIKT
...'cause the next noise you hear is gonna be the sound of your own severed head hitting the--
That's enough, Logan.
Unless you wanna give that healing factor a real workout.

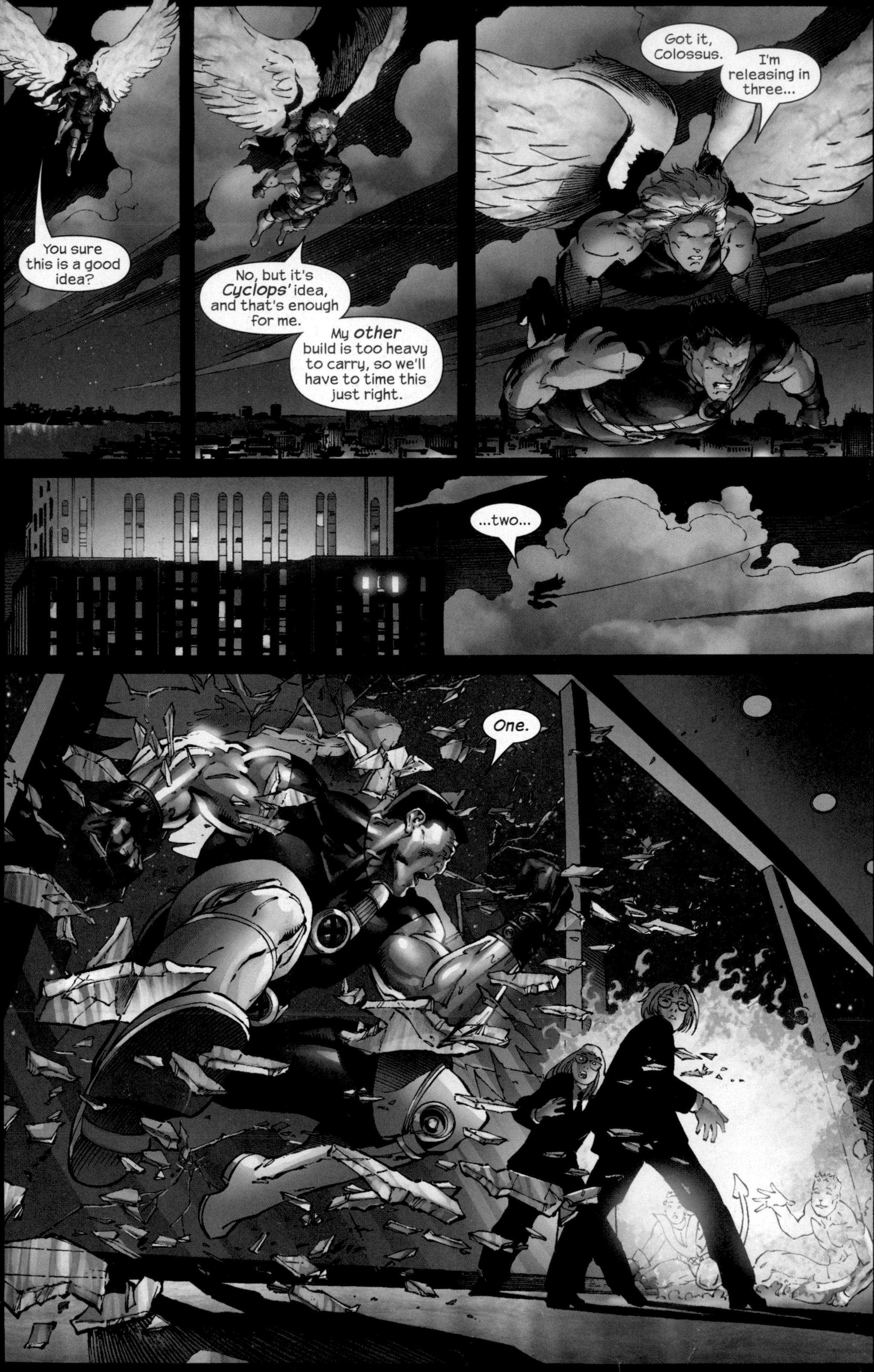

You sure this is a good idea?
No, but it's *Cyclops'* idea, and that's enough for me.
My ***other*** build is too heavy to carry, so we'll have to time this just right.
Got it, Colossus.
I'm releasing in three...
...two...
One.

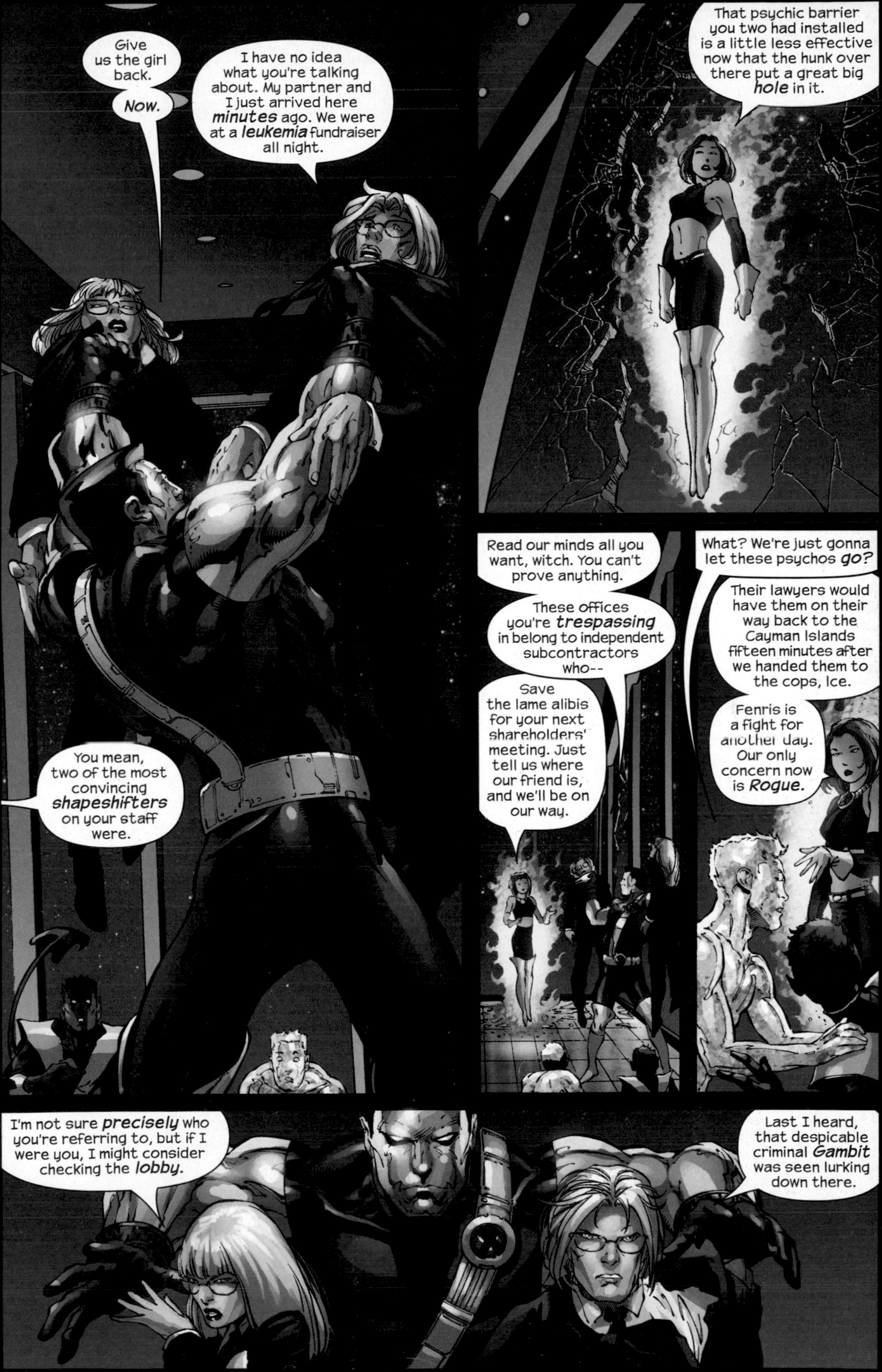
Give us the girl back.
Now.
I have no idea what you're talking about. My partner and I just arrived here minutes ago. We were at a leukemia fundraiser all night.
You mean, two of the most convincing shapeshifters on your staff were.
That psychic barrier you two had installed is a little less effective now that the hunk over there put a great big hole in it.
Read our minds all you want, witch. You can't prove anything.
These offices you're trespassing in belong to independent subcontractors who--
Save the lame alibis for your next shareholders' meeting. Just tell us where our friend is, and we'll be on our way.
What? We're just gonna let these psychos go?
Their lawyers would have them on their way back to the Cayman Islands fifteen minutes after we handed them to the cops, Ice.
Fenris is a fight for another day. Our only concern now is Rogue.
I'm not sure precisely who you're referring to, but if I were you, I might consider checking the lobby.
Last I heard, that despicable criminal Gambit was seen lurking down there.

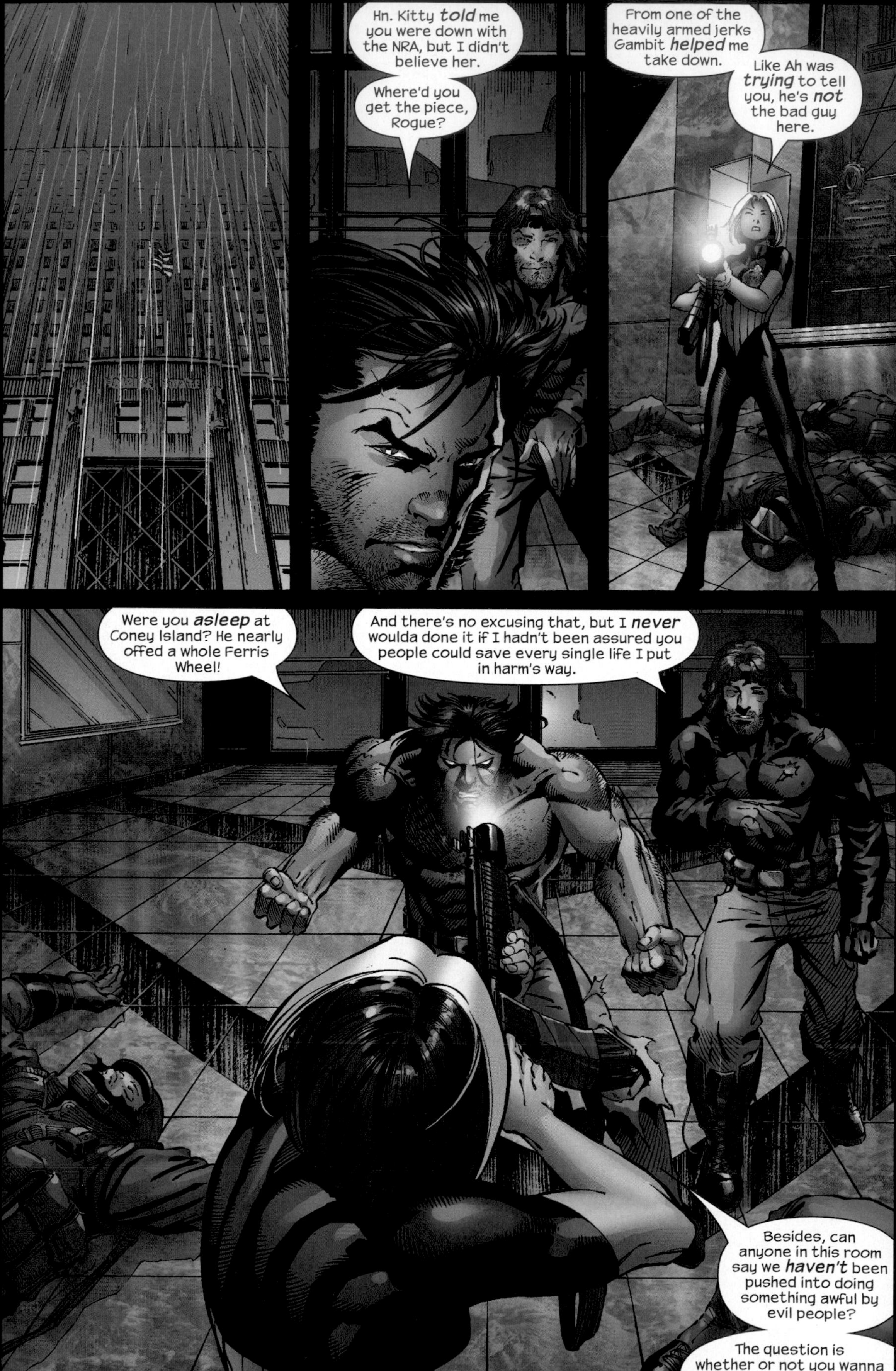
Hn. Kitty told me you were down with the NRA, but I didn't believe her.
Where'd you get the piece, Rogue?
From one of the heavily armed jerks Gambit helped me take down.
Like Ah was trying to tell you, he's not the bad guy here.
Were you asleep at Coney Island? He nearly offed a whole Ferris Wheel!
And there's no excusing that, but I never woulda done it if I hadn't been assured you people could save every single life I put in harm's way.
Besides, can anyone in this room say we haven't been pushed into doing something awful by evil people?
The question is whether or not you wanna atone for what you done.

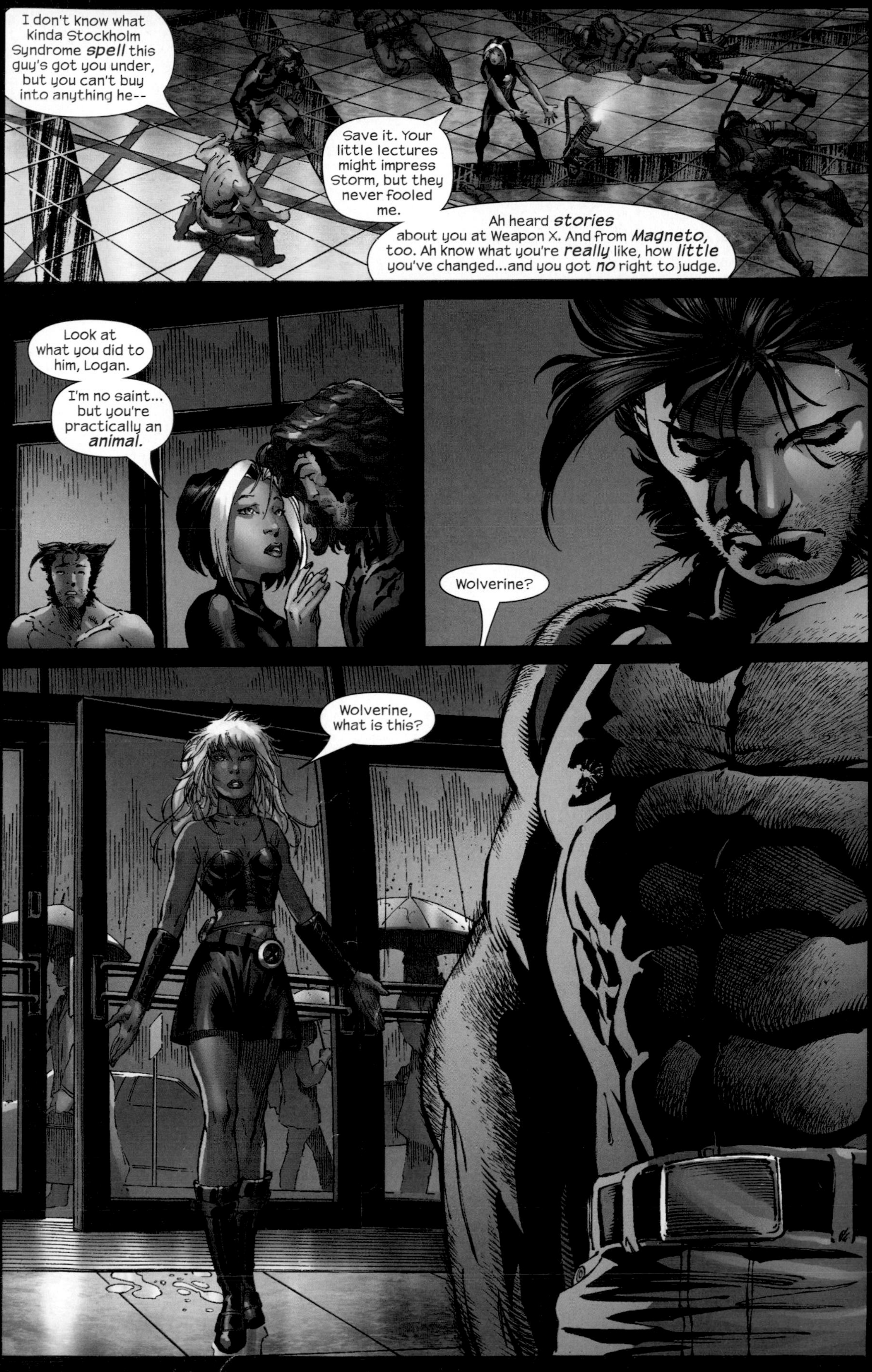

I don't know what kinda Stockholm Syndrome spell this guy's got you under, but you can't buy into anything he--
Save it. Your little lectures might impress Storm, but they never fooled me.
Ah heard stories about you at Weapon X. And from Magneto, too. Ah know what you're really like, how little you've changed...and you got no right to judge.
Look at what you did to him, Logan.
I'm no saint... but you're practically an animal.
Wolverine?
Wolverine, what is this?

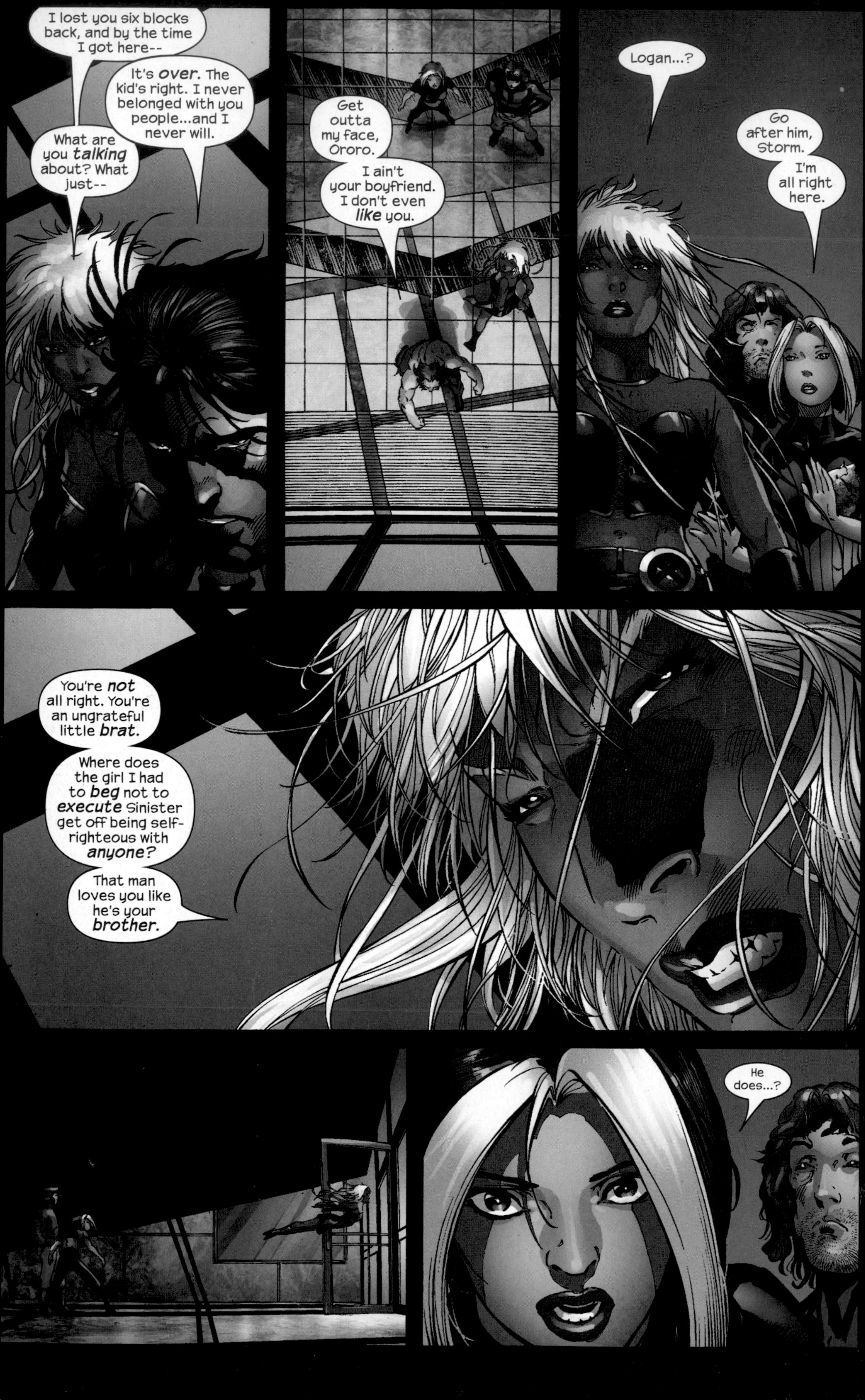
I lost you six blocks back, and by the time I got here--
It's over. The kid's right. I never belonged with you people...and I never will.
What are you talking about? What just--
Get outta my face, Ororo.
I ain't your boyfriend. I don't even like you.
Logan...?
Go after him, Storm.
I'm all right here.
You're not all right. You're an ungrateful little brat.
Where does the girl I had to beg not to execute Sinister get off being self-righteous with anyone?
That man loves you like he's your brother.
He does...?

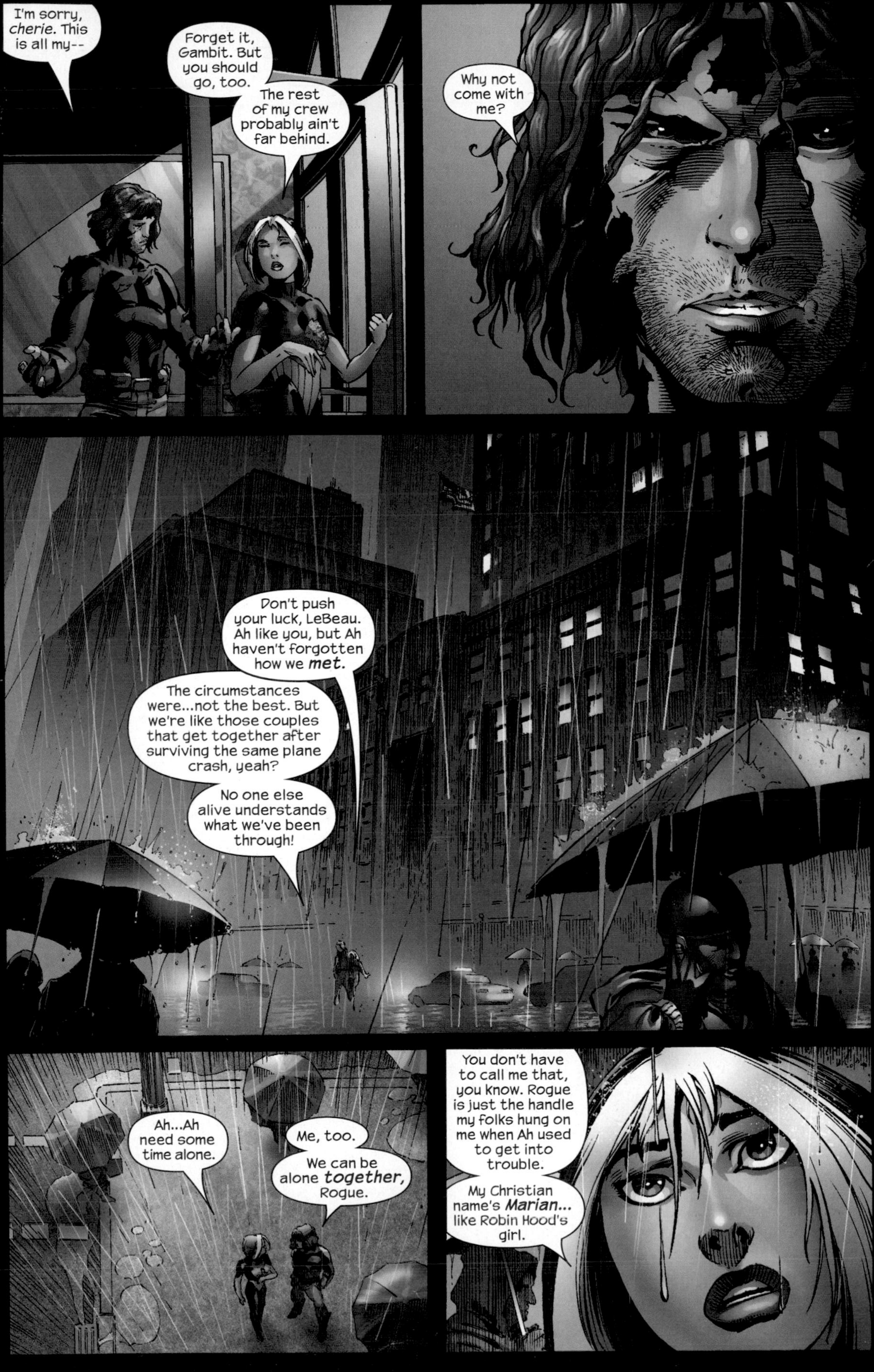
I'm sorry, *cherie*. This is all my--
Forget it, Gambit. But you should go, too.
The rest of my crew probably ain't far behind.
Why not come with me?
Don't push your luck, LeBeau. Ah like you, but Ah haven't forgotten how we ***met.***
The circumstances were...not the best. But we're like those couples that get together after surviving the same plane crash, yeah?
No one else alive understands what we've been through!
Ah...Ah need some time alone.
Me, too.
We can be alone ***together,*** Rogue.
You don't have to call me that, you know. Rogue is just the handle my folks hung on me when Ah used to get into trouble.
My Christian name's ***Marian...*** like Robin Hood's girl.

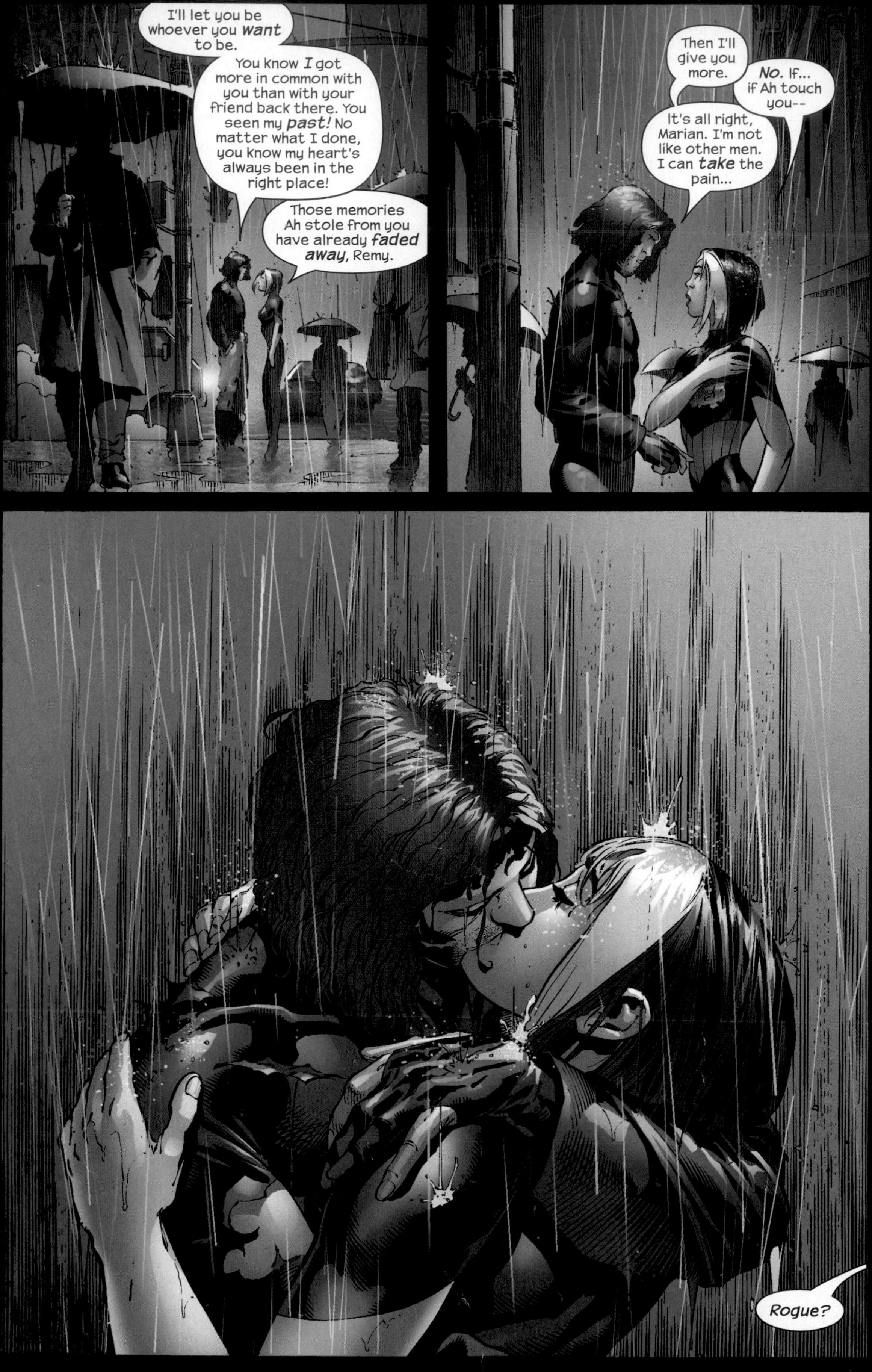
I'll let you be whoever you *want* to be.
You know *I* got more in common with you than with your friend back there. You seen my *past!* No matter what I done, you know my heart's always been in the right place!
Those memories Ah stole from you have already *faded away*, Remy.
Then I'll give you more.
No. If... if Ah touch you--
It's all right, Marian. I'm not like other men. I can *take* the pain...
Rogue?

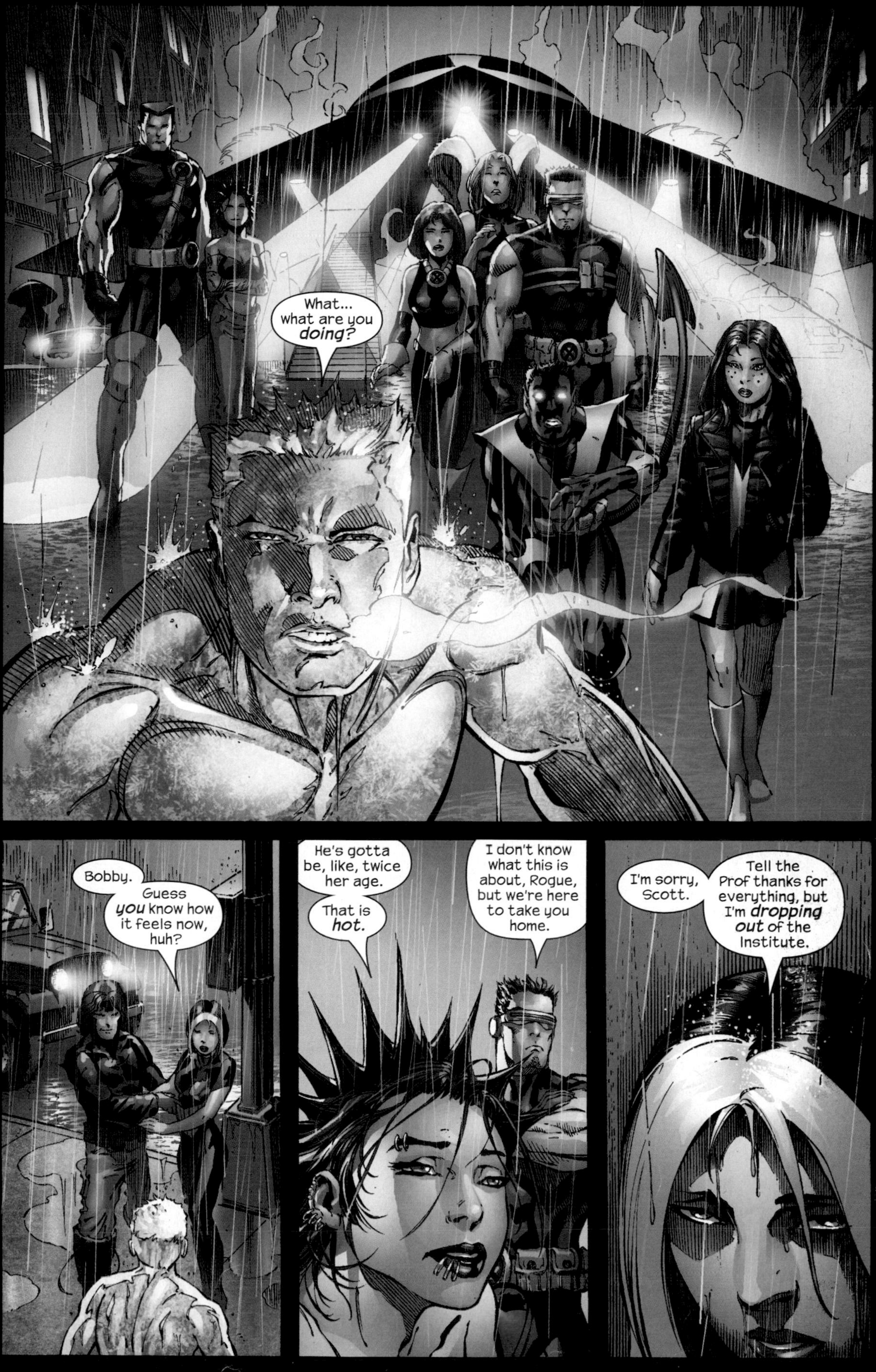
What... what are you doing?
Bobby.
Guess you know how it feels now, huh?
He's gotta be, like, twice her age.
That is hot.
I don't know what this is about, Rogue, but we're here to take you home.
I'm sorry, Scott.
Tell the Prof thanks for everything, but I'm dropping out of the Institute.

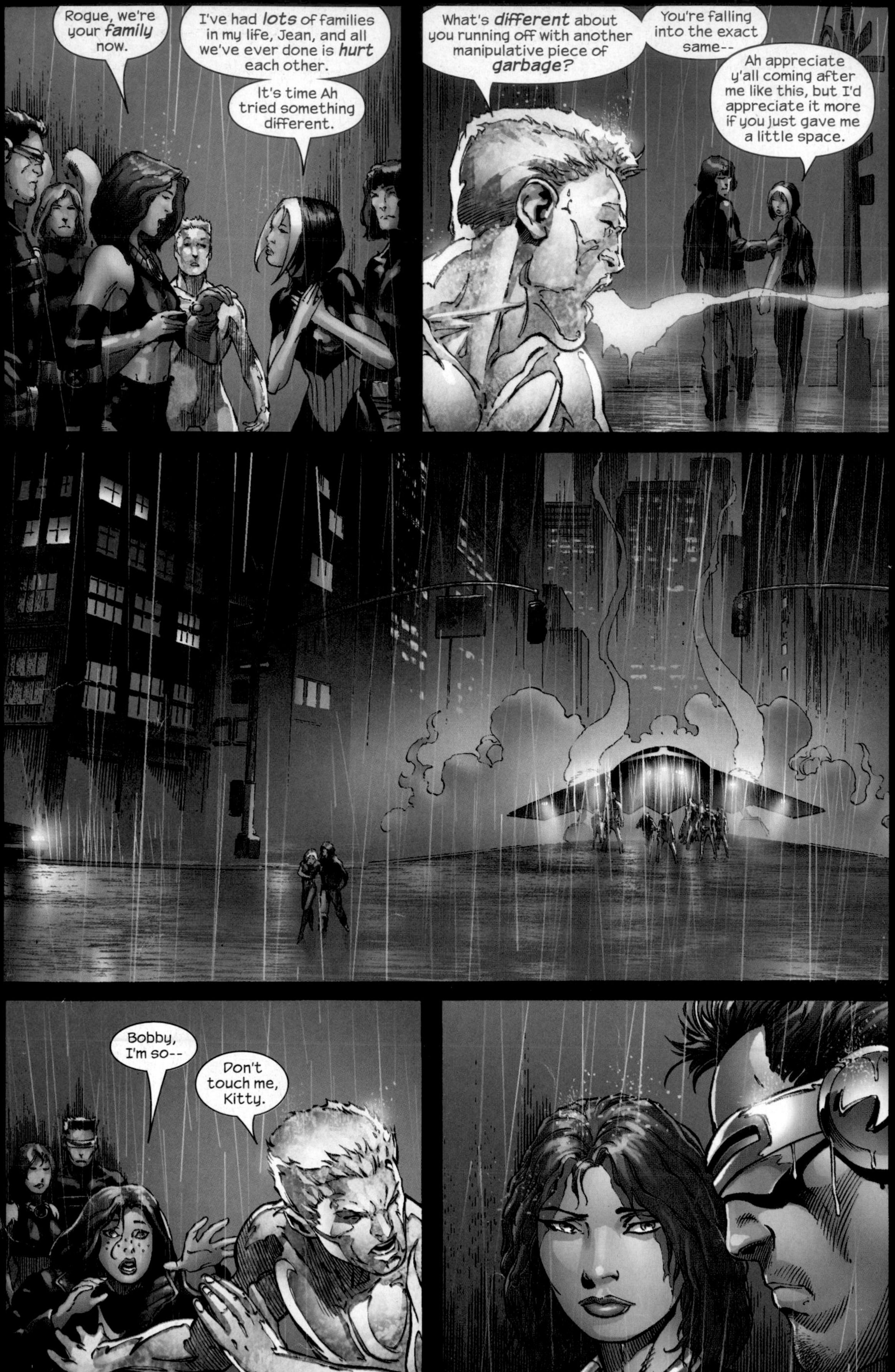
Rogue, we're your family now.
I've had lots of families in my life, Jean, and all we've ever done is hurt each other.
It's time Ah tried something different.
What's different about you running off with another manipulative piece of garbage?
You're falling into the exact same--
Ah appreciate y'all coming after me like this, but I'd appreciate it more if you just gave me a little space.
Bobby, I'm so--
Don't touch me, Kitty.

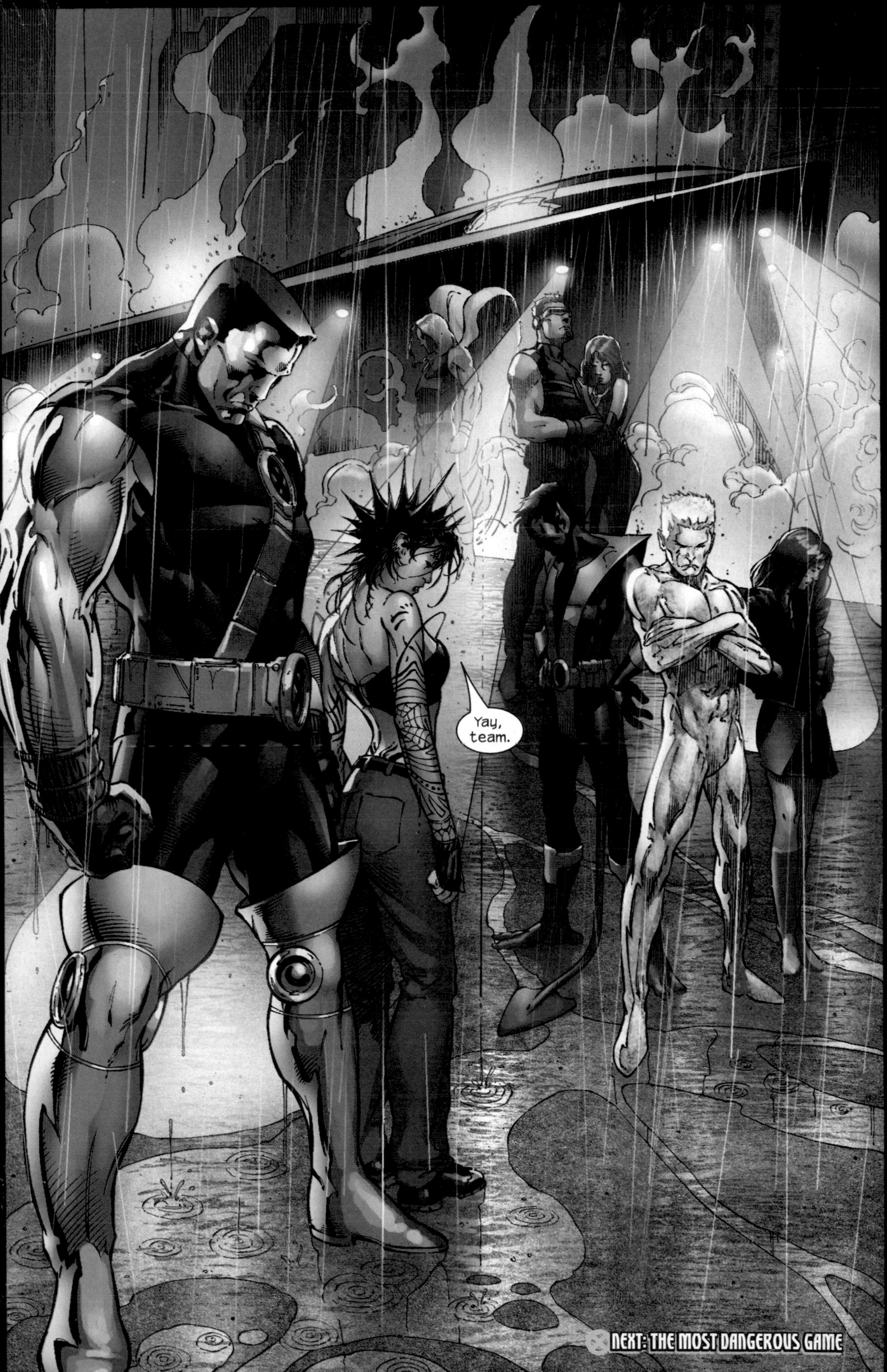
Yay, team.
NEXT: THE MOST DANGEROUS GAME

Cover #53 Pencils
By Andy Kubert

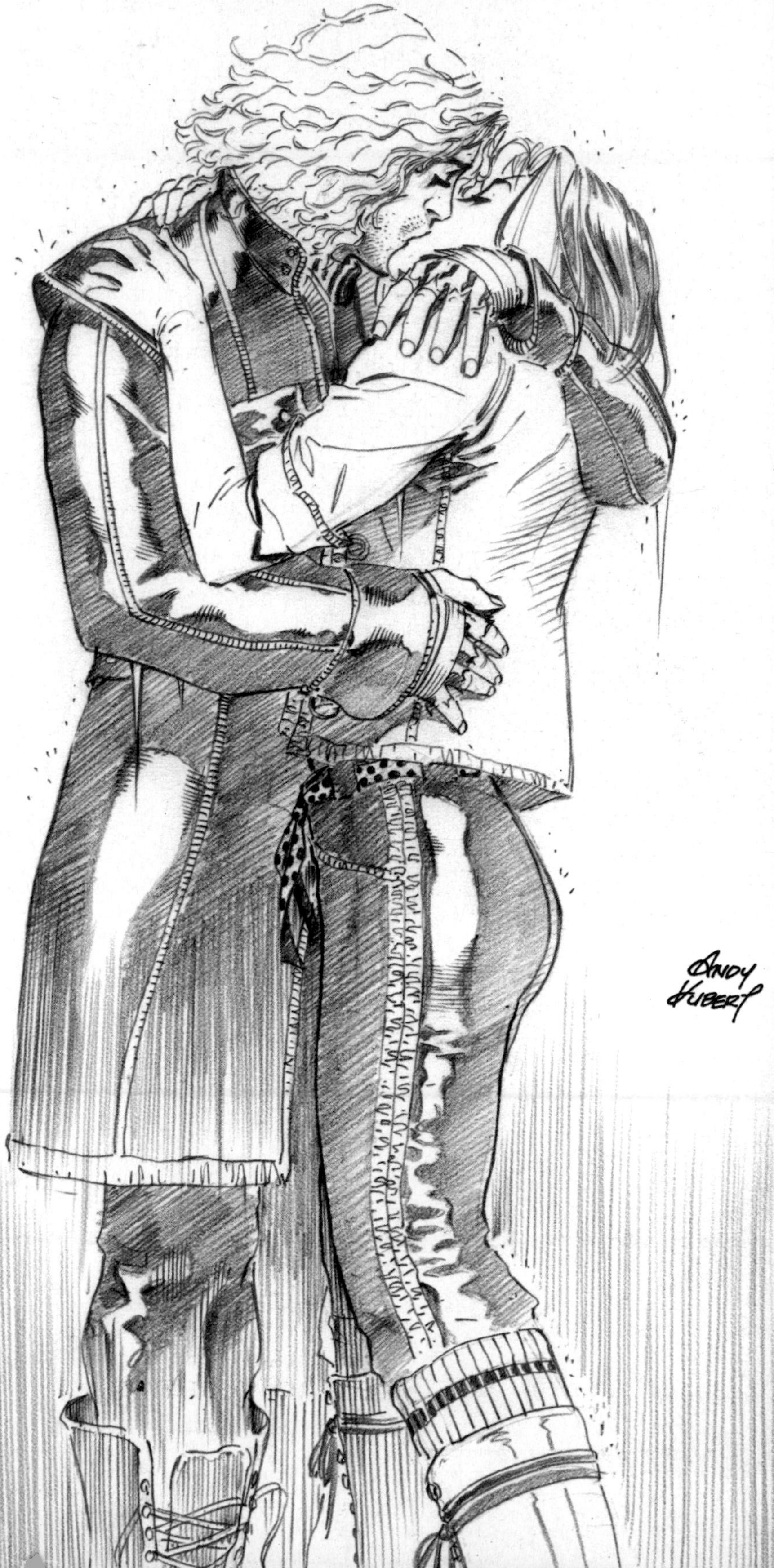
ANDY
KUBERT